INSIGHT GUIDES

Created and Directed by Hans Höfer

BURMA
MYANMAR

Updated by Wilhelm Klein

Managing Editor: Jessamyn Cheam Gwynne

Executive Editor: Scott Rutherford

Editorial Director: Brian Bell

Houghton Mifflin

APA PUBLICATIONS

For decades Burma has been a kind of secret in traveller circles. Entry was restricted, and of a tourist infrastructure, there was near to none. The government was not interested in foreigners roaming its soil. That's how the country looked when this book appeared for the first time in 1980. Many things have changed in the meantime and this book has changed with them. This edition presents Burma as it is in the middle of the 1990s. Open for tourists, as enchanting as ever.

The romance and adventure of Burma lends itself especially well to the approach taken by the *Insight Guide* series, created in 1970 by **Hans Höfer**, founder of Apa Publications and still the company's driving force. Each book encourages readers to celebrate the essence of a place rather than to try to tailor it to their expectations, and is edited in the belief that, without insight into a people's character and culture, travel can narrow the mind rather than broaden it.

The books are carefully structured: the first section covers a destination's history, and then culture, in a series of magazine-style essays. The main Places section provides a comprehensive run-down on the things worth seeing and doing. Finally, a fact-packed listings section contains all the practical information you'll need.

Höfer

Austrian author **Wilhelm Klein**, former co-editor of a German political magazine and one-time publisher, has travelled extensively to Asia since the early 1960s.

In the late 1970s, Klein approached Apa founder-publisher **Hans Höfer** with the project, and one of Klein's first steps was to find a photographer with sufficient sensitivity to catch the mystery and diversity of Burma on film. He found the ideal candidate in **Günter**

Klein

Pfannmüller, a graduate of Germany's Darmstadt Academy of graphic design. Pfannie, as he is known to friends, worked at that time for. Gruner and Jahr, the publisher for *Geo, Stern* and *Brigitte* magazines.

He had never been to Burma, but upon hearing Klein's wondrous tales of this extraordinary land, he and his Nikon did not need further convincing. Two years and many week-long visits later, Klein and Pfannmüller had thoroughly combed all the regions of Burma regarded as accessible to visitors.

Apa's first edition of this book went to print, appearing at a time when visitors were permitted to stay for only one week in the country, and the most scenic regions were off-limits. But the authors soon found ways to go beyond the trodden tourist tracks. Since then the two have been back to Burma year after year. They have travelled to remote locations such as the Kyaik-tiyo "Golden Rock", the Ayeyarwady (Irrawaddy) delta capital of Pathein (Bassein) and the little-known lost cities of Rakhine (Arakan).

At the beginning of the 1990s, Klein and Pfannmüller cruised along the entire Ayeyarwady, and in 1993 they were the first foreign photojournalists to go to the still-besieged city of Myeik (Mergui), and were also permitted to visit the recently-pacified Kachin State – a region with a huge, untapped tourist trade potential. 1994 and 1995 saw them in the remote Chin hills and the ruby mines of Mogok.

Pfannmüller

Especially after the violent incidents at the end of the 1980s – when Burma's name was officially changed to Myanmar – the contemporary section of the guide had to be re-written.

Apa received some critical opinions that the present political state of the country is not evaluated more thoroughly in this book. Klein suggests, however, leaving the final assessment to world-wise visitors themselves, thus stating mainly dates and facts that stand the test of history without any ideological or biased point of view.

A similar approach has been taken regarding the geographical names in this book. Since visitors will be confronted with the new designations (actually the local Burmese way of pronunciation) wherever they go, this book has been amended, using the new names with the former ones in parentheses wherever deemed necessary. Thus, instead of stating a point of view, this book does what a travel guide is made for: it helps the visitor to easily find the way.

When the SLORC (Social Law and Order Restoration Council) officially changed the name from Burma to Myanmar in 1989, the democratic opposition and most of the minority people of the country opposed this move. For the minority people whose mother language is not Myanmar (Burmese), it meant a subtle kind of domination. Since some of them are still striving for independence or autonomy, they see in *Burma* a word that somehow indicates that the country is multi-racial, and that other people, with a different historical, religious and cultural background from the Bamars (Burmans), live there.

Most international institutions and organizations are using the word Myanmar. Many publications, however, particularly in North America and Europe, continue to use the name Burma. The reasons are diverse – sometimes pragmatic and sometimes philosophical. Apa has chosen to use Burma, while using new spellings for place names in the country.

Nevertheless, visitors will have to get their visas at a Myanmar embassy, and they will use Myanmar Airways.

During the later 1990s, Burma expects a yet unprecedented influx of foreign visitors that will soon reach several hundred thousand. The magic of the country, however, with its 1000-year-old history, a culture and a faith that is more than twice as old, will remain unshaken by the social transformation now taking place.

Sherry Cox, a University of Hawaii graduate in Burmese music and one of the very few young Westerners fluent in the Burmese language, prepared the section on "Survival Burmese".

While Pfannmüller was responsible for the majority of photographs in *Insight Guide: Burma*, others who also made important contributions include **Wilhelm Klein, Karl Ammann, Kal Müller, Jan Whiting, Joseph Lynch, Ronni Pinsler** and **John Anderson**.

Anderson

Thanks are also due to **Mi Seitelman**, who provided the World War II photographs from the U.S. Army archives, and to **Leo Haks**, for allowing us to reprint the 19th-century photographs from his collection.

Several Burmese assisted in making the book a reality. They include the late **U Bokay** in Bagan (Pagan), **Win Myint** in Taunggyi, **Freddie Khin Maung** and **Ba Ky** in Yangon (Rangoon), **U Tin Htway** in Heidelberg, and **U Gye Myint** and **U Win Aung** in Bonn.

Of institutions there were **Myanmar Travels & Tours (Tourist Burma)**, the **Myanmar Directorate of Archaeology**, the **U.S. Army**, the **Imperial War Museum** in London, the **Asia Record** and the **University of Hawaii Center for Asian and Pacific Studies**.

This edition of *Insight Guide: Burma* has been shaped into true Apa style by **Jessamyn Cheam Gwynne** of Apa's Singapore editorial office.

—Apa Publications

CONTENTS

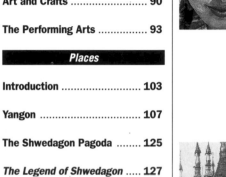

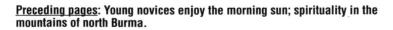

Preceding pages: Young novices enjoy the morning sun; spirituality in the mountains of north Burma.

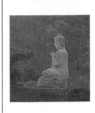

Maps

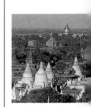

INTRODUCTION

Any visitor to Burma (Myanmar) will be spellbound. It is the atmosphere, the varied scents, the ambience and the feeling of another world, that envelopes him here.

While the country experiences traumatic changes in its political and social structure, the visitor, when approaching the main platform around the ancient Shwedagon pagoda's golden stupa, takes his first steps toward a fairy-tale Burma, lifting him above the mercurial reality encountered in the streets below.

The Shwedagon is a constant reminder of the transience of all things, a sign that Buddhism recognizes man's sorrowful plight. Yet in making its silent statement, it produces in devotees an almost imperceptible joy which can most readily be felt at the sunset hour among the pagoda's prayer halls and pavilions.

Burma fascinates the visitor with one unexpected surprise after another, from the leg-rowers of Inle Lake to the pagoda-speckled plain of Bagan (Pagan); from the *nat* dancers of tiny Taungbyon to the remarkable "giraffe women" of the Padaung tribe.

The number of western visitors to Burma is increasing once again due to new travel regulations that now permit them to stay in Burma for up to four weeks. Also, a new type of visitor is now seen in the streets of Yangon (Rangoon): the foreign businessman. With the introduction of a market economy after decades of a stagnant socialist order, Yangon has become a boom-town attracting Southeast Asian investors and some Western businessmen. New hotels, restaurants and businesses are mushrooming, and previously-unknown traffic congestion now jams Yangon and Mandalay.

Soon, the world will witness a struggle of different values taking place in this otherwise peaceful land. The government is taking pains to modernize the country (while, however, trying to minimize the influx of western ideas). Energy plants, fertilizer factories, oil refineries, assembly plants, road construction, government-controlled television channel and many other infrastructure projects – all have left their marks on a society on the threshold of modernity. Change seems inevitable and irrevocable in a country where the majority of people still live in a timeless fashion.

For the most part, though, Burma's colours are still natural. Monks are clothed in a variety of shades from saffron to purple. Women, wearing pale yellow *thanaka*-bark makeup and smoking green or white cheroots, conjure up images of the last century. The visitor to Burma is constantly reminded of past ages – even of images which may not even have really appeared. This, perhaps, is what makes Burma the thoroughly fascinating country it is.

Much of the historical material in this book has come from the British scholars of the colonial period, though during the last decades, a wealth of research by Burmese scholars has emerged and

Preceding pages: early birds ply a village road near Bagan; modern Myohaung in the morning mist; a native craft glides down a tranquil Rakhine river; lone devotee before the radiant Shwedagon in Yangon; young Buddhist monks. **Left**, Shwezigon Pagoda, Bagan.

is about to change part of Burmese history as we know it.

On June 18, 1989, the orders from the State Law and Order Restoration Council (SLORC), signed by Lieutenant General Khin Nyunt, changed many well-established English names, so as to be in accordance with the Burmese pronunciation. Since then, many, but not all foreign news media, have begun to use these new designations, which in fact are the indigenous names that the Bamars (Burmans) have always used.

The most important of the changes is the new name of the country itself, which has officially changed from the "Union of Burma" to the "Union of Myanmar." The same is true with "Rangoon", which became "Yangon", a name given to the city as far back as 1755 by Alaungpaya when he captured and renamed the city of Dagon. It was the British who changed this name and many others into the colonial names most Westerners are familiar with.

The river Irrawaddy is now the Ayeyarwady, the Sittang changed to Sittoung, the Chindwin to Chindwinn, and the Salween to Thanlwin.

Of the cities, Pegu became Bago, Pagan has changed its name to Bagan, Tavoy to Dawei, Prome to Pyay, Moulmein to Mawlamyine, Maymyo to Pyin-U-Lwin, Magwe to Magway, Bassein to Pathein, Mergui to Myeik, and Sandoway to Thandwe.

Tenasserim is now Tanintharyi and Arakan became Rakhine. Burmans are now called Bamars, the Karen became the Kayin, and the Arakanese are called Rakhines.

In this book we will use the new names, with the corresponding previous names in parentheses in the first reference of each chapter. The name of the country will remain as Burma, as will the language still be described as Burmese, since it is derived from the internationally-accepted word "Tibeto-Burman."

This book draws a distinction between the Bamar (Burman) people, the country's majority ethnic group, as well as those people who speak a Tibeto-Burman language, and the Burmese (Myanmars), a term that represents all peoples of Burma. Indigenous terms used are from the Burmese (Tibeto-Burman) language, except for Pali language words in religious contexts.

For many visitors, Burma is known only through its disputed politics. Behind this, however, hides a country and a people that should not be forgotten, deeply religious and dignified. A country of ancient charm not yet infected by western values. It is the aim of this book to present just that, an eternal beauty beyond the controversy of the day.

Paddy work is a family matter in Burma

LAND OF RICE AND RIVERS

Burma (Myanmar). The Ayeyarwady (Irrawaddy). For millennia, these names have been almost synonymous.

As the centre of the rice culture on which Burma's economy has always been based, the Ayeyarwady is the lifeblood of the land. Rising in the southern Himalayas, the river traverses the country from north to south for 2,170 kilometres (1,350 mi), emptying into the Andaman Sea through a nine-armed delta. Called "the Road to Mandalay" by British colonialists, the broad river has always been the land's major transportation route.

The traveller who follows the Ayeyarwady's entire course, will find it possible to sample the full range of Burma's climatic zones. Beginning at the far north, the river runs through the rugged Kachin Hills, foothills of the mighty Himalayas. At Bhamo, the furthest point to which the Ayeyarwady is navigable by steamer (1,500 kilometres, [930 mi] from the delta), the Ayeyarwady enters the Shan Plateau region. Further downstream, it emerges on the broad dry plain of central Burma, the centre of classical Burmese civilization. The Ayeyarwady then cruises past sandbars to the ruins of Bagan (Pagan) and Sri Ksetra, and enters the moister southern stretch of the course. In its vast delta, 240 kilometres (150 mi) wide and 290 kilometres (180 mi) long, the river opens up to seemingly endless rice paddies.

The "kite" and its string: Indeed, the Ayeyarwady is the string controlling the "kite" that is Burma. Thinking of a kite is a good way to envision the country: it is roughly diamond-shaped, with long, narrow Tanintharyi (Tenasserim) as its tail. A surface area of 676,577 square kilometres (261,228 sq mi) makes Burma the largest Asian mainland country east of India and south of China. Despite its former colonial ties to India, it is usually grouped geographically with Southeast Asia.

Burma's population is estimated at about 43.1 million (1994) of whom about 75 per-

cent live in rural villages. After Yangon, with its population of more than 3 million, the major population centres are Mandalay (about 600,000), Pathein (Bassein) (about 350,000) and Mawlamyine (Moulmein) (about 220,000).

Bounded by Bangladesh and India on the northwest, the People's Republic of China on the northeast, Laos and Thailand on the east, the Andaman Sea on the south, and the Bay of Bengal on the southwest, Burma is located between 10°N and 28°N. The Tropic of Cancer traverses the country 160 kilometres (100 mi) north of Mandalay.

The most agreeable season is the winter. From November through February, the average mean temperature along the Ayeyarwady plain is between 21°C and 28°C (70°F and 82°F), although in the northern Kachin mountains and on the Shan Plateau the temperature can drop below freezing point.

March and April are the hottest months in Burma, with central Burma's temperatures sometimes reaching a stifling 45°C (113°F). In May, however, the rainy season begins. It is a time of high humidity, somewhat more bearable in Mandalay than in Yangon. From May through October, one must reckon with daily afternoon and early evening showers.

The "horseshoe mountains": This seasonal rainfall, as in all of South and Southeast Asia, is a result of the monsoon winds of the Indian Ocean, which move from the southwest in summer and from the northeast in winter. Burma gets its heaviest rains between June and August, but is protected by its "horseshoe mountains" from the severe flooding which plagues much of the region.

Burma's central river system is ringed by a series of peaks – several over 3,000 metres (10,000 ft) – which create profound if predictable effects on the nation's climate. There are the Rakhine, Chin, Naga and Patkai hills in the west, the Kachin hills in the north, and the Shan Plateau, extending to the Tanintharyi Coast ranges, in the east.

The coasts of Rakhine (Arakan) and Tanintharyi receive 300 to 500 centimetres (120 to 200 in) of rain per year, with the Ayeyarwady Delta getting 150 to 250 centimetres (60 to 100 in). On the leeward sides of

Preceding pages: dancers at the Manao Festival in Myitkyina; rain saturates the paddies in central Burma. **Left**, climbing a golden mountain of harvested paddy at a Hlegu workers' cooperative.

the mountain ranges and on the Shan Plateau, annual precipitation ranges from 100 to 200 centimetres (40 to 80 in), while central Burma's Dry Zone varies from 50 to 100 centimetres (20 to 40 in). It is largely due to the protection of the 2,000-metre (6,500-ft) peaks of the Rakhine Yoma that central Burma is Southeast Asia's driest region – and that Bagan's (Pagan's) priceless buildings have remained so well preserved through the centuries.

The seasonal monsoons nourish Burma's rice crop with abundant rainfall. But it is the melting snows of the Himalayas, far to the north, which feed Burma's great rivers.

Two rivers besides the Ayeyarwady are

important to Burma's inland navigation and irrigation. One, the Chindwinn (Chindwin), is a tributary of the Ayeyarwady, joining the larger river about 110 kilometres (70 mi) downstream from Mandalay. Readily navigable for 180 kilometres (110 mi) upstream from its confluence – and for 610 kilometres (380 mi) during the rainy season – it opens up remote stretches of the Sagaing Region.

In eastern Burma, the Thanlwin (Salween) River slices through the Shan State in a series of deep gorges. Like the Mekong, which comprises the Burma-Laos border, the Thanlwin flows for long stretches through areas controlled by anti-government rebel

forces. It has few tributaries between its source in the Himalayas and its exit to the Andaman Sea at Mawlamyine (Moulmein), despite a 2,816-kilometre (1,749-mi) course. It is navigable only for about 160 kilometres (100 mi) upstream because of its dangerously fast current and 20-metre (65-ft) fluctuations in water level. It used to play an important role in the Burmese economy – as the route by which teak was rafted from the Shan Plateau, where it is harvested, to Mawlamyine, its export harbor. But teak is now mostly exported via Yangon.

One other river has traditionally been of great importance in Burmese history – the Sittoung (Sittang). It is a relatively short river which marks the lower boundary between the Bago (Pegu) Region and the Mon State. But it has silted up badly in the past three centuries, to the extent that it is now navigable only by flat-bottomed boats, and only on certain stretches.

Geographically, Burma can be divided into several zones. In the far north, as noted, are the Kachin hills, reaching heights of 3,000 metres (10,000 ft). On the Tibetan border is Hkakabo Razi, the highest peak in Southeast Asia at 5,887 metres (19,314 ft). Deep valleys, many of them harbouring subtropical vegetation and terraced rice, separate the mountain ridges. The chief inhabitants are the Kachin people; tribes of Lisu are also common in the Chinese border region. The administrative centre of Myitkyina (pronounced *myit-chee-na*) is the terminus of the railway from Yangon and Mandalay.

If future political events were to allow for a direct overland route between Europe and Southeast Asia, it would pass through the Kachin State. In ages past, the Ledo Road and several old caravan routes were of inestimable importance to commerce in the region. Today the Ledo Road is closed except for use by the established minorities of this otherwise impassable region. Due to the recent cease-fire agreement between the government and the Kachins, this stretch might soon be opened for outside visitors.

The Kachin Hills are linked to the Shan Plateau in the south, a vast area averaging about 1,000 metres (3,200 ft) in elevation. Deep, incisive valleys intersect the undulating surface of the plateau, and the powerful Thanlwin (Salween) flows through it like an arrow. Once popular as a site for "hill stations" where British colonials could escape the daunting heat of central Burma, the region still offers the flavour of a bygone era in its administrative centres of Taunggyi, Pyin-U-Lwin (Maymyo), Kalaw and Lashio. A modern tourist centre has also been developed around Inle Lake in the southwestern part of the plateau.

With an almost European climate, fruits, vegetables and citrus crops thrive on the Shan Plateau, as does timber. Burma is the world's leading exporter of teak, and most of that valued wood is harvested in the Shan State. Other crops include rice, peanuts, potatoes, tea, tobacco, coffee, cotton ... and opium. The notorious Golden Triangle en-

only in the coastal areas of Mawlamyine, and Dawei (Tavoy) does one come across more densely populated farming settlements. Strewn off the Tanintharyi coast are the isles of the Myeik (Mergui) Archipelago, one of Southeast Asia's few remaining untouched island groups. Because of its isolation, it thrives as the centre of the flourishing smuggling trade between Thailand and Burma – and for security reasons is therefore still off-limits to most Burmese and foreigners.

West of the Ayeyarwady, on the seaward side of the Rakhine Yoma, is the state of Rakhine. This flat coastal strip is broken by numerous small rivers flowing out of the east-lying mountains – chief of which is

compasses much of the eastern part of the Shan Plateau.

East of the Gulf of Martaban, the Shan Plateau funnels into the Tanintharyi coastal range which forms the natural border between southern Burma and Thailand. The long tongue of coastland which follows this range down to the Isthmus of Kra – the "tail of the kite" – is not easily accessible, and

Left, the monsoon-type rigging of boats in the Bay of Bengal is much the same as in the 17th century when pirates ruled the seas. Right, the roadless jungles near Mawlamyine (Moulmein) depend on a different form of transportation.

Mount Victoria, elevation 3,053 metres (10,016 ft). Several untouched, long and sandy beaches grace the coastline.

Then there is the central belt of the nation, or "Burma Proper," as the British called it. Extending around the Ayeyarwady, its tributary the Chindwinn, and the Sittoung, it is the settlement area of the Bamar (Burman) race. The region is generally subdivided into two parts – Upper Burma, that area surrounding Mandalay, north of the towns of Pyay (the former Prome, now also called Pyi) and Toungoo; and Lower Burma, focusing on Yangon, and south of the Pyay-Toungoo line. Not only do Upper and Lower Burma have distinctive climates; their historical development in colonial times was markedly different as well.

Upper Burma is a region of low rainfall, with farmers employing traditional methods of irrigated and dry cultivation in rice-growing. A complicated system of lakes and canals made it possible for the earliest Burmese civilizations to exist here. Today, 607,000 hectares (1.5 million acres) of land are under irrigation and devoted to rice farming. But crop failures nevertheless occur with alarming regularity at least once a decade, and before rice was available from Lower Burma, famines were common in this region. Because the delta is now Burma's "breadbas-

19th century, the delta was uncultivated jungle and tall grass. The monsoon rains attracted colonists from the Dry Zone, who cleared the jungle and planted it with wet-rice fields. For the most part of the 20th century, until 1962, Burma was the world's largest exporter of rice. The population, though, has grown faster than production, so that the annual amount exported – more than 3 million tons annually in the pre-war years – dropped to 600,000 tons in 1976. In 1994/95 the export of rice has risen above the 1 million tons mark, and with the introduction of high yielding strains of paddy, substantial land reclamation and improved irrigation, it is on a perpetual rise.

ket," an impressive 1.5 million hectares (3.7 million acres) of irrigated land in the Dry Zone are now devoted to the farming of cotton, tobacco, peanuts, grain sorghum, sesame, beans and corn.

If Upper Burma's agricultural area is impressive, that of Lower Burma is astounding. The Ayeyarwady Delta contains 3.6 million hectares (9 million acres) of irrigated rice farms, with a carrying capacity great enough to feed the entire population of Burma by itself. The delta is expanding into the Andaman Sea at a rate of about 5 kilometres (3 mi) a century, the result of silt deposits.

When the British arrived here in the mid-

Other crops grown in Lower Burma, for export as well as for home consumption, include cotton, sugar cane, rubber, tea and jute. In addition to teak, two other hardwoods – ironwood and padauk (Andaman redwood) – are coveted export items. Recently, minable gold was found between the Ayeyarwady and Chindwinn rivers.

Burma also has a tremendous untapped mineral wealth. Oil, found in the central Ayeyarwady basin, is most important; in recent years, test drilling for natural gas in the Gulf of Martaban has resulted in a US$ 2 billion investment by the French/American Total/Unocal company. The government revenue of about US$ 200 million will by far exceed the lacking OECD assistance, while further concessions for gas, oil and gold will bring direly needed foreign currencies into the country. Iron ore, tungsten, lead, silver, tin, mercury, nickel, plutonium, zinc, copper, cobalt, antimony and gold are found in significant quantities in various parts of the country. World-renowned rubies and sapphires are mined in Mogok in western Shan State, and quality jade is extracted in the vicinity of Mogaung in Kachin State.

Burma's natural vegetation varies according to regional rainfall. Nearly half of the country's surface area is still covered by vast unexploited forests; 15 percent is given over to stands of teak and other hardwoods.

In wetter districts, tropical rainforests climb the hills to about 800 metres (2,625 ft) above sea level; bamboo, used extensively in house construction, is common here along with teak. From this elevation to the snow line at about 3,000 metres (9,842 ft), oaks, silver firs, chestnuts and rhododendrons thrive. In the Dry Zone of central Burma, cacti and acacia trees are common sights.

The *taunggya* (slash-and-burn) cultivation through much of upland Burma has resulted in the depletion of a great deal of the original forest cover, now replaced by a second growth of scrub forest. In *taunggya* agriculture, large trees are felled and the jungle burned over to prepare it for planting – often with 40 or more different crops. When crops and torrential rains have depleted soil fertility in a year or two, the clearing is abandoned and left to the "elephant grass" for 12 to 15 years while the soil regains its fertility. Villages therefore, often change their sites when the accessible land has been exhausted. About 2.5 million of Burma's population still pursue this agricultural method.

Elephants, tigers and leopards: In the remaining virgin forests, a rich variety of wild animals make their home. Elephants, tigers, leopards, wild buffalo and red deer are often hunted today, along with the Himalayan black bear, Malayan sun bear, civet cat, wild boar, several species of monkeys, mountain goats, flying squirrels, porcupines, and even rhinoceros. There is a great variety of birds,

Left, a boat is laden with lake weed used to fertilize floating gardens. Right, an amazing fig tree on the banks of the Ayeyarwady (Irrawaddy).

insects and reptiles, but the most dreaded of all are the snakes.

Deadliest of Burma's snakes is the *mweboai*, or Russel's viper, with a temper so nasty that it attacks to kill without aggravation. It reaches a length of about 170 centimetres (5.5 ft). Also feared is the infamous Asiatic King Cobra, which reaches 425 to 550 centimetres (14 to 18 ft) in length when fully grown.

There is little domestication of animals in Burma, save for the beasts of burden – the oxen in the Dry Zone, buffalo in the wet regions, and elephants in the mountains. Devout Buddhists do not kill animals. The Mon people of the southeast, however, do

have domesticated animals, including cattle, swine, horses, dogs and poultry. The Kayin (Karen) are also noted for their domesticated animals, and some tribes, especially the Kayah, specialize in breeding horses.

No discussion of Burma's fauna could be complete without mentioning the famed Burmese cat. This exotic domestic breed, noted for its short brown hair, is actually from Thailand, and not from Burma at all. In fact, the so-called "fixed" characteristics of the pedigreed feline, according to Western cat breeders, was established only after a period of experimental cross-breeding with the more established Siamese cats.

RUBIES AND JADE

The first mental image many Westerners have of Burma is of precious stones – gems sparkling green, red and purple.

The reputation is not undeserved. The northern mines of Mogok (now open to Western visitors) and Mogaung boast large quantities of rubies, jade, sapphires and other stones.

Ludovico di Varthema, an Italian merchant who visited Burma in 1505, was the first European to report this wealth to the West. "The sole merchandise of this people is jewels," wrote di Varthema. "Large pearls and diamonds are worth more there than with us, and also emeralds."

Di Varthema was also the first Westerner to

become rich by successfully dealing in gems in Burma. He presented the king of Bago some corals, and was rewarded with 200 rubies – worth about 100,000 ducats (approximately US$150,000) in Europe at that time.

Today, it is not so easy to prosper in the gem market. But each February for some decades now, hundreds of gem dealers from all over the world have gathered in Yangon for the "Gems and Pearls Emporium" at the Inya Lake Hotel.

Most prized of all Burmese gems is the ruby, the stone of which Burma virtually holds a monopoly on the world market. Rubies of the colour of pigeon blood, apparently unique to Burma, fetch the highest prices.

However, it doesn't require an alchemist's recipe to produce a fake. False rubies can be created in a flame fusion process from purified ammonia alum and small amounts of chrome alum, with a dash of chrome oxide tossed in for the deep colour. These synthetic stones, deceptively labeled, are popular attractions at markets wherever tourists congregate.

Mogok, where Burma's largest ruby mines are situated, lies about 110 kilometres (70 mi) northeast of Mandalay as the crow flies. In earlier times, the kings of Burma confiscated the wealth recovered here, leaving the miners only with small stones of lesser value.

When the British annexed Upper Burma in 1886, a year of frenzied digging ensued, as the Burmese were now unhindered by royalty. But the colonials were able to occupy the Mines District in 1887, and the London firm of Messrs. Streeter & Co. received sole buying rights for whatever the ground yielded. It made the company's shareholders and the government revenue office significantly rich. Today however, the mines have been nationalized.

In the far north, west of Myitkyina in the Kachin State, is the town of Mogaung, the centre of a jade-mining district. The rich soil of this region was well known to the Chinese in 2000 BC.

As most of Burma's natural wealth is found in the region where the minorities live, how this wealth is distributed between the central government and the states is crucial for the country's future. During the past decades, these natural resources have been the main source of income for the rebellious ethnic tribes, and are an important factor for the future economic independence of the nation. If the forthcoming constitution finds an appropriate way to share this wealth between the regions and the central government, then there is also opportunity for peace in these far off hills. Rubies, jade and teak are commodities in huge demand on the world market; Burma could supply them so that what seemed to be a lawless region could prosper. But that has yet to happen.

Since peace has come to Kachin State, the jade district has been experiencing what California saw during the gold rush. Burmese from all over the country have flocked there in search of fast wealth. Many have succeeded, and their stories are told all over the country, but most end up as day labourers in the larger pits that are often controlled by Chinese groups. Since the government is not yet in complete control of the region, the stories that seep from this "off limits" area tell of a lawless situation beyond a Westerners' imagination.

Rubies and jade are only the most evident examples of Burma's precious mineral wealth. Star, blue and colourless sapphires, Oriental aquamarine and emeralds, topaz, amethysts and lapis lazuli are among other stones for which buyers flock to the Gems Emporium Hall. ∎

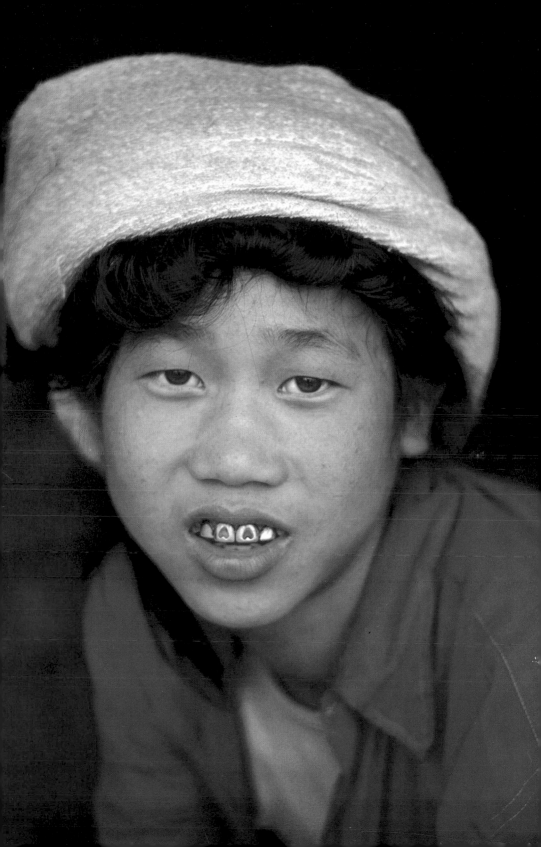

P. KLIER RANGOON

BURMESE IN FESTIVAL DRESS.

Brahma, the world of the gods. This is from where the names *Myanmar* and *Burma* derive, and it is where the Burmese symbolically consider themselves to live. The word has taken many forms in past centuries – Mramma, Bamma, Mien, Burma, Myanmar (as the nation is now officially called) – but always with the same meaning.

According to *The Glass Palace Chronicle of the Kings of Burma* – the 19th century history-mythology of the country – the first kingdom on Burmese soil was founded in pre-Christian times by Sakyan immigrants from India.

However, ethnologists generally agree that the present Bamar (Burman) inhabitants of Burma are the descendants of immigrants that originally came from what is today's Gansu province in northwestern China.

"The land of gold": The Mons were the first group to reach Burma, several centuries before the birth of Christ. These people, whose language belongs to the Mon-Khmer family and who are still to be found in parts of Thailand and Cambodia today, probably came from Central Asia. They settled on the estuaries of the Thanlwin (Salween) and Sittoung (Sittang) rivers, and their settlement area, which they called *Suvannabhumi* ("the land of gold"), is mentioned in ancient Chinese and Indian texts.

Legend says it was the Mons who laid the foundation stone of the Shwedagon Pagoda as far back as 2,500 years ago. While the pagoda has been altered so often in ensuing centuries that the legend would be difficult to prove, it is known that the Mon race established the Buddhist tradition in Burma. In the 3rd century BC, the Mons had already made close ties with the realm of King Ashoka in India through their port city of Thaton.

About 2,000 years ago, the Pyu people settled in Upper Burma. Unlike the Mons, they belonged to the Tibeto-Burman language family. The Pyus set up their first

capital at Sri Ksetra, near present-day Pyay (Prome). The brick ruins of Sri Ksetra still clearly display extensive evidence of their brand of religious architecture – mainly Buddhist in style, but with a noticeably strong Brahman influence.

About the 8th century, the Pyus relocated their capital north to Halin, in the region of Shwebo. At about the same time, the Tai people were pressing southward from their ancestral home in Yunnan. As a part of the powerful Nan-chao dynasty, the Tais subju-

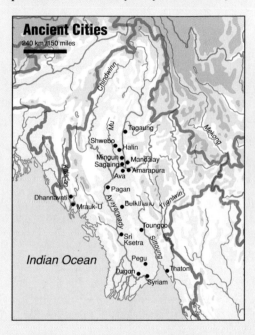

Ancient Cities

240 km/150 miles

Indian Ocean

gated Upper Burma in the 9th century, attacking Halin in 832, and enslaving the population. Very little mention of the Pyus in a historical literature can be found from that time onwards.

It was also in the 9th century that the Mramma people, now known as the Bamars, first made their appearance. Coming from the China-Tibet border area, they moved down the Ayeyarwady (Irrawady), overran the Kyaukse plain, and established themselves as the major power in the rice-cultivating region of the north. From Bagan (Pagan), which they built into a fortified town, they could control the Ayeyarwady and

Sittoung river valleys as well as the trade routes between China and India.

According to the *Glass Palace Chronicle*, Bagan had actually been founded in AD 108. But the town's first nine centuries of recorded existence are viewed with some skepticism because the *Chronicle,* which tells its story, did not appear until 1829.

Anawrahta established the First Burmese Empire in 1057 when he suddenly and overwhelmingly conquered the Mon capital of Thaton. He returned to Bagan with 30,000 prisoners, including the Mon royal family and many master builders.

Other Mon and Pyu settlements submitted to Anawrahta's dominance over Burma, and

Pagoda in Nyaung U (near Bagan), as well as other shrines on the dry plain.

Bagan's golden age: It was only under Anawrahta's second successor, Kyanzittha (1084–1113), that the golden age of pagoda-building began. Kyanzittha, whose name means "soldier lord", came to power after his troops had crushed a Mon rebellion during which Anawrahta's son and successor, Sawlu, was killed.

Like Anawrahta, Kyanzittha was a highly religious man. He ordered the construction of the Ananda Temple, and sent a ship filled with treasures to Bengal to assist in the restoration of the famed Mahabodhi Temple in Bodhgaya, the place of Buddha's enlight-

the king reigned for 33 years.

Ironically, despite the Mons' defeat, their culture became supreme in the Bamar capital. The Mon language replaced Pali and Sanskrit in royal inscriptions, and the Theravada Buddhist religion became predominant. Through the close relations maintained by the Mons with Sri Lanka – at that time the center of Theravadin culture – "the way of the elders" spread throughout the whole of Southeast Asia.

Under this new influence, especially from the monk Shin Arahan, Anawrahta became a devout convert to Theravada Buddhism. He commissioned the building of the Shwezigon

enment. Kyanzittha gave his daughter away in marriage to a Mon prince, and chose their son, Alaungsithu, as his successor to preserve the unity of the Burmese Empire.

Bagan's golden age came during the 12th century, a time in which it acquired the name "city of the four million pagodas." This civilization was supported by rice cultivation, made possible by a highly developed system of irrigation canals.

But in the middle of the 13th century, the empire began to crumble. The culturally sustaining power of Buddhism quickly abated, and the Shan – descendants of the Tai – threatened from northern Burma. And to hasten the end of the empire, there arose the Mongol army of Kublai Khan.

The Khan and his forces, whose homeland was in Central Asia, had occupied the Nanchao Empire in Yunnan. They now expected payment of tribute by the Bagan emperors. King Narathihapate, overestimating the strength of his own forces, refused.

When Khan's forces invaded Burma in a series of battles, advancing as far as present-day Bhamo, it is said that in desperation, Narathihapate pulled down 6,000 temples to fortify Bagan's city walls. Despite his attempts to defend his empire, Narathihapate was branded with the title *Tarok-pyemin*, which means "the king who ran away from

After the fall of Bagan, Burma was divided into several states of varying sizes for almost 300 years. In Lower Burma, the Mons founded a new kingdom in the town of Bago (Pegu). Although they lost their grip on Tanintharyi (Tenasserim) during a mid-14th century invasion by the Thais (Siamese) from Ayutthia, they managed to hold the rest of the realm together.

In Upper Burma, the Shans established sovereignty over a Burmese kingdom with its capital at Innwa (Ava). And in the west, along the Bay of Bengal, Rakhine spread north to Chittagong inwhat is present-day Bangladesh.

Between 1385 and 1425, the Mons and

the Chinese". The unfortunate king died soon after, poisoned by his son, the ruler of Pyay. The end result was the annihilation of the Burmese armies in the battle of Vochan, and the subsequent conquest of Bagan by the Mongols in 1287.

The Mons, supported by the Shan leader Wareru, withdrew from the First Burmese Empire, and the Rakhines (Arakanese) on the Bay of Bengal did the same.

Left, Bagan in the 13th century when the Mongols invaded. **Right**, a galleon typical of those on which the Portuguese arrived along the Rakhine coast during the 16th century.

Shans engaged in a long war. Despite the conflict, Theravada Buddhism underwent a revival in the court of Bago (Pegu), to where monks and scholars from all over Southeast Asia flocked.

It was in the 15th century that Europeans began to make inroads into Burma. In 1435, a Venetian merchant named Nicolo di Conti visited Bago and remained for four months. Decades later in 1498, the Portuguese seafarer Vasco da Gama discovered the sea route from Europe to India, and his countrymen were very quick to take advantage of his great success.

The Portuguese period: Alfonso de Albu-

WHEN THE EARTH SHAKES

Earthquakes are as much a part of Burmese history as Buddhism. From the earliest times, the Burmese people have lived with earthquakes which have caused rivers to flow upstream, entire coastal regions to emerge from the sea, and golden *pyathat* to tumble from stupas and pagodas.

In contrast to the scientific Western mind, the Burmese see hidden meanings behind these "catastrophes." The Buddha told his followers that earthquakes occurred upon the conception of a future Buddha, at the time of a Buddha's birth, his enlightenment, his first sermon, and his death and entrance into nirvana. The coming

of a *chakravarti* (universal monarch), his coronation and death were also believed to be signaled by great upheavals in the earth's crust.

In addition, Burmese cosmology dictates that the physical world and all planes of existence comprise a single indivisible unit. The shaking of the earth is a reminder that inhabitants of the Asian "island" constitute only a small part of the cosmic whole. In this framework, earthquakes are viewed as physical evidence of major occurrences on other planes of existence, and therefore indicative of great changes in the making.

One legend tells of an enormous tremor which could have occurred during the 5th century BC (perhaps at the time of the Buddha's entry into nibbana). The soil on which Sri Ksetra was later built rose from the seabed; two new rivers began

to flow; and Mount Popa, Burma's sacred mountain, bulged from the central plain.

Another legend well-known among the Burmese people relates the fall of the 9th century Pyu capital of Halin. It is said that the Pyu king's brother had a smile so wonderful, it was always followed by a shower of gold over the city. When the kingdom's coffers were exhausted, all it took was a smile to refill them.

One day, the king needed gold and ordered his brother to smile. Unfortunately, the brother, who had just heard about the imminent destruction of Halin, was only able to cry. The king shouted in anger, and his great rage instigated a massive earthquake which swallowed up the whole city as well as its inhabitants.

Many major earthquakes have been recorded through the centuries. Whenever stupas were destroyed by movements of the earth, stone inscriptions erected on the renovated sites told of these quakes – and named the Burmese who gained merit by doing the repair work.

Every temple and pagoda in Burma today has suffered damage by earthquakes. Be it the Shwedagon, the Shwemawdaw, or the Ananda, all have lost their *htis* (upper "umbrellas") or have collapsed at one time or another during centuries past. It has been left to faithful Buddhists to restore the stupas, increasing their karma at the same time.

In the 20th century, there have been two major earthquakes which have left scars that are still clearly visible today. On May 5, 1930, a tremor shook the whole of southern Burma. Its epicentre was at the old Mon city of Bago, and most of the community's ancient monuments, including the Shwemawdaw and Mahazedi pagodas and the Kalyani Sima, were utterly destroyed. It has taken five decades, but the Shwemawdaw and Kalyani Sima have been rebuilt, and reconstruction work on the Mahazedi was completed only in the early 1980s.

The most recent of the major earthquakes occurred on July 8, 1975, when the jewel of Burma – the ancient city of Bagan – was shaken as never before. Initially, it was feared that the damage to the monuments had been so severe that reconstruction would have been impossible. That, however, was not the case.

Today – thanks to an international effort initiated by the United Nations Educational, Scientific and Cultural Organization (UNESCO) – most of Burma's great buildings have been restored to their former splendour. The Burmese government gladly accepted all financial assistance from outside sources, but no foreign architect or structural engineer was permitted to lay a hand on the monuments of Bagan. The ancient temples and pagodas were reconstructed with the same care and in the traditional Burmese fashion just as they had been built centuries ago. ∎

querque conquered Goa in 1510, and within a year Malacca, the spice centre of the Orient, was in his grasp. It was from these two ports that the Portuguese managed to controll all of their Indian colonies.

Antony Correa arrived in Martaban in 1519 and signed a trade and settlement treaty with the town's viceroy. The treaty gave the Portuguese a port of trade with Siam without making the long sea journey through the Straits of Malacca.

Bago's King Tabinshweti however, would not tolerate the Portuguese presence in his vassal state. In 1541, he laid siege to Martaban, and surprisingly was joined by 700 Portuguese who opposed their country-

Portuguese era in Burma was Philip de Brito y Nicote. De Brito came to Asia as a cabin boy and later accepted a post in the royal court of King Razagyi of Rakhine, who had conquered Bago.

De Brito was entrusted with the job of running the customs administration in Syriam (then called Thanhlyn). Before long, de Brito had constructed forts and placed the town under Portuguese sovereignty. After a trip to Goa, during which he married the viceroy's daughter, he returned to Syriam with supplies and reinforcements to withstand native sieges (as Bamars and Rakhines had already attempted), and proclaimed himself king of Lower Burma.

men's decision to side with the viceroy of Martaban. When Tabinshweti was successful and solidified his grip on the Second Burmese Empire, the Portuguese maintained their hold on Martaban as a trading settlement until 1613. Meanwhile, the Portuguese also allied themselves with the king of Myohaung (Mrauk-U) in Rakhine, thereby controlling the sea routes of the Bay of Bengal, often as pirates, for 100 years.

The most remarkable character from the

Above left, a Burmese prince and **right**, princess of Upper Burma's long-reigning Konbaung dynasty period.

De Brito's superior naval power forced all seagoing trade to his port of Syriam. During his 13-year reign, 100,000 native people were said to have been converted to Christianity. But his religiousness was limited only to Christianity. He displayed utter contempt for Buddhist monuments and relics, destroying and plundering them wherever he went. The Buddhist holy leaders condemned him to eternal damnation in the deepest hell of the Buddhist cosmos – and, indeed, he came to a horrific end.

In 1613, Anaukhpetlun of Toungoo stormed Syriam with a force of 12,000 men. The 400 or so Portuguese and their followers defended the town for 34 days until they ran out of gunpowder. De Brito was captured and impaled: it took three days for him to die. The rest of the Portuguese and Eurasians in Syriam – called *Bayingyis* – were exiled to villages near Shwebo in Upper Burma, where they established a settlement.

Rise and fall of an empire: In north Burma meanwhile, hill tribes had attacked and burned down the Shan capital of Innwa in 1527. The Bamar population withdrew to the town of Toungoo, where Tabinshweti established his empire before moving it to Bago. After his victory over Martaban, he extended his control down the Tanintharyi coast to Dawei (Tavoy), and west to Pyay on the

deported the French to Bayingyi, and burned down the British trading posts. Mon resistance ceased entirely, and the Mon people either fled to Siam or became assimilated with the Bamars.

Alaungpaya's second successor, Hsinbyushin, attacked Ayutthia in 1767 and returned to Innwa with artists and craftsmen who gave a fresh cultural impetus to the Burmese kingdom. Bodawpaya, who took the throne in 1782, conquered Rakhine, bringing the borders of his kingdom right up against the British sphere of influence in Bengal. On the advice of his soothsayers, he moved his capital to Amarapura, not far from Innwa.

Because Burma and British India now

central Ayeyarwady. His son-in-law and successor, Bayinnaung, overwhelmed the Shans and conquered the Tai kingdoms of Chiangmai and Ayutthia, thus extending Burma's boundaries to the maximum.

During the 17th century, the Dutch, British and French set up trading companies in ports along the coast of Burma. When the country's capital was transferred back to Innwa, it was retaken by the Mons in 1752 with the help of French arms. As a result, the Second Burmese Empire foundered and dissolved.

Soon afterwards, however, Alaungpaya, a Bamar from Shwebo, founded the Third Burmese Empire. He defeated the Mons,

shared a common boundary, the number of border incidents increased. Royal Burmese troops frequently pursued rebels over the border and deep into Indian territory.

Serious conflict was sparked after King Bagyidaw came to the throne in 1819. The Raja of Manipur, who previously had paid tribute to the Burmese crown, did not attend Bagyidaw's coronation. The subsequent punitive expedition took the Burmese into the Indian state of Cachar, and this intrusion was used by the British as a pretext for what is now called the First Anglo-Burmese War.

The Burmese badly underestimated the strength of the British, and were soundly defeated. In the Treaty of Yandabo (1826), the Burmese were forced to cede Rakhine and Tanintharyi, plus Assam and Manipur border areas taken in 1819, to the European victors. The British thereby succeeded in making secure their exposed flanks on the Bay of Bengal, which had been their aim all along in fighting the war.

The Burmese were without a capable ruler through the first half of the 19th century. Part of the reason for this was that no institutionalized system had been set up for transfer of power upon a ruler's death. Since this weakened the kingdom during the period of rapid European colonial expansion, when British and French interests collided in Southeast

It was about this time that King Mindon (1853–1878) came to power in Amarapura. His was an enlightened rule. Mindon was the first Burmese sovereign to attempt to bring the country more in line with Western ideas. He readily sent young men to be educated in Europe, reformed the structure of his government, and made halting first steps toward industrialization.

Mindon's Mandalay: In 1861, commemorating the 2,400th anniversary of the preaching of the Buddha's first sermon, Mindon transferred his court to the new city of Mandalay.

Mandalay was sacred to the Buddhist faith, and in 1872 Mindon hosted the Fifth Great Synod of Buddhism. In the threatening

Asia, Burma's days as an independent kingdom were rapidly nearing an end.

In 1852, two British sea captains registered a complaint about unfair treatment in a Burmese court. The British Empire responded by sending an expeditionary force to Burma. In the Second Anglo-Burmese War, this force quickly conquered Lower Burma.

Left, Burma's wars have varied as much in method as in result. Elephants were used in the 1767 invasion of the Siamese capital of Ayutthia. **Right**, Burmese troops sought refuge behind Yangon stockades during the First Anglo-Burmese War.

shadow of British expansionism, this synod – the first such gathering in nearly 2,000 years – was staged as a means of unifying all Burmese people under a single creed. It was during the Fifth Synod that the text of the *Tipitaka*, the Buddhist scripture recognized today as authentic, was written. Until then, the Buddhist scriptures had been written on perishable palm leaves.

King Mindon wanted the sacred scriptures to be conserved in a way that they would be available until the end of Buddha's religion – another 2600 years. Hence, some 2,400 scribes worked on the text, which was then chiseled onto 729 tablets of stone. In addition, a pagoda was built over each of the tablets at the base of Mandalay Hill. The scriptures are so lengthy that a book version consists of 38 volumes of 400 pages each. But even this appeal for a return to the values of Buddhism, which would thereby sustain the Burmese state and people, could no longer alter the course of history.

Mindon was succeeded by King Thibaw, who wasted little time in alienating the British. When a smallpox epidemic struck Mandalay in 1880, soothsayers recommended the capital again be transferred – but Thibaw rejected this as unfeasible.

The French, meanwhile, were negotiating an agreement with Thibaw for shipping rights

on the Ayeyarwady. They sought a direct trade route to China, but this was clearly contrary to the interests of the British. When a British timber company became embroiled in a dispute with Thibaw's government, the king was issued an ultimatum. In no time, British troops had invaded Upper Burma, and with virtually no resistance, easily overwhelmed the capital.

On January 1, 1886, Burma ceased to exist as an independent kingdom. Thibaw and his queen, Supyalat, were forced to leave the country, and Burma was annexed as a province of British India.

In order to facilitate their exercise of power over the whole of Burma, the British permitted the autonomy of the country's many racial minorities. As early as 1875, they had enforced the autonomy of the Kayin (Karen) states by refusing to supply King Mindon with the arms he needed to put down a Kayin revolt. The repercussions of this and similar political moves by the British are still influencing modern Burma.

Throughout Upper and Lower Burma, the British assumed all government positions down to the district officer level. In the bordering states where Chins, Kachins, Shans and other minorities predominated, the British relied on indirect rule, permitting the respective chieftains to govern in their place. Military forces were largely recruited from India and the northern hill tribes. Throughout most of the colonial period, Bamars were, under British decree, barred from admission to the armed forces, hence greatly intensifying the already strained interracial tensions in Burma.

British interest in Burma was principally of an economic nature. So it is understandable that an economic upswing took place after 1886. The Ayeyarwady Delta had been opened up for rice cultivation and colonized following the British occupation of Lower Burma in 1852.

A generation later, this move began to pay back big dividends. The economic growth was to the advantage both of the British, who controlled the rice exports, and the Indian money lenders and merchants, who were far ahead of the Burmese in familiarity with a money economy. In particular, the *chettyars*, a caste of moneylenders from south India, profited a great deal from Burma's agricultural expansion.

In the five years following annexation of Upper Burma, a quasi-guerrilla war tied up some 10,000 Indian troops in the country's regions. The guerrillas were led by *myothugyis*, local leaders of the old social structure. But this resistance fell away after 1890, and from then on, the Burmese attempted to keep pace peacefully with the far-reaching social and economic changes that were taking place.

Left, the only portrait of King Mindon, founder of Mandalay, hangs today in the Kyauk-Tawgyi Pagoda. **Right**, a nostalgic portrait of a Burmese man and traditions past.

A BURMESE MAN
438

P. KLIER RANG

449
BURMESE FESTIVAL CART
P. KLIER. RANGOON.

47

The first important nationalist organization of the 20th century was the Young Men's Buddhist Association (YMBA), founded in 1906 when a group of London-trained lawyers merged with the Buddhist elite of Burma. It played an important role in the nation's politics in years to come.

Following World War I, India had been granted a degree of self-government by its British sovereigns. But Burma remained under the direct control of the Colonial Governor. This led to extensive opposition within the country, highlighted by a lengthy boycott of schools beginning in December 1920. Finally, in 1923, the same condition granted India – known as the "dyarchy reform" – was extended to Burma as well.

A major revolt took place in the Tharrawaddy region north of Yangon between 1930 and 1932. Saya San, a former monk, organized a group of followers called *Galons* (after the mythical bird), and convinced them that British bullets could not harm them. In a subsequent battle, 3,000 of his supporters were killed and another 9,000 were taken prisoner, of whom 78, including Saya San, were executed.

Throughout the early 1930s, opinion was divided in Burma as to whether the country should be separated from British India or whether it should remain as part of that dominion. The question was resolved in 1935 when the "Government of Burma Act" was signed in London. Two years later, Burma became a separate colony with its own Legislative Council. This council dealt only with "Burma Proper" however, and not with the indirectly-ruled border states.

However, as Burma was gaining a greater degree of autonomy, the underground nationalist movement was gaining momentum. In 1930 at the University of Yangon, the All Burma Student Movement emerged to defy the British system. The young men who spear-headed this group studied Marxism

Preceding pages: Burmese festival cart in scene from the past. **Left,** statue of modern Burma's founding father Bogyoke Aung San, near Yangon's Royal Lake. **Right,** a British soldier marvels at a Buddha in the Shwedagon.

and called each other *Thakin*, a title of respect (like the Hindi *Sahib*) previously used exclusively in addressing Europeans. In 1936, the group's leaders – Thakin Aung San and Thakin Nu – boldly led another strike of university and high school classes in opposition to the "alien" educational system.

The success of their movement in bringing about major reforms helped to give these young men the confidence in the following decade to come to the forefront of the nationalist movement.

Meanwhile however, war was brewing. The "Burma Road" made that inevitable. Built as an all-weather route in the 1930s to carry supplies and reinforcements to Chinese troops attempting to repulse the Japanese invasion, it was of extreme strategic importance. As Allied forces moved to defend the road, the Japanese made plans for an all-out attack on the Burmese heartland.

The colonial government unexpectedly played into the Japanese hands when it arrested several leaders of the Thakin organization in 1940. Aung San escaped by disguising himself as a Chinese crewman on a Norwegian boat. He arrived in Amoy seek-

majority of the votes (60 percent) that would have resulted in its domination of the *Pyithu Hluttaw*. However, according to the *tatmadaw*, the role of the elected members was never clearly stated before the election. Hence, the military demanded that a new constitution had first to be drafted by a national convention in which different groups, including the military, should have a say. In spite of the free elections and the clear democratic vote, the *Pyithu Hluttaw* could not be convened.

In 1993, assisted by pressure from China, the KIO, the Kachin Independence Organisation, signed a cease-fire agreement with the Yangon government, thus ending a 30-year

war in the north of the country. This was soon followed by agreements with 14 other insurgent groups. Most important for the region was the faltering of the BCP, once an eminent contender for power and the fiercest foe of the armed forces.

By 1995, only Khun Sa's forces and the Kayin KNU had not signed cease-fire agreements with the government. With most of the insurgent groups returning to the "legal fold," the national convention, in which Aung San Suu Kyi, the spiritual leader of the NLD, is not taking part, is about to be concluded. In the draft form of the new constitution, the *tatmadaw* reserves for itself the final say in all matters of national unity, as is the case with some other Southeast Asian nations, especially with the Indonesian *dwifungsi* system. In this system, the military and the civilian sector of society share power, but the military reserves for itself "a leading role in national politics." It will depend on the final content of this new constitution and its acceptance by the Burmese if peace and prosperity will return to the country.

In spite of the quasi-boycott of Western nations barring Burma from loans of the World Bank and assistance of the International Monetary Fund, the *tatmadaw* has managed to get the economy going by attracting Southeast Asian, Chinese, French and American capital. The GDP has grown by 6.5 percent, though the per capita GDP is still at US$235, about half of India's.

New banknotes have been issued, the tourist visa period extended to four weeks and FECs are issued at the value of the former black-market rate. Nevertheless, Western nations, led by the United States, are pressing for the return to a purely civilian and democratic government. The "National Coalition Government of the Union of Burma," which sees itself as the legally elected body to represent the country, has set up its exile office in Washington, DC.

In July 1995 Aung San Suu Kyi was freed from six years of house arrest. In one of her first press interviews, she indicated her willingness to work together with the *tatmadaw* to find a peaceful solution of the constitutional impasse.

After Aung San Suu Kyi's release, Burma was officially invited to the annual ASEAN meeting in Brunei. There, Burma signed the Treaty of Amity and Cooperation, which gave it an automatic observer status in this regional group. ASEAN has opted for a constructive engagement policy to support the present government's stated intention of a slow but peaceful transformation.

SLORC secretary Lieutenant General Khin Nyunt has indicated that as soon as the new constitution has been drawn, the *tatmadaw* will hand over power to a civil government. If that should indeed happen, Burma might attain the status of a full member of ASEAN by the year 2000.

The dream of democracy has had a turbulent past.

TEARS OF THE POPPY

Throughout the 1970s and into much of the 1980s and 1990s, photographs in Western news media depicted caravans of 200 or more mules, stretching for miles through the roadless hills of Southeast Asia, carrying up to 20 tons of raw opium.

It is believed that this drug, destined for the high schools, military barracks and ghettos of the industrial nations, is produced in this mountainous region known as the Golden Triangle. The largest part of the area falls in Burma's Shan State, encompassing parts of Thailand, Laos, and China's Yunnan province.

With an average elevation of more than 1,000 metres (3,280 ft), the Triangle offers ideal growing conditions for *papaver somniferum*, commonly called the Eurasian poppy. This is the raw material from which heroin is derived.

Opium, known in Burma as "the tears of the poppy," has been in use locally as medicine and as a relaxant ever since the present inhabitants of Southeast Asia immigrated here from the great plains of Central Asia.

Burmese kings prohibited the use of the drug, and meted out punishment by pouring liquid lead down the throats of offenders.

During the British administration of Burma, opium usage constituted no problem. The British even fought two colonial wars in support of the sale of opium, and it was not until 1906 that the House of Commons in London declared the opium trade "immoral."

Decades later, Southeast Asia's struggle for independence from colonial powers brought opium sharply to the forefront of world attention in the mid-20th century. The Western nations' fear of communism in the 1950s and 1960s was so great, they gave tacit approval to anything which could stop the spread of the ideology. In order to pay local mercenary troops fighting for them, the French and the Americans encouraged a multi-million dollar opium business under the charge of Kuomintang (Nationalist Chinese) troops, who had settled in the Golden Triangle after fleeing the communist takeover of China, and Shan rebels. The latter used their revenues to support their revolutionary struggle against Burma's new government.

By the end of the 1960s, it had become obvious that the only way to stop the cultivation and distribution of opium would be to alter the entire political landscape of the Golden Triangle region. The various tribes who had become involved as producers or middle men, including the Wa, Lisu, Lahu, Akha and Lu, had become so used to the easy money from this commodity that no other cash crop, neither coffee nor tea,

would be a satisfactory substitute.

Meanwhile, the new governments of Indochina have outlawed the opium trade, and are fighting a rigorous war against hill tribes which have not complied with the new regulations.

The Burmese government confirmed that it would raze every cultivated field it could find – if it could assert any political authority over the Golden Triangle region. Growing poppy is the main occupation of the population in the Trans-Salween region which, until recently, has been under the control of the BCP (Burma Communist Party); the area still lacks the sway of law and, it seems, will remain so for some time to come.

Khun Sa, called the kingpin of the Golden Triangle and head of state of the self-proclaimed independent Shan State, controls the Mong Tai Army. In trying to appear as a political figure, he

has offered that he would stop any opium growing and trade if the western nations would recognize his Shan State as an independent nation, thus involuntarily confirming that he runs the opium theatre.

It is unlikely that the opium trade in the country will fade for a long time. A form of highly refined heroin, called No.4 or Double Uoglobe, is currently being produced at the laboratories in the Shan border region. This strain is so concentrated, it takes up about one-tenth of the space of raw opium – thus reducing logistical problems during shipment and transportation. The newest strain from the region is so potent that it doesn't even have to be injected – it can be sniffed or smoked, thus posing an increased danger to the developed nations. ∎

By the old Moulmein Pagoda, lookin' lazy at the sea,
There's a Burma girl a settin', and I know she thinks o' me . . .
An' I seed her first a-smokin' of a whickin' white cheroot,
An' a wastin' Christian kisses on an 'eathen idol's foot . . .
—*Rudyard Kipling (1889)*

A BURMESE LADY, BY
P. KLIER RANGOON

"Burma...is peopled by so many races that truly we know not how many; nor who they are, nor whence they came. In no other area are the races so diverse, or the languages and dialects so numerous..."
– C.M. Enriquez, *Races of Burma* (1933)

The old name "Union of Burma" implies that the nation is a federation of many peoples. But it is an uneasy federation. "Burma Proper," (as it was called by the British) chief settlement area of the Bamar (Burman) majority, is encircled by separate minority states of the Chin, Kachin, Shan, Kayin (Karen), Kayah (Red Karen), Mons and Rakhines (Arakanese). Through the centuries, there have been mistrust, antagonism, and frequent wars among the various races. The situation is no different today.

The current administrative divisions were built into Burma's 1948 constitution, based on the model devised by the British. During the colonial era, the British – with their principle of "divide and rule" – made a distinction between "Burma Proper" and "Outer Burma," the latter comprising the settlement areas of the ethnic minorities. "Burma Proper" was placed under the direct rule of British India, but the minorities were left with much greater autonomy under an indirect rule.

While the Bamars were denied a place in the colonial army, the various minorities were heavily depended upon for their fighting skills. The racial enmity between the Bamars and the minorities festered just beneath the surface until independence was granted. Since that time, more than a generation of violent domestic confrontations have played havoc with the nation's hopes of internal peace.

No less than 67 separate indigenous racial groups have been identified in Burma, not including the various Indians, Chinese and Europeans who make the country their home. A survey in the late British colonial period determined that 242 separate languages and

Preceding pages: taking a photographic journey through a nostalgic Burmese portrait gallery. **Left**, a lacquer worker in Myinkaba.

dialects were spoken.

Traces of prehistoric man: Long before ancestors of the modern Burmese moved east and south from central Asia and Tibet, prehistoric people inhabited the area that is now known as Burma.

Caves and rock shelters in the mountains and fertile river valleys were home for these proto-Australoids. Not yet acquainted with agricultural techniques, they lived by hunting and gathering. Stone chips and other vestiges of their primitive culture have been

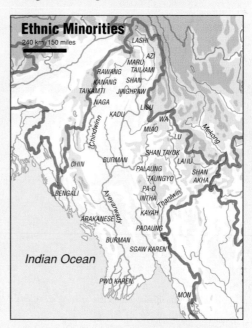

found in western Shan State.

These aborigines gradually mixed with the Austronesians, and eventually moved on toward what is today Indonesia. No trace of them is found in the present-day population of Burma. The Andaman Islanders, who live in the middle of the Bay of Bengal south of Burma, and the Semang of the Malay Peninsula might be direct descendants.

In historic times, three separate migrations are important in Burma's history.

First to arrive were the Mon-Khmer people. They came from the arid, wind-swept plains of Central Asia, and it is not difficult to imagine their motivation. Anyone who has seen the mountains of golden rice, piled high at harvest time, will understand why the first Mon-Khmer kingdom was called Suvannabhumi, the "Golden Land."

Then came a second wave of immigrants, the Tibeto-Burmans, who pushed the Mon-Khmer people further to the south and east, away from the middle reaches of the Ayeyarwady (Irrawaddy). First the Pyus, then the Bamars moved down the valleys of the Ayeyarwady and Sittoung (Sittang) rivers, establishing their magnificent empires at Sri Ksetra and Bagan (Pagan).

Between the 12th and 14th centuries, the third migration took place. The Tais (known today in Burma as Shans), a Sino-Tibetan

race who had settled in Yunnan in the 7th century, began moving south down the river valleys. When they tried to force the Bamars out of the Ayeyarwady Valley, centuries of warfare followed – with mixed success on both sides. In the end, the Bamars clung to their home-land. The Tais established themselves in the Shan Hills and the Menam (Chao Phraya) River valley in present-day Thailand.

Even today, there remains a tendency of the mountain peoples to migrate toward the south. The Kachins were moving in that direction when the British assumed administration of northern Burma late in the 19th century. The quest for better living conditions and, in very remote areas, the simple search for arable land - inspire such movement, and underlie the antagonism dividing the races of Burma.

The Bamars in control: As the majority racial group and the predominant landholder, as well as the group holding the reins of the present government, the Bamars bear the brunt of much interracial hostility.

Their settlement area is in the divisions of Yangon (Rangoon), Ayeyarwady, Pathein (Bassein), Bago (Pegu), Magway (Magwe), Mandalay and Sagaing, as well as Rakhine (Arakan) State, Mon State and Tanintharyi (Tenasserim). It is this in these regions that 70 percent of Burma's peoples live.

Most of the cultural forms described in later sections of this book are most representative of the Bamars, who typically live in thatched dwellings and work as wet-rice farmers. Perhaps their greatest cosmetic trademark is the pale yellow powder, made from *thanaka* bark, which their women apply to their cheeks and foreheads as a protection against the tropical sun. Traditional dress is the wrap-around *longyi*, which is not unlike the Malaysian sarong.

The once-great Mons: Nestled mainly around the cities of Mawlamyine (Moulmein) and Bago are the Mons. Before the Bamars came, they were the most powerful group in Burma. In 1995, after decades of armed resistance, they signed a cease-fire agreement with the *tatmadaw.*

Today, the Mons - who number just over 1 million – are largely assimilated in the mainstream of Burmese culture, although they continue to use their own distinct language, and have retained their own state within the Burmese union.

The Mons are at home in the monsoonal plains of Burma's southeast. Far from being slash-and-burn agriculturists, they prefer an area with plenty of rain to pursue wet-rice growing. They also produce crops such as yams, sugar cane and pineapples, as well as catch fish and snare birds. Ardent Buddhists, they observe their own ceremonial calendar of Theravadin festivals.

Burmese Mons constitute only a small part of the Mon-Khmer race. The majority of their "cousins" live further east on the Indochinese peninsula – in Thailand, Cambodia and Vietnam.

North of the Mon State, firmly ensconced in Shan territory, is another large group of Mon-Khmer speakers – the Palaungs. Unlike their southern cousins, they are hill dwellers and dedicated dry-rice agriculturists. Tea is their principal cash crop. Devout Buddhists and *nat* worshipers, their stockaded villages traditionally contain not only a monastery, but also spirit shrines.

The Padaung "giraffe women": Among the smaller minority groups belonging to the Mon-Khmer language family are the Padaungs and the Wa. Both groups have gained a certain fame – or notoriety – that far exceeds their meagre numbers.

There are only about 7,000 Padaungs, all

six. Year after year, new rings are added, until by the time of marriage, their necks are 25 centimetres (10 in) long.

Despite the illusion, the women's necks have not been elongated at all. In fact, their collarbones and ribs have been pushed down. But the resulting effect is essentially the same. Since no muscles can develop where the heavy rings support the head, the rings become a permanent necessity. If the rings are cut off as they were in the past as a punishment for adultery, the head can actually flop over and suffocation can follow unless a neck brace is worn.

It is conjectured that this unusual custom dates from a time when the Padaungs were

of whom live in the vicinity of Loikaw, capital of Kayah State. Their "giraffe women" have been highly publicized by various ethnographers of the 19th and 20th centuries, as well as by *National Geographic*.

Padaung women's necks give the appearance of having been elongated by the 9 kilograms (20 lbs) of copper or brass rings which rest around their throats. Young girls receive their first neck rings - as well as rings for the arms and ankles – at the age of five or

Left, painting a pretty picture of the physical deformity of a Padaung "giraffe woman". **Right**, playful young novices of the Sangha.

subject to frequent slave raids from larger tribes. By deforming their women in this manner, they were able to dissuade would-be captors from stealing them away. Some even claim the rings served as protection against tiger bites. As time passed, the original purposes became superfluous. But the custom has remained.

The wild, wild Wa: The other Mon-Khmer people of special interest are the Wa, the notorious frontier inhabitants of Burma's northeast flank.

About 300,000 Wa people live in remote habitats on both sides of the border with China. Until the 1940s, there was little known about them – except that they were head-hunters who offered human skulls as sacrifices to their gods. They too, have signed a peace agreement with the *tatmadaw*. However, it will take a long time until they are integrated into mainstream Burmese life.

In the 1960s, due to the political turmoil ravaging Indochina, the Wa came into the focus of world attention, the reason being that they were the main suppliers of raw opium in the "Golden Triangle."

Originally, the Wa had been dry paddy agriculturists, using traditional slash-and-burn methods to grow their staple rice crop. But their numbers outgrew their ability to support themselves. Hence the opium poppy,

nist raids. The CIA bought their opium poppies to finance the mercenary units which fought during the Vietnam War. And last but not least, the Peking-supported Burmese Communist Party recruited them to fight in their ranks against the Yangon government.

Today, the KMT units have resettled in northern Thailand or have flown to Taiwan. Meanwhile, substitute cash crops like coffee and tea have (with only little success) been introduced in the Golden Triangle.

At the beginning of the 1990's, the Peoples Republic of China stopped supporting the BCP whose forces have been dismantled or have gone across the border into China. Most of them are now in the United Wa State

until then a secondary product, became the Wa's principle cash crop.

After the post-World War II communist takeover in China, the Wa people were courted by many interest groups. The Kuomintang (KMT), or Chinese Nationalists, who had to flee the new People's Republic; the American Central Intelligence Agency (CIA); the communist rebels in Burma; they all sought to employ the Wa to serve their own purposes.

Because their settlement area was so secluded, the Wa were able to penetrate China's Yunnan province without detection, and thus were used by the KMT in anti-commu-

Army that signed a peace agreement with the SLORC government and opposes Khun Sa's Mong Tai Army.

All this means that difficult times are ahead for the Wa. Their methods of planting and harvesting are outmoded, and they will have to find new ways to survive.

"Free people" with a feudal past: Most of the Burmese Wa live in the eastern part of the Shan State. But their numbers are small compared to the 3.9 million Shan people (1989 census) of this vast district.

Thanaka-**bark makeup is a traditional part of the Burmese woman's beauty regime.**

THE PATH OF LIFE

There are few countries in the world today in which tradition has such a strong influence on everyday life as it has in Burma. The colonial period did not pass without affecting the Burmese; rationalism, science and realism profoundly altered commerce and national affairs. But daily life is still dominated by old values, and the path of life that a typical Burmese goes through has undergone little change over the generations.

Childhood years, from birth to marriage: Seven days after birth, the baby's parents invite friends to a naming ceremony. The youngster is given a name based on astrological calculations, and it need bear no relation to that of the parents.

The child is sent to school at the age of five. However, despite a system of compulsory education and strenuous efforts by the government since independence to ensure education for all, there are still areas with no state schools. In these places, the local *kyaung* (monastery) takes charge of the child's elementary education.

When a boy is nine years old, his *shin-pyu* takes place. This is an initiation ceremony marking the end of his childhood and the beginning of a period of monkhood. Girls of the same age participate in an ear-piercing ceremony called the *nahtwin*, which also symbolizes a farewell to the unburdened life of the child.

A number of social psychologists see this abrupt transformation from childhood to adulthood as the cause of the characteristic Burmese excitability – quickly passing, but ever present.

However, as two-thirds of the population still work on the arable land, the transition from school to adult life is relatively easy for most young people: during their school years, they help out with the harvest in their parents' fields.

Burmese tend to get married relatively young. The marriage itself requires no religious or civil ceremony, although it should be registered for the purpose of any future division of property.

Women, despite their lower status in Buddhist doctrine, have a secure place in society. Their rights were almost always equal to those of men, and are guaranteed by an uncomplicated divorce law. A woman does not change her name when married. If her marriage does break up, she can return to her parents at any time.

Traditional dress – longyi and gaung-baung: Burmese emphasize their feeling of national identity through the clothes they wear. Most evident is the *longyi*. Similar to the Malaysian sarong, it consists of a kilt-like piece of cloth worn from the waist to the ankle. Together with the *eingyi*, a transparent blouse which is also worn with a round-collared, long-sleeved jacket,

the *longyi* still takes precedence over the imported style Western garments.

The traditional headgear of the men, the *gaung-baung*, today is seen only on special occasions. During the colonial period, it was wrapped around the head like a turban, with different styles and colours according to one's social position. Today, it is superseded by a ready-made cap.

Burmese women attach great importance to jewellery. As rubies, sapphires, jade and pearls are found in significant quantities in Burma, it is common at festivals to see peasant women richly adorned with precious stones and such. The Burmese still regard the purchase of gems as the safest form of investment.

"Crossing the river" to old age and death: Not many young Burmese remain in the monkhood

for more than a few months or years after their *shin-pyu*. Some become *pongyis* and devote their entire lives to meditation and the teachings of the Buddha. To most adult Burmese, however, the Sangha is not merely a religious brotherhood. It is also an institution providing social insurance and old-age support.

Death has a different meaning for a Buddhist than it has for a Christian. When a Burmese dies, he is either buried or cremated. A coin is put in his mouth so he can pay the "ferryman" who transports him "across the river" into the next life. All persons close to the deceased are invited to the funeral. It is generally accepted that the dead person himself takes part in these rites, and that his spirit remains in his family's house for a week afterward. ∎

Shan. Siam. Assam. All three geographical names have the same root meaning – an indication of the widespread migration and settlement area of this race. The word means "free people," a theme which might have been the guiding force behind their medieval move down the alluvial plain of the majestic Chao Phraya river.

From the 15th century – when they were pushed back onto the Shan Plateau after early success in establishing an Ayeyarwady kingdom – until 1959, 34 *sawbwas*, or hereditary princes, ruled separate feudal principalities in medieval splendor, with serfs, slaves and mistresses. Their alliance of small states was recognized by the 1948 constitu-

cause of U Nu's apparent inability to deal with this problem (and others), Ne Win staged his military coup in 1962, and subsequently imprisoned some Shan leaders who had not fled Burma. They were released in 1968, but by that time their era had definitely passed. Some of them are now in self-imposed exile; others, highly educated scholars, teach at universities in Yangon and elsewhere; and those who responded to the 1980 amnesty have returned to their Shan homes.

In the 1990's, Khun Sa, who has been indicted in the United States as a drug dealer, declared an independent Shan State. He leads the MTA, the Mong Tai Army, a faction of which rebelled, disassociating itself from

tion, and was granted the right to withdraw from the "Union of Burma" after 10 years of membership therein.

But in 1959, the *sawbwas* signed an agreement with the Ne Win caretaker government, renouncing all their hereditary rights and privileges. In exchange, they accepted a payment of 25 million kyats (over US $4 million at 1991 exchange rates), a sum approximately equal to their revenues over a 15 to 25-year period.

Some of the *sawbwas* and their followers founded the Shan Independence Army, and in ensuing years attempted to wrest the Shan territory away from the government. Be-

Khun Sa's opium dealings, and set up its own SSNA, the Shan State National Army.

These groups are now under constant military attack from government forces and the Wa State Army. SLORC's Khin Nyunt, who lead most of the cease-fire agreements with the other rebelling minorities, declared that there would no longer be any negotiations with drug dealers.

Most Shans are Buddhists. This in itself distinguishes them from animistic hill people, who generally occupy the mountaintops and steep slopes. Burma's 3.9 million Shans make their homes in valleys and on high plains. After the Shan State, the Shans' next largest concentration is in Kachin State, but they can also be found throughout the nation.

With residences at an average altitude of 1,000 metres (3,280 ft) above sea level, the Shans are Burma's leading growers of fruit, vegetables and flowers. They have also developed stunning irrigation systems in the river valleys.

Shans are easily recognizable by their bathtowel turbans, worn by men and married women. Men generally dress in baggy, dark-blue trousers rather than in *longyis*, perhaps indicative of their Western outlook and related dependence on the smuggling trade from Thailand. Girls wear trousers and blouses until the age of 14, at which time they don colourful petticoats. As they get older, their costumes get less colourful, until – at age 40 – the women put away their bright garments and dress in sober black clothes for the rest of their lives.

The many faces of the Kayin: The Kayin people belong linguistically to the Tibeto-Burman-speaking majority of Burma. There are presently 2.7 million members of this race living in Burma. Although they have their own separate administrative division – the Karen (Kawthule) State – only about one-third of the Kayin population lives there. Other large numbers populate the Ayeyarwady division around Pathein, as well as the Kayah State (actually the realm of the so-called Red Karen), the Mon State and Tanintharyi.

There are three generally recognized groups of Kayin: the Pwo, who prefer lowland or delta homes; the Sgaw, including the Paku (White Karen or Kayin), Pa-O and other hill tribes; and the Bwe, whose subgroups include the Kayah (Red Karen), Karennet (Black Karen) and other remote mountain-dwelling peoples.

The Pwo in particular are conspicuous in the Ayeyarwady Delta, and are practically indistinguishable from the Bamars. They have to a high degree assimilated themselves into Burmese society, living in Bamar-style houses and devoting their energies to wet-rice farming. Even so, the "Karen Independence Movement" has gathered a force of

about 1,000 men in the delta region.

The Sgaw are less integrated into Burmese society than their Pwo cousins. Of all the many ethnic groups rebelling against the SLORC government, the "Karen National Liberation Army" is the best organized. Under the leadership of Bo Mya, the army has 8,000 well-equipped and trained soldiers.

In January 1995 the *tatmadaw* started its final offensive against the Kayin stronghold at Manerplaw. According to official statements it was the split between the DKBO, the Democratic Karen Buddhist Organization, which sided with government troops and the Christian dominated KNU that sealed the Karen's fate. On 21 February, their last

stronghold at Kawmoora fell. Consequently, thousands of Kayin refugees streamed into Thailand. The quasi-independent Karen State with its own administration, schools, infirmaries and social services had ceased to exist. Kayin leaders vowed to carry on the struggle in a guerrilla fashion, though negotiations between them and the SLORC are currently taking place.

Since the Kachin, the Kayinni (Karenni) and the Mon have withdrawn from the struggle against the central government, the Kayin and the Shan are now the only significant foes in the eastern border area. Thailand's "constructive engagement" policy towards

Left, a group of animistic Nagas from the isolated mountain country of northwestern Kachin State pose in ceremonial dress. **Right,** an elderly Kachin woman savours a puff on a local cheroot.

Yangon has also greatly diminished the support the Kayins once had.

For the simple slash-and-burn hilltop peasants, the rebel activities have little effect on daily life. They fight a continuous battle against drought and food shortages. As their population increases, the soil they farm is becoming unproductive and depleted of nutrients. Many Kayins now seek other jobs as *mahouts* (elephant riders) with woodcutters, or as miners in the tin mines. With few industries in the region, choices are slim.

Kayins are said to have migrated to Burma by stages from an original homeland in the Gobi Desert region of Mongolia, where they lived about 4,500 years ago. In tribal legends

that survive today, they still call the desert "the River of Sand".

Uncanny parallels between the Kayin legends and Bible stories led many colonial era missionaries to believe they had found one of the lost tribes of Israel. The name "Y'we," the name for their creative power, is remarkably similar to that of the Hebrew God, "Yahweh." Included in the Kayin scriptures is the story of a seven-day creation period, and of a serpent who persuaded the first man and woman to eat a forbidden fruit, after which they were subject to suffering, aging and death.

The missionaries found the Kayin eager to embrace the Christian religion, and today the Kayin are by far the largest Christian group within Burma.

Among the more unusual subgroups of the Sgaw Kayin are the Pa-O. These people, who number about 200,000, make their principal home near Taunggyi in the Shan State, to where they fled during Anawrahta's 11th century attack on Thaton. Their language is an older, purer tongue than standard modern Kayin; the written language of the Pa-O is unique.

The Red Karen of Kayah State: The Kayahs, or Red Karen, have the smallest state in Burma, in terms of area as well as population. Virtually all members of this ethnic group - about 75,000 – reside here.

During the British colonial era, the Kayahs were never officially incorporated into the Burma colony, instead maintaining autonomy in several feudal principalities known as the Karenni States. Given the same hereditary rights as Shan princes according to the 1948 constitution, the Kayah princes – whose territory was united as Kayah State in 1951 – relinquished their special rights at the same time as the Shans in 1959. During the 1960s, the feudal estates were split up and allotted to small farmers.

The Kayahs are primarily hill people, making their living through dry cultivation of rice, millet and vegetables. They are probably nicknamed the "Red Karen" because the colour is a favourite in the wardrobe of both men and women. However, the most startling aspect of their dress has nothing to do with colour. Women tie their calves with many garters of cord or rattan, often to a thickness of two inches, and these are then decorated with beads and seeds. Although walking and sitting thus become very difficult, this fashion is considered graceful.

The Kachins and other mountain people: Kachin State is the real hodgepodge of hill tribes in Burma. Throughout this large, heavily mountainous district in the nation's far north, Jinghpaws (Kachins), Shans and Bamars share space with Maru, Lashi, Azi, Lisu, Rawang, Tailiami, Tailon, Taikamti, Tailay, Kadu and Kanang villagers without any recognizable settlement pattern.

Mohamed Musa, South Indian manager of a biryani chicken restaurant in Yangon, serves a customer.

HOT AND SPICY

The menu in a standard restaurant in Burma is dominated by Indian curries and Chinese noodle and rice dishes. That isn't really surprising, given that Burma is located on the ancient India-China trade routes, and immigrants from both countries have influenced Burma with their famed cuisines.

There are traditional Burmese dishes, which in the past were hard to find. Fortunately, several traditional restaurants have opened recently. In Yangon, the Golden View Restaurant, the Royal Rose Restaurant and the Karaweik Restaurant cater to the more affluent. Otherwise, one must befriend a Burmese and get invited home for a truly native-style dinner.

Burma's geographic and cultural seclusion has contributed to a culinary tradition all its own. Because the people are not stock breeders, beef is not a major element in the diet, and milk is used only sparingly. However, the rivers and long coastlines have made fish the most important source of protein.

Large quantities of rice are the core of any Burmese meal, usually prepared with a curry. But the meal will invariably be served with *ngapi* or *nganpayay*, fermented fish or shrimp paste with a reputation as the "national dish." Because of its strong smell, *ngapi* is not ordinarily served to Westerners. Kipling described it as "fish pickled when it ought to have been buried long ago," and Sir James George Scott said: "An old herring barrel smells strong, but there is nothing in nature that more than *ngapee* hath an ancient and a fish-like smell." Used in small quantities, however, it is not unpleasant.

Another typical dish is *mohinga*, a soup with fish and rice noodles, eaten mainly at breakfast and lunch. More common is *hingyo*, a clear soup served with green leafy vegetables for dinner.

Fish or prawns, and frequently chicken, constitute the main course, along with the rice. Especially popular is *kaukswe*, a chicken and noodle dish prepared with coconut milk. In the Ayeyarwady Delta, it is normally prepared with onions, ginger, garlic and chilies. Tastes vary regionally, however, and on the Shan Plateau it is likely to be prepared in a very different fashion.

A variety of delicious fruits is available in Burma. Bananas, oranges, limes, mangoes, papayas and pomeloes (Chinese grapefruit) are easily found; other fruits, such as the highly-prized mangosteen and the notorious durian, are shipped to the capital from Mawlamyine (Moulmein) and Tanintharyi (Tenasserim). Of the durian, Scott once wrote: "Some Englishmen will tell you that the flavour and the odor of the fruit may be realized by eating a "garlic custard" over a London sewer; others will be no less positive in their perception of blendings of sherry, delicious custards, and the nectar of the gods..."

On street corners in Burma's larger cities, small food stalls hawk shrimp chips, sweet pancakes, fried pumpkin, Shan sausage, and – for a strong stomach – fried grasshoppers. Ice cream should be avoided, and likewise water unless it has been thoroughly boiled, but sugar cane juice, soft drinks, tea and coffee are easily obtainable. (Most Westerners find Chinese tea preferable to Burmese tea.)

There is also betel chewing. In Yangon, although selling betel nuts has recently been prohibited, the fading red stains on streets and on house walls remain as a sign that the betel nut is still popular and cherished.

Betel chewing was once even a treasured

royal pastime, and betel boxes, bowls and trays were part of royal regalia. Kings were followed by their own betel-box carriers wherever they went, and even today, lacquer or silver boxes indicate the wealth of a family. No matter how poor the family, betel nut was always offered to every visitor to the home.

Each chewer prepares his own mixture. Betel nuts, cloves, cutch, anise seeds, tobacco, shredded liquorice, lime and fresh betel leaves are the main ingredients. Even the folding of the leaves to form the perfect quid is an art in itself, as is chewing, as well as spitting it out without offending anyone. Burmese women have always used betel nuts to redden their lips, but reddened teeth and soiled streets are now becoming an unwelcome sight. ∎

The label "Kachin" is often indiscriminately applied to all inhabitants of this state. In fact, the only true Kachins are the Jinghpaw people. Traditionally hilltop dwellers, their lifestyle and social structure are distinctly different from those of the Shans, who have generally populated the valley floors.

The dominant Kachin group plants dry rice in a shifting cultivation scheme, alternating with buckwheat, millet and barley. When possible, they plant wet paddy in hill terraces, and trade with the Shans and Bamars for other necessities.

The Jinghpaws' religion is animistic, a trait they have in common with nearly all of Burma's hill tribes. Their concept of the

based. Contrary to the norm elsewhere, it is the youngest son and not the eldest who inherits the father's position (including chiefdom). Jinghpaws maintain that the younger a son is, the greater the chance that he is of the same flesh and blood as his father.

Since peace has come to Kachin State, the cross-border-trade with China has developed tremendously. A new road between Bhamo and Zhangfeng in Yunnan Province was inaugurated in 1993. Additional border crossing points have been opened, although crossing the border is not yet possible for individual foreign tourists. The region has great potential as a tourist destination since both sides of the border, in China and Burma,

supernatural involves a hierarchical pantheon of gods who wield a mystic power over the lives of humans. The spirits must be propitiated with generous offerings and sacrifices, of which they consume the "breath," or essence; the remainder is left by the gods for mortals to eat.

Witchcraft and sorcery are a part of the Jinghpaws' daily lives. Nothing "good" or "evil" can just happen. There is always a spirit behind every action who must be thanked or appeased, often by tribal shamans, who perform rites at village shrines.

Heredity is important in the kin-based clan structures upon which Jinghpaw society is

are inhabited by some of the most colourful tribes of Southeast Asia.

The notorious Nagas: Another group of people who prefer high mountain terrain to establish their homes is the Nagas. While their homeland is not only Burma – they have their own state of Nagaland in eastern India – a sizeable number (perhaps 50,000) of the 400,000 Nagas make their home in the upper Chindwinn River area of the Sagaing Region, as well as in the neighbouring Kachin and Chin states.

In past decades they were notorious for warfare and headhunting. Today Nagas lead a more tranquil existence, in which their agricultural and religious habits are similar to other highland peoples of Burma. Their social structure is also archaic, with no group hierarchy, and there are no legal institutions above the village level.

The main concern to the SLORC government in this region is that dissident Nagas from India, waging a guerrilla war of independence there, occasionally cross the border into Burma for training and weapons.

Burma's Chins held high: The Chins are the least known of Burma's major ethnic groups, and the least affected by foreign influence. While the majority of Chins – about 850,000 – live in India and Bangladesh, some 350,000 of them speak 44 mutually unintelligible

dialects in Burma.

Over 60 percent of Burma's Chins live in the Chin State, with most of the rest settled in the Rakhine Yoma and the Magway division. Because of their relative isolation, they were largely overlooked by the medieval rulers of Bagan and other empires. By colonial times however, they had developed such a solid reputation as extraordinarily brave soldiers, that they were heavily recruited to

Left, affluent Chinese newlyweds stand with in-laws at the Strand Hotel in Yangon after a wedding reception. **Right**, a Rakhine woman carries pots of water from the Kaladan river to her kitchen.

join the British armed forces.

The Chins are swidden agriculturists, like other hill peoples, with their settlements built at an average elevation of 1,200 to 1,500 metres (4,000 to 5,000 ft). Northern Chins, who have an elaborate social hierarchy, construct permanent homes of wooden planks and raise corn as their staple crop. Southern Chins, whose clan system is less formal, build their homes of bamboo and rattan, frequently pulling up stakes and moving. Their principal crop is rice. Both groups of Chins are heavily animistic.

The proud people of Rakhine: Ever since King Bodawpaya swept south from his capital at Innwa (Ava) and annexed the Kingdom of Rakhine two centuries ago, the Bamars have had their hands full dealing with this coastal race. On the other hand, the Rakhines (Arakanese) still look back with pride and dignity on the many centuries of independence they enjoyed.

Although of the same Tibeto-Burman stock, Rakhines are slightly darker in complexion than the Bamars. The region's 2,000-year history of contact with Indian traders, sailors and Brahman settlers has left its lasting mark upon the physical appearance of the Rakhine people.

There are several significant differences between the lifestyles of the coastal Rakhines and the Ayeyarwady basin Bamars.

Rakhine gets far more rain and has higher humidity than does the inland regions, due to its exposure to the monsoons. This has required that Rakhine's entire transportation system be dependent on boats. Cultivated land is always situated only a short distance from navigable rivers, creeks, channels and tidal waters for easy access.

Two roads that will connect northern and southern Rakhine with the Ayeyarwady basin are now being upgraded for year-round use. One will connect Minbu with Kyauktaw, while the other which connects Padaung with Taungup will continue south to Ngathaingchaung thus reducing the isolation of the state.

Most Rakhines are devout Buddhists. But a fairly large number of people in the capital city of Sittwe (Akyab), and along the northern coast, are Muslims of Bengali descent. The ancestors of most of these people settled in Rakhine during the British colonial era, when movement between India and Burma was not restricted.

In the 1970s, the population explosion in neighbouring Bangladesh led to massive movements by illegal immigrants entering Rakhine. When the Burmese army moved to the border area many of the Rakhines fled into Bangladesh. A similar situation developed again in 1992 when again more than 200,000 Rakhines of Bengali descent went fleeing into Bangladesh. By 1995 most of them had been repatriated.

In both city and country areas, Muslims and Buddhists lead separate lives and have little to do with one another. In Sittwe, many Muslims have their houses along the Kaladan River and work as fishermen – a profession no devout Buddhist would ever take up because it would involve taking life.

Rural and urban Chinese: For millennia, Chinese have travelled overland into Burma, down the northeastern trade routes and along the great rivers. In centuries past, many Chinese settlements were established along these routes. The descendants of these early settlers still live in Upper Burma.

There are two groups of Chinese who inhabit Burma, with very different histories and lifestyles. The first group is made up of the Shan Tayok and the Kokang Chinese. They came over the border of Yunnan during the time when the Shan principalities were under British administration.

The urban Chinese have an entirely different background. Most of them came to Yangon by sea to work as small merchants and restaurant owners during the British colonial era. Working hard and diligently, sending their sons and daughters to be educated in Western-type schools and universities, they soon occupied the middle and higher strata of modern society.

Despite the nationalization of private businesses under Ne Win, these Chinese remained strong, although some have turned to the arts or even vegetable farming as alternative occupations. With the market economy now taking roots in the country, many Chinese are once again in business.

Estimates of the number of Chinese in Burma today range from 100,000 to 400,000. At the height of Mao's Cultural Revolution, many young Chinese in Yangon undertook to import the revolution to Burma; with minimum instigation from the federal government, the Burmas reacted violently, ram-

paging through the city's Chinese sector. Since then, the Chinese have kept a low profile in Burma, adapting themselves more strictly to local customs.

The industrious Indians: The Indians and their culture have a 2,000-year history in Burma, predating even the Bamar majority.

However, it was not until the 19th century, when Burma became a part of the British India colony, that they began to settle in Burma in such quantity that a purely Indian community developed. In fact, they came in such great numbers that by 1939, about 58 percent of the Yangon's population was Indian, and an estimated 1 million Indians were living in Burma at that time.

The Indians were largely well-educated, and occupied middle and higher levels of administration and business during the British era. Those who were not so well-educated came to Burma as contract labourers for government projects. These ranged from railway and road construction to the extension of urban areas.

Many of the immigrants were from southern India, and brought with them their beliefs and regional village social structure, which included the caste system, Hindu deities and moneylenders.

These moneylenders (*chettyars*) quickly became so entrenched in Burmese society that they bought up more than half of the arable land in the Ayeyarwady Delta region. The tide soon turned however. Many were forced to return to India during the wartime Japanese occupation of Burma, and those who endured were soon faced with the land reforms of the new independent government of the "Union of Burma". Businessmen who remained in Burma during the U Nu years staged a mass migration when Ne Win installed his nationalization program.

Today, there are fewer than half a million Indians still living in Burma, perhaps only 100,000. Most are of the poorer classes and make their living doing menial jobs. Those born in Burma are generally Muslims, but have tried hard to adopt the Burmese lifestyle. The majority of those born in India are Hindus, and are employed in various trades and professions.

Sister Luise-Marie, a lowland Kayin, is a Roman Catholic nun serving at St Peter's Cathedral in Pathein.

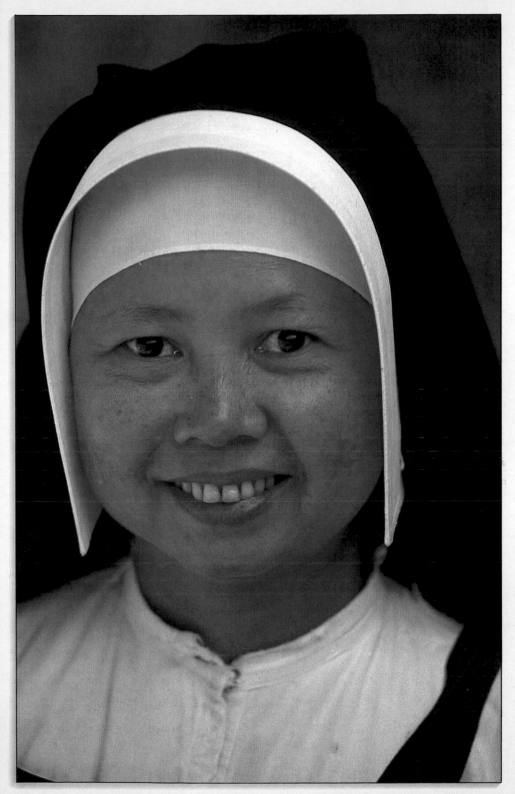

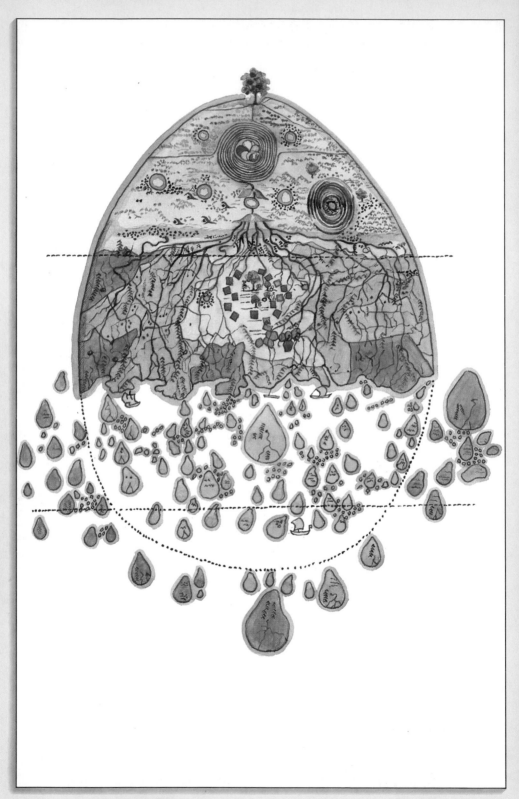

It has often been said that Burma is the most profoundly Buddhist country in the world. That may well be true. But the brand of Buddhism practised in this isolated land is unique on the face of the globe.

Burmese Buddhism, theoretically, is Theravada or Hinayana Buddhism, that sect of Buddhism adhering most closely to the Buddha's teaching, and is the dominant form of Buddhism throughout Southeast Asia. It was preceded in Burma, however, by the animistic beliefs of the hill tribes and by the Hindu-Brahmanism of early traders, which has had a profound effect on the cosmological concept of the land.

Burmese cosmology – 31 planes of existence: Strictly speaking, Burmese cosmology is Buddhist cosmology. But it has been shaped by millennia of influences from other cultures, particularly that of the Brahmans.

According to the Burmese, the European-Asian continent is called Jambudipa. It is the southern of four islands situated at the cardinal points surrounding Mount Meru, the centre of the world.

This southern island is the only place where future Buddhas can be born. This is because Jambudipa is a place of misery, compared to the other abodes of this universe. The inhabitants of the northern island, for instance, have lives of only joy and pleasure. There, everything one needs can be found growing on trees – the finest food already cooked, glittering garments waiting to be plucked from bushes. The northerner lives for 1,000 years in perfect, youthful shape. But because life for him is so pleasurable, there is no way he can gain merits.

Despite their sufferings, the Buddhist inhabitants of Jambudipa would not change places with the northerner. Only in the land of humanity can one gain sufficient merit in good deeds to rise through the vertical states of existence and attain the state of nibbana.

There are, in fact, 31 planes of existence

Preceding pages: the holy temples of Bagan; the 37 *nat* form an integral part of the religious beliefs of the Burmese. **Left**, cosmology's physical world centred on Mount Meru. **Right**, a *nat* in his temple alcove.

on, above, and below Mount Meru. They can be divided into three main groups: the 11 planes of *Kama-Loka*, the realm of the sensuous world; the 16 planes of *Rupa-Loka*, the realm of subtle material matter; and finally, the four planes of *Arupa-Loka*, the realm of formlessness.

Of the 11 planes of *Kama-Loka*, four are beneath the human plane of existence. These are demon and ghost worlds, the animal world, hells and purgatories. This is the sphere of punishment. A human being who

collects demerits for bad deeds and who fails to counterweight them with good deeds will be reborn in one of these four lower worlds.

Still within the sensuous realm, but above the place of humanity, are the six planes of sensual bliss on and above Mount Meru. Their inhabitants – *nat, deva, naga, garuda*, and gods of many kinds – exist in the realm of pleasure. The duration of their lives is much longer than that of human beings. But these entities still need the inhabitants of Jambudipa to share in their merits, and thereby prolong their blissful existences. Once the power of the entities' merits – which led to their being reborn on this plane – has subsided, they must once again be reborn on Jambudipa to collect more merit for new opportunities in future existence.

The inhabitants of the 16 planes of *Rupa-Loka* are already free from sensual desire. They are born without the aid of parents, feed on joy, and are luminous. This realm is sometimes called the "16 heavens of Brahma," because it is on this level that refined and beautiful beings exist. Indeed, the higher the place of existence, the more refined and beautiful the beings become. The five uppermost *Rupa-Loka* planes are called the "pure abodes." Still, they belong to the material world.

It is different in the highest heavens, the

four planes of *Arupa-Loka*. Here, the inhabitants are disembodied intellects. They no longer belong to the material world. These planes of existence are no longer places; they comprise (in order) the infinity of space, the infinity of consciousness, nothingness, and at the highest level, "neither perception nor non-perception."

The 31 planes of existence into which a human being can be reborn reach far beyond Mount Meru. The peak of the sacred mountain, in fact, is only the No.7 plane (Jambudipa is No.5) in this cosmic description.

The distance between the different worlds of heavens cannot be measured in earthly terms. According to the Burmese, heavens are millions of *yuzena* (28,000 cubits, about nine miles) apart, and many *kappa* divide the worlds. A *kappa*, the duration of a single universe, lasts 4,320 million years. Single universes are destroyed and recreated on a regular basis; in fact, it is considered that precisely 10,100,000 universes of the same type as our own currently exist. These universes come and go, and at times, when all other worlds have dissipated, only the four upper planes remain. Their inhabitants have lifespans of over 20,000 *kappa*.

Within this cosmos, every aspect of life interacts with every other. Animals, man, *nat*, gods and demons – they are all bound to the wheel of life. They all exist and are a part of the Burmese Buddhist's world.

It is only the various Buddhas of history who are free from this wheel of *samsara*, or rebirth. The Buddha of our era, Gautama, left his Dhamma, his teaching, for the inhabitants of Jambudipa so they could learn how to achieve enlightenment and escape the 31 planes of existence. Even the beings of the highest plane – that beyond consciousness – cannot directly reach nibbana. They must first be reborn in Jambudipa, the world of misery, and the only world with a direct link to the state of "un-becoming."

The 37 *nat* – respect and honour, or else: Since long before the introduction to Burma of Buddhism, there has been a pronounced belief in animism among the native peoples. Even today, the 37 primary *nat* are an integral part of the religious beliefs of the Burmese people. Essentially demons and evil spirits, they make life difficult for those who do not accord them sufficient respect and esteem. The people of Burma appease and honour them with offerings of flowers, money and food, placed on special altars.

Originally, each village had its own spirits. Each tree and field was inhabited by a local *nat*. There were harvest *nat*, *nat* of the wind, and *nat* of the rain. Some of the isolated tribes of northern Burma still have localized beliefs, manifested annually at the great Manao Festival in Myitkyina.

For most Burmese, however, there are specific *nat* recognized throughout the country for their individual powers. It has been so for more than 1,500 years.

The brass head of a Buddha.

SHIN-PYU

The most important moment in the life of a young Burmese boy is his *shin-pyu* – his initiation as a novice in the order of monks. Until a Buddhist has gone through the *shin-pyu* ceremony, he is regarded as no better than an animal. To become "human," he must for a time withdraw from secular life, following the example set forth by the Buddha when he left his family to seek enlightenment, and later by the Buddha's own young son, Rahula.

Unlike his illustrious predecessors, the novice monk will probably carry his alms bowl for a short period, then return to his normal lifestyle. But his time spent as a monk, studying Buddhist scriptures and strictly following the code of discipline, makes him a dignified human being.

During the period between his ninth and twelfth birthdays, a boy is deemed ready to don the saffron-coloured robes of the Sangha and become a "son of the Buddha." If his parents are very pious, they may arrange to have the *shin-pyu* staged on the full moon day of *Waso* (June/July), the beginning of the Buddhist Lent. This arrangement ensures that the novice can remain in the monastery throughout the entire rainy season, until Lent ends with the Festival of Light in October.

Once the ceremony has been arranged, the boy's sisters announce it to the whole village or neighbourhood. Everyone is invited, and contributions are collected for a festival which will dig deep into the savings of the boy's parents.

Traditionally, a *shin-pyu* is a time of extravagance. The boy is dressed in princely garments of silk, wears a gold headdress and has a white horse. These objects are meant to symbolize the worldly goods that the novice monk must renounce in accepting the rules of the Sangha.

The night before a *shin-pyu* is a busy one. A feast is prepared for all the monks whose company the young boy will join, and they are elaborately fed early on the morning of the ceremony. Next, all male guests are fed, then the women.

Later in the morning, the novitiate monk's head is shaved in preparation for his initiation. The boy's mother and eldest sister hold a white cloth to receive the falling hair, and later bury it near a pagoda. This head-shaving is a solemn moment; when completed, the boy looks appropriately like a "son of the Buddha."

In the weeks before the ceremony, the boy has been familiarized with the language and behaviour befitting a monk. He has learned how to address a superior; how to walk with decorum, keeping his eyes fixed on a point 2 metres (6 ft) in front of him; and how to respond to the questions put to him at the novitiation cer-

emony. He has also learned the Pali language words he must use in asking to be admitted to the Sangha.

His instruction serves him well when it is time for the ceremony. "Reverend Sir, I request admission to the novice-hood in view of the perfect liberation from the cycle of suffering transmigration. Reverend Sir, I request for the 10 Precepts to be observed by a novice. Would you be kind enough to counsel me on the precepts."

During his novice-hood, he will not take any food after noon, sing or play, use cosmetics, sit on elevated seats, possess any money, interfere in the business of other monks, create dissension amongst them or abuse them.

He must not kill or steal, or have sex, must not tell a lie and must not be intoxicated. He must not blaspheme the Buddha, the Sangha or the

Dhamma, must not listen to heretical doctrines and must not implicate the nuns.

When the boy's request to enter the monkhood is approved, he prostrates himself three times. He is robed, and now he is ready to walk the path of perfection first trodden by the Buddha. If he is steadfast enough, he might even reach nirvana.

Once the *sayadaw* – the abbot who has presided over the ceremony – hangs the novitiate's *thabeit* (alms bowl) over his shoulder, the boy's innocent childhood is left behind. He has now been accepted as a monk.

During the time he spends in the monastery, the boy's parents must address him in honorific terms. He will call them "lay sister" and "lay brother," the same names he calls others who are not in the monkhood. ∎

According to the *Glass Palace Chronicle*, King Thinlikyaung (ca. 344–387 AD) united 19 villages in the vicinity of present-day Bagan (Pagan) to found the town of Thiripyitsaya. Within this coalition of communities, there arose the need for an inter-regional system of religious beliefs. Hence, the king had a tree that was reputed to be carrying brother and sister *nat* from the north of the land, fished from the Ayeyarwady River. Two figures were carved from the tree; they were borne to the top of Mount Popa, where they remain enshrined to this day. They are known as the Mahagiri Nat.

King Anawrahta, founder of the First Burmese Empire, also devoted his attention to

original group have been replaced by historical figures through the centuries.

For the Burmese, these 37 *nat* serve nearly the same purpose as the saints of the Roman Catholic Church. In both cases, they are called upon in times of need. Theravada Buddhists cannot beseech the Buddha. When regarded from this perspective, the animism prevalent today within the framework of Burmese Buddhism is not as archaic as it may first seem.

The 22 *nat* originating from the pre-Bagan (pre-Pagan) period are:
(1) Thagyamin, king of the *nat*, known as Indra in Hindu mythology, sometimes called Sakka;

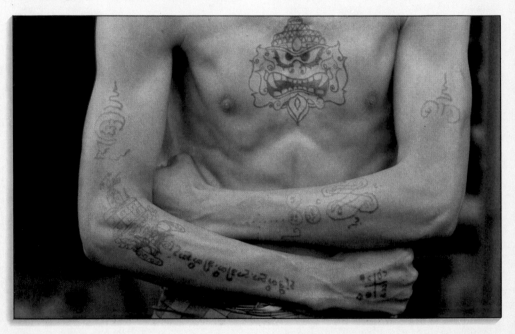

simplifying spiritual beliefs. When he introduced Theravada Buddhism into Upper Burma as the national religion, he was unable to eliminate the animistic beliefs of his people. Despite radical measures, 36 of the countless *nat* survived in the people's daily activities. So Anawrahta introduced a 37th figure – Thagyamin – and made him king of the *nat*. He thereafter tolerated the popular worship of these 37 *nat*, once it had been established that they were also followers of the Buddha's teachings.

However, not all of the 37 *nat* worshipped today are the same 37 as those worshipped during Anawrahta's time. About 15 from the

(2) Nga Tin De, or Min Mahagiri, the Lord of the Great Mountain;
(3) Shwemyethna, Princess Golden Face, his sister;
(4) Lady Golden Sides;
(5) Lady Three Times Beautiful;
(6) The Little Lady With the Flute;
(7) The Brown Lord of Due South;
(8) The White Lord of the North;
(9) The Lord With the White Umbrella;
(10) The Royal Mother (of No. 9);
(11) The Sole Lord of Pareim-ma;
(12) The Elder Inferior Gold;
(13) The Younger Inferior Gold;
(14) The Lord Grandfather of Mandalay;

(15) The Lady Bandy Legs;
(16) The Old Man by the Solitary Banyan;
(17) Lord Sithu;
(18) The Young Lord of the Swing;
(19) The Valiant Lord Kyawswa;
(20) Captain of the Main Army Aungswa;
(21) The Royal Cadet; and
(22) His Mother, the Lady Golden Words.
The 15 *nat* who took their places after the reign of Anawrahta are:
(23) The Lord of Five Elephants;
(24) The Lord King, Master of Justice;
(25) Maung Po Tu;
(26) The Queen of the Western Palace;
(27) The Lord of Aungpinle, Master of White Elephants;
(28) The Lady Bent;
(29) Golden Nawrahta;
(30) The Valiant Lord Aung Din;
(31) The Young Lord White;
(32) The Lord Novice;
(33) Tabinshweti;
(34) The Lady of the North;
(35) The Lord Minhkaung of Toungoo;
(36) The Royal Secretary; and
(37) The King of Chiangmai.

Each of the 37 *nat* carries a tragic tale associated with him or her, in some way connected with the history of Burma. It is through these tales that the Burmese masses are introduced to their country's history, legend, myth and drama. The *nat*, in fact, essentially provide Burma with a national history comprehensible to one and all, splendid yet marvelously simplistic.

There is a widespread superstition in Burma that ailments can be cured and the future predicted by those with proper channels to the *nat*. Soothsayers, prophets and miracle healers are offshoots of this belief. With a tradition of thousands of years of *nat* worship, these beliefs are deeply ingrained in the lives of the country people even today, and a reeducation program by the government does not seem likely to succeed.

The beatitudes of Buddhism: Theravada Buddhism is recognized as the principal religion of about 80 percent of all Burmese people. While there are significant numbers of Hindus, Muslims, Christians and primitive ani-

mists (among the northern hill tribes), it is safe to say that over 99 percent of the Bamars (Burmans), Mons, Shans and Palaungs are Theravadins.

Indeed, Buddhism permeated the everyday lives of Burma's people during the past decades far more than did "The Burmese Way to Socialism." Every Burmese village supports at least one *kyaung* (a monastery, usually linked with a school); and the yellow, orange or red-clad *pongyi* (monks, whose title literally means "great glory") are an established part of the street scenes in the villages and urban areas alike.

Another name for Theravada Buddhism is Hinayana ("the lesser vehicle"). This is not

to imply that Theravada Buddhism is less powerful than its counterpart, Mahayana ("the greater vehicle"), dominant in most of East Asia. Rather, Theravada is a more conservative, more orthodox, form of Buddhism, adhering strictly to the original Pali scriptures. It places a great emphasis on individual achievement, and allows fewer options to those seeking to attain nibbana (thus, "the lesser vehicle"). It does not, as Mahayanists sometimes claim, ignore the salvation of all but the individual; rather, it is through service to other beings that a human being enhances one's own status.

The division between Theravada and

Left, Many popular tattoos represent animistic deities. **Right**, a woman in prayer at one of the Shwedagon's eight planetary posts.

Mahayana, while developing for some time, actually occurred in 235 BC when King Ashoka convened the Third Buddhist Synod at Pataliputra, India. The Buddhist elders (Theravada means, "the way of the elders") held tight to their literal interpretation of the Buddha's teaching; they were opposed by a group which sought to understand the personality of the historical Buddha, and its relationship to one's salvation. This latter group became known as the Mahayana school. It established itself in Tibet, Nepal, China, Korea, Mongolia, Japan and Vietnam, where its further development varied greatly from region to region.

The Theravada school, meanwhile, has

thrived in Sri Lanka, Burma, Thailand, Laos and Cambodia. Buddhaghosa, the famous Indian monk, in AD 403 carried the Pali scriptures to Thaton (where a form of Buddhism was already practised). Buddhaghosa had summarized and interpreted the *Tipitaka* – the "Three Baskets" of Theravada scripture, composed of the *sutra* (discourses), *vinaya* (rules and regulations of the Sangha, the order of monkhood), and *abhidhamma* (interpretations of the Buddha's teachings) – and took this body of knowledge with him to the Mon capital.

In recent years, in synods at Mandalay in 1872 and Yangon in 1954, there have been efforts to give Theravada Buddhism a new impetus. At the former synod, the entire *Tipitaka* was recited and recorded on stone tablets, and at the latter, an Institute for Advanced Buddhistic Studies was founded.

No god, no self: There is no all-powerful god in Theravada Buddhism. In contrast to Mahayanism, even the Buddha himself cannot be invoked to intervene benevolently in one's life. It is up to the individual to work out his own salvation. Life and death are two sides of the same "coin" of existence. All living things, including plants and animals, are included in the perpetual round of *samsara*, or rebirth. According to Buddhist doctrine, this is an endless cycle of suffering from which there is but one escape: faithful adherence to the Dhamma, the Buddha's teaching, and following the paths of *arhat* (saints) and *bodhisattva* (future Buddhas) to reach nibbana.

In practice, Theravada Buddhism has developed a higher and a lower form of teaching. The pure form of Buddhism has largely been left to the monks. The masses engage in a hodgepodge of Buddhism and their ancient *nat* worship, coupled with cosmological beliefs; most Burmese Buddhists seem to be more desirous of making merit for a better rebirth in a higher heaven than they are in taking the direct path to nibbana to escape the cycle of suffering.

There are 227 rules (officially, but there are many more according to the scriptures) by which all monks must guide their lives; but there are only five precepts of Buddhist morality which are truly relevant to the masses. These are restrictions against killing, stealing, lying, adultery, and the consumption of intoxicating liquor.

As there is no true form of worship in Theravada Buddhism, the only ritual to which monks and laity submit themselves is the thrice-daily recitation of the "Three Jewels," the *Triratna*:

"I take refuge in the Buddha. I take refuge in the Dhamma. I take refuge in the Sangha."

The formula of the "Three Jewels" offers solace and security. These are needed for strength, if one understands the "Four Noble Truths" expounded upon by Gautama Buddha in his first sermon:

(1) Life always has in it the element of suffering. (2) The cause of suffering is desire. (3) In order to end the suffering, give up

desire, give up attachment. (4) The way to this goal is the Noble Eightfold Path.

The Eightfold Path consists of right views, right intent, right speech, right conduct, right means of livelihood, right endeavour, right mindfulness, and right meditation.

This "path" is normally divided into three: views and intent are matters of wisdom; speech, conduct (action) and livelihood are matters of morality; and endeavour, mindfulness and meditation are matters of true mental discipline.

The Buddha denied the existence of a soul. There is no permanence, he explained, to that which one perceives to be self – one's essence is forever changing. The idea of re-

then extinguish the first, it could not be said that the new flame was the same as the previous one; but its existence would be due to that of the previous flame.

The Noble Eightfold Path, therefore, does not lead to salvation in the Judeo-Christian sense. By pursuing matters of wisdom, morality and mental discipline, one can hope to make the transition into nibbana, which can perhaps best be defined as extinction of suffering, cessation of desire. It is not heaven, nor is it annihilation. It is a simply quality of existence.

Popular Buddhist practice: These then, are the tenets of Theravada Buddhism. But the vast majority of Burmese Buddhists do not

birth, therefore, is a complicated philosophical question within the structure of Buddhism. When a Buddhist (or any person, for that matter) is reincarnated, it is neither the person nor his soul which is actually reborn. Rather, it is the sum of one's karma, the balance of his good and evil deeds: one is reborn as a result of prior existence.

One popular metaphor used to explain this transition is that of a candle. Were a person to light one candle from the flame of another,

Left, a nun studies the *Tipitaka* in Sagaing.
Right, a monk rests between periods of meditation in a monastery.

actively pursue the goal of nibbana in this lifetime. To them, "extinction" is not as desirable as rebirth. They seek a reduction in suffering in this life and the next – a goal which can be accomplished through participation in merit-making activities, and by avoiding sinful actions.

Sinful acts are those which violate the five precepts of Buddhist morality, as well as those which create greed, anger or delusion. Good Buddhists must keep the five precepts and strive above all for compassion, equanimity and wisdom.

Other activities earn additional merit. The single best deed is sponsorship of the construction of a pagoda or reliquary stupa. It is commonly believed that a person with the ways and means to build a pagoda will ensure his rebirth at the time of Maitreya, the Buddha of the future, and in Maitreya's presence, will achieve enlightenment. This is why there are so many pagodas in Burma. Relics and many images of Gautama Buddha are believed to contain an innate power that can be drawn upon by those who worship them, and every pagoda builder fervently hopes to obtain one of these "magic" relics for veneration at his own pagoda.

There are many other acts which earn lesser, but important, amounts of merit. Of these, becoming a monk and performing charitable acts for the Sangha are deemed most worthwhile. Worship, meditation, pilgrimage, preaching or listening to sermons on the Buddha's teachings, showing respect to elders and superiors, and sharing merit with others (through certain ritual acts) are other ways of earning merit.

In addition to advancing one's chances for a more prosperous future life, these acts can improve one's worldly prestige (pagoda builders earn a special title for life), as well as contribute to the gratification of physical pleasures – as at the annual temple festivals, where great feasting and pageantry abound.

The Sangha: There are no priests in Theravada Buddhism. But the faithful still need a model to follow on the path to salvation. This model is provided by the colourfully clad Southeast Asian monks.

In Burma, there are about 800,000 monks. Most of these are students and novices who put on the monk's robe only temporarily; nearly all male Burmese devote a period – from a few weeks to several years – in their lifetime to the monkhood. There are now vows such as those of Roman Catholicism. Indeed, the *pongyi* can leave the order at any time. Nevertheless, about 100,000 have dedicated their entire lives to the Sangha, a Buddhist brotherhood which has renounced our world. There are three fundamental rules to which the monk must subscribe:

(1) the renunciation of all possessions, except these eight items – three robes, a razor (for shaving), a needle (for sewing), a strainer (to ensure that no living thing is swallowed), a belt and an alms bowl;
(2) the vow to injure no living thing and to offend no one;
(3) the vow of complete celibacy.

The *pongyi* must make his livelihood by begging. He sets out two hours before dawn, begging for food from door to door. He does not thank the donor for alms received, for it is the donor who must be grateful: the monk has given him an opportunity to earn merit by doing a good deed for one in the Buddha's service. The food received at this time is the monk's only meal of the day.

The vow to injure nothing came about as a reaction to the animal sacrifices of Brahmanism. It is also valid, to a certain extent, for lay Buddhists. With few exceptions, Burmese fishermen and butchers are non-Buddhists.

The law of celibacy is based on the assertion that sexual union with a woman takes up a great deal of physical and psychic energy, which must instead be directed toward meditation. Women, therefore, are expected to avoid any contact with a *pongyi*. They should not touch his alms bowl, tread on his mat, or speak to him.

According to Buddhist belief, the fate of being born a woman is the price one must pay for having led a poor life in a prior existence. There is, however, an order of Buddhist nuns, easily recognizable with their pink robes and close-cropped heads. But they are not accorded the same respect as the monks.

A young Burmese begins his novitiate at around the age of nine. He is brought to the *kyaung* and handed over to the monks, who teach him the basic Pali scriptures and the 10 basic Buddhist rules of conduct. At the time of this initiation (called the *shin-pyu*), the boy is given an old Pali name and may only be addressed in revered tones, even by his parents. He is then a "son of Buddha," and addresses his father as "lay brother" and his mother as "lay sister."

For the majority of Burmese, their period of novitiate does not last long. Most have left the monkhood before their 20th birthday, which is the minimum age at which one can become a member of the Sangha and submit oneself to the 227 rules of the order.

Those who do become ordained have all the hair shaved off their bodies. They then devote the rest of their lives to meditation, the study of the Pali scriptures, and the instruction of the laity.

Yangon monks pause during their daily alms-collection rounds.

From Yangon's Bogyoke Aung San Market to Mandalay's renovated Zegyo Market, and at all local bazaars beyond and between, the visitor to Burma finds a remarkable variety of native handicrafts.

Stalls display lacquerware, metalwork, brass and marble sculpture, wood carvings, embroidered textiles and more. The craftsmen of Burma may not have achieved the same international renown as artisans of other parts of Southeast Asia, but they are no less skilled at their specialties.

with the air, it turns hard and black.

In times past, extraordinarily fine lacquerware bowls were produced around cores of horsehair and bamboo, or even pure horsehair. This gave such great flexibility that one could press opposite sides of the bowl's rim together, without the bowl breaking or the lacquer peeling off.

Today, two other techniques of manufacture prevail. Inferior products have a gilded lacquer relief on a wooden base. Better quality wares have a core of light bamboo wicker-

Lacquerware: Lacquerware in particular has developed into an art form of refined quality. Its history can be traced to China's Shang dynasty (18th to 11th centuries BC). The craft reached the area of present-day Burma in the 1st century AD by way of the Nanchao Empire (modern Yunnan), and is believed to have been carried to Bagan (Pagan) during King Anawrahta's conquest of Thaton in 1057. Today it thrives in northern Thailand and Laos as well as in Burma.

Raw lacquer is tapped from the thitsi tree (*Melanorrhoea usitatissima*) in the same way as latex is taken from the rubber tree. As soon as the sticky-gray extract comes in contact

work, assuring elasticity and durability.

This basic structure is coated with a layer of lacquer and clay, then put in a cool place to dry. After three or four days, the vessel is sealed with a paste of lacquer and ash, the fineness of ash determining the quality of the work. It may come from sawdust, paddy husk or even cow dung. After this coating dries, the object is polished until smooth.

Over time, it is given several successive coats of lacquer to eliminate irregularities.

At this stage, the ware is black. But the artist isn't finished: ornamental and figurative designs must still be added. Cheaper articles are simply painted, while the more expensive ones are embellished by means of engraving, painting and polishing. A similar effect can be produced with coloured reliefs, painted and partially polished. Red, yellow, blue and gold are the colours usually used. The production of multi-coloured lacquerware takes about six months, going through 12 or more stages of production.

Bagan and Pyay (Prome) are Burma's main lacquerware centres, where visitors can select from a wide variety of and purchase quality vases, jewel boxes, dinnerware sets and other items.

Metalwork: The most frequently seen evidence of Burmese metalwork is probably the gold leaf, pasted by Buddhist devotees on pagodas and Buddha images all over the country. The industry is especially prevalent in Mandalay.

The gold comes from the north of Burma in nuggets, which are flattened on a slab of marble until paper-thin. These sheets are then alternately cut and pounded between layers of leather and copper plate until they are almost transparent. Then they are picked up with pincers, placed between sheets of oiled bamboo paper, and neatly packaged in two-centimetre-long stacks of 100 leaves for sale at pagodas and bazaars. An ounce of gold can produce enough gold leaf for an area of 10 square metres (12 sq yds).

Burmese silverwork dates to the 13th century, when palace bowls, vases and betel-nut boxes, as well as daggers and sheaths, were made from this metal. Today, work done at Ywataung village near Sagaing rivals the earlier silverwork.

While silverwork is not as prominent as it once was, work in copper and brass has never seriously declined in importance. It remains a major cottage industry in Mandalay for about 300 families. Bago (Pegu) is another centre. Here, Buddha images, orchestral gongs, bells for pagodas and monasteries, and small cattle bells are in constant demand.

Buddha images made of marble are also very popular. Good quality marble is taken from a quarry at Sagyin, 34 kilometres (21 mi) north of Mandalay. It is then transported to a district in southern Mandalay city, where carvers use chisels, mallets and files to create their works of religious art.

Wood carving is among the most ancient of Burmese handicrafts, although evidence of ancient artisans has been destroyed. Significant 19th century works still remain in Mandalay, particularly in the ornamentation of monasteries. Today, *nat* images are among the objects most commonly made. The artisans sketch, in charcoal and chalk on a solid

block of wood, the figure they wish to carve. They shape the rough outline with chisel and saw, and complete details with knives and other fine instruments.

Embroidery, on the other hand, is a highly respected art form. Fine gold thread, silver sequins and coloured glass (imitation jewels) were traditionally stitched into cotton or wool garments for royalty and other dignitaries. Today, silk *longyi* often display peacock figures or broad belts of floral design; and applique work of coloured cloth cuttings on black velvet are sold as pictures. Blankets and shoulder bags woven by tribal groups are also popular souvenir items.

<u>Left</u>, **Bhamo pottery with a modern touch.**
<u>Right</u>, **an Intha weaver.**

"The description of the Burmese as a happy and smiling person is borne out on the stage more than one would think possible."
– James R. Brandon, *Brandon's Guide to Theatre in Asia*, 1976

To the people of Burma, a festival or fair of any kind means a *pwe*. It is a time to gather the entire family and go to watch a marvelous mixture of dance, music, comedy and recreation of epic drama.

Burmese theatre has its audience shrieking, sobbing and rolling with laughter. Lively carefree dancers, as resplendent as tropical birds in their dazzling plumage, leap and whirl before the awed eyes of spectators of all ages. Clowns cavort across the stage, their antics and acrobatics inspiring fits of happy hysteria. An orchestra of drums and gongs beats out a strange melody, as the stage becomes "a fairyland peopled by ravishingly handsome princes and vivacious princesses," in the words of Asian theatre authority Brandon. Certainly, no one in Burma between November and May should miss an opportunity to take in at least one form of the Burmese performing arts.

There are several types of *pwe*. Most popular is the *zat pwe*, the ultimate melange of music, dance and dramatics. *Anyein pwe* is a more "folksy" theatrical form presenting episodes from everyday life, along with dancing and story telling. *Yein pwe* is pure dance, solos alternating with group numbers. *Yokthe pwe*, or marionette theatre, is a uniquely Burmese theatrical form not often seen today. *Nat pwe* is ritual spirit-medium dance, never performed in public except at animistic festivals, and rarely seen by Westerners.

Among other forms of theatre, *pya zat* is frequently seen preceding *zat pwe* performances. A dance-play with a mythical theme, it is generally set in a fantasy world where a heroic prince must overcome the evil-doings of demons and sorcerers.

From the mid-18th to the mid-19th centuries, a masked dance-drama called *zat gyi* flourished in royal courts under the patronage of Burmese kings. Today, public per-

A Burmese actor during a break in a *pwe*.

formances are rare, although papier-mache replicas of *zat gyi* dance masks as souvenirs can be purchased at souvenir stalls along the stairs leading to the Shwedagon Pagoda. (Marionettes and orchestral drums and gongs are also sold.)

Burma has a National Theatre, a company of 14 dancers and musicians who went on a highly acclaimed concert tour of the United States in late 1975. Other troupes are trained in the State Schools of Music and Drama in Yangon and Mandalay. Countless troupes travel from village to village, from pagoda festival to pagoda festival throughout the countryside during the dry season.

These troops present their time-proven repertoire to village throngs, performing on temporary bamboo structures, under a makeshift awning or (more often than not) in the open air. Audiences of hundreds or even thousands sit on mats spread in front of the stage. Many bring their children and babies, as well as food and beverage in baskets, bowls and jugs. Performances often last from sunset to sunrise; many spectators doze off for a couple of hours in the middle of the show, hoping to be nudged awake for their favourite dance sequence or story.

The history of Burmese dance troupes dates to 1767, when King Hsinbyushin returned to Ava after his conquest of the Thai capital of Ayutthia. Among his captives were the royal Siamese dancers. It was from these exquisitely trained performers that the Burmese developed the dance movements which prevail on stage today.

During the dominance of Bagan in the 11th through 13th centuries, a form of dance resembling Indian dance had been popular at pagoda festivals and royal audiences. This had disintegrated into popular drama after the fall of Bagan, and took a back seat to the highly refined Thai classical dance. But it still wielded some influence in shaping a uniquely Burmese dance form.

Burmese dance reached its zenith in the late Konbaung dynasty era in Mandalay. Although the leaps and turns of Western ballet were introduced and assimilated during the years of British colonial rule, enthusiasm for dance went into a period of decline.

Only since independence has Burma's government made efforts to revive the theatre arts. The program has been quite successful.

To the unknowledgeable Westerner, Burmese dance appears awkward, even double-jointed. Wrists, elbows, knees, ankles, fingers and toes are bent in stylized directions with seeming effortlessness.

Setting the mood is an orchestra, called the *saing*, akin to the Javanese *gamelan* and dominated by percussion instruments. Its centre-piece is a circle of 21 drums, the *patt-waing*. (Smaller orchestras have only nine drums.) Around this are a gong section (*kye-waing*), a single large drum (*patt-ma*), cymbals (*lingwin*), bamboo clappers (*wah let*

khok), an oboe-like woodwind instrument (*hne*), a bamboo flute (*palwe*), and a bamboo xylophone (*pattala*).

Occasionally, an orchestra will employ the most delicate of all Burmese instruments, the 13-stringed harp. Shaped like a toy boat covered in buffalo hide, with silk strings attached to a curved wooden "prow," it is a solo instrument usually played by a woman, unlike other musical instruments. When used in a *pwe*, it accompanies solo singing.

Burmese music lacks a chromatic scale, or even chords. But the melody pounded out on drums and gongs is mellowed by the other instruments, and love songs are as touching as they would be on violins.

Traditionally, the Burmese compare their music to the rustling of the wind through the leaves of the rose-apple tree, and the splash of its fruit falling into a sacred river. Legend explains that King Alaungsithu of Bagan, who reigned from 1112 to 1167, encountered Thagyamin, king of the *nat*, under the shade of a rose-apple tree "at the end of the world," where he was told the secret of the Burmese tonal system.

Legendary performances: Ancient legends permeate all aspects of the theatre in Burma. Nearly all performances are based either on the Hindu epics (the *Ramayana* in particular), or on the *Jataka* tales of the Buddha's 550 prior incarnations.

The *Ramayana* is the best known saga in South and Southeast Asia; it tells the story of the capture of the beautiful Princess Sita by the demon king Dasagir, and of her heroic rescue by her husband, Prince Rama.

The *Jataka*, meanwhile, are familiar to every Burmese schoolchild or adult. The tales relate, in quasi-historial moral fashion, how the Buddha overcame the various mortal sins to earn his final rebirth and enlightenment. The 10 tales of incarnations immediately preceding Buddhahood are regarded as especially important.

Because the stories are generally well known beforehand, it is up to the troupe and its individual dancers to bring them to life for audiences. The highlight of a *zat pwe* performance usually comes about 2.30 in the morning, when the stars of the show let go with a breathtaking exhibit of their song-and-dance skills. The more imaginative an actor or actress can be during a performance, the more the crowd will roar its appreciation.

An exception to all other forms of theatre is the *yokthe pwe*, or marionette theatre. A single puppeteer manipulates 28 separate doll figures, some with as many as 60 strings for different dances and gestures (although most require only 20 strings). He presents the dialogue simultaneously, while getting help from only two stage assistants.

Puppet theatre in Burma had its foundation not long after Hsinbyushin's return from Ayutthia with the Siamese dancers. The king's son and successor, Singu Min, created a Ministry for Fine Arts in his court, and gave the minister, U Thaw, the specific task of developing a new art form.

In 18th century Burma, and to some extent even today, modesty and standards of etiquette forbade the depiction of intimate romantic scenes on the stage. Further, many actors refused to portray the future Buddha in the *Jataka* tales, considering this to be sacrilegious. U Thaw saw a way around these obstacles. What human beings could not do in public, wooden figures could do without prohibition. And thus the *yokthe pwe* was born.

The *yokthe pwe* has been standardized more than any other Burmese dramatic form. The stage setting is always the same: a throne on the left for court scenes, a primeval forest of branches on the right, and a sofa in the

Then (in order) a parakeet, two elephants, a tiger and a monkey come on stage.

The imagination of the audience is stirred with the entrance of two giants, a dragon as well as a *zawgyi* (sorcerer) who always flies on stage. These figures prepare onlookers for the magical world of Brahman-Buddhist belief, which provides the plot for almost all puppet plays.

According to traditional Buddhist belief, each organism consists of 28 physical parts. U Thaw, seeking to be consistent with this teaching, directed that there be precisely 28 marionettes. Each of them is almost a metre high, faultlessly carved and with costumes identical to the originals U Thaw specified.

centre, with the action taking place before a monochrome wall.

The order of the various scenes is likewise predetermined. The orchestra opens with an overture to create an auspicious mood. Then two ritual dancers appear, followed by a dance of various animals and mythological beings to depict the first stage in the creation of the universe. Next, making its appearance alone, is the horse, whose heavenly constellation brings order to the primeval chaos.

Left, a classical dancer re-enacts traditional stories of popular *nats*. **Right,** A one-man percussion orchestra in a Mon State village.

Each of the figures derives from some mythological figure. In addition to those previously mentioned, the puppets include a king, two older princes, four ministers, an old woman, a Brahman priest, a hermit, two clowns and two heavenly beings. The two principal figures are a prince and princess – Mintha and Minthami – around whom the romantic plot always revolves.

The *yokthe pwe* is fast disappearing in modern Burma. Few puppeteers perpetuate the art, and there are no established texts – only a prescribed order of events. It can be seen occasionally at temple festivals, including Yangon's Shwedagon Pagoda festival.

Burma (Myanmar)

240 km /150 miles

102

PLACES

A journey through Burma is a journey through history. The visitor arrives in Yangon, where contemporary and colonial Burma (19th and 20th centuries) continue to coexist decades after the British departure. Travelling north to Mandalay, one encounters living reminders of the Konbaung dynasty, which dominated in the 18th and 19th centuries here and in neighbouring Amarapura. In Innwa (Ava) and Sagaing, the Burma of the Shan sovereignty (14th through 16th centuries) is predominant. And in enchanting Bagan (Pagan), one can marvel at more than 2,200 stone buildings constructed during the First Burmese Empire (11th to 13th centuries).

Following the route just described – Yangon to Mandalay to Sagaing to Bagan – the visitor can make a direct journey into the past. It is not an easy journey; it demands one to call constantly on one's imagination to make the ruins come to life, and it requires an advance historical perspective. The tourist who goes "temple-hopping" without these will wind up either exhausted or jaded...or both. What is true everywhere else, is also true in Burma: One has to bring the excitement along before the imagination can flourish.

Bagan itself can be overwhelming; but if the visitor makes a careful selection of temples to focus on, he will be able to trace the history of an incredible era. At the same time, he can observe in the structures of Bagan the development of an architectural style born 1,000 years earlier in India, then maturing on the plains of Bagan.

These destinations are far from all that Burma has to offer, either historically or scenically. Bago (Pegu), Tagaung, Mrauk-U (Myohaung) and many other places are steeped in history, offering the visitor insights into past centuries.

Burma's important destinations are placed along the Ayeyarwady (Irrawaddy) river like a string of pearls. Enjoying the sights of Thayekhittaya (Sri Ksetra), Bagan and Mandalay from the comfort of a modern river boat will certainly be one of Southeast Asia's great tourist pleasures. For the eager traveller who cannot wait, this trip can already be made today on the regular Ayeyarwady boat, though luxury steamers start their service in 1996.

Many trips that could not have been done a few years ago are now within reach for the adventurous traveller. The north of the country is now open, and may soon rival Thailand's "tribal tourism". Mogok, Mawlamyine (Moulmein), Bhamo, Myitkyina, Lashio, Kalemyo are other new destinations. All one basically needs is time and a versed local travel agent to cut the red tape. For many regions one will still need permission, a tour guide, and the ability to stay in places with little or no tourist infrastructure. But that, for some, is the challenge and the intrinsic beauty of travel. Once the visitor falls for Burma, he is likely to depart with the heavy heart of a lover who must leave a beloved behind.

Preceding pages: Bagan at dusk; standing room aboard a local ferry; day tripper.

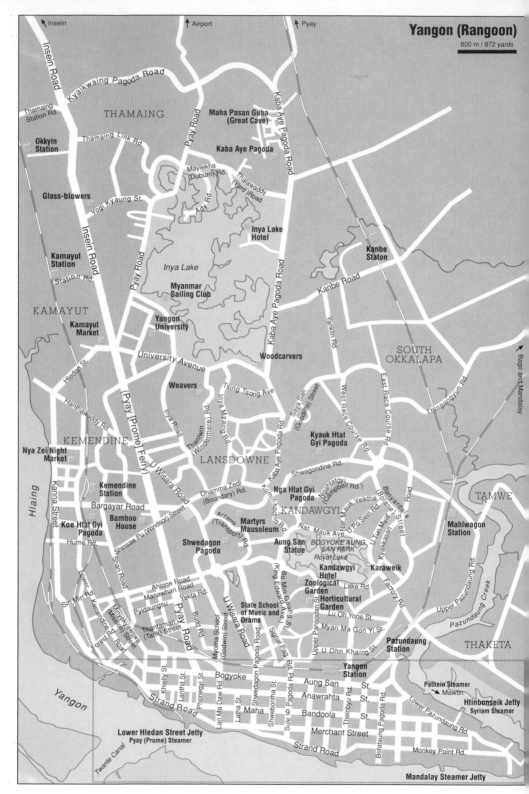

Yangon (Rangoon)

800 m / 872 yards

↑ Insein   ↑ Airport   ↑ Pyay

Insein Road

Kyaikwaing Pagoda Road

THAMAING

Thamaing Station Rd.

Thamaing Link Rd.

Okkyin Station

Glass-blowers

Yogi Kyaung St.

Pyay Road

Maha Pasan Guha (Great Cave)

Kaba Aye Pagoda

Kaba Aye Pagoda Road

Maylekha (Duburn) Rd.

Thalawaddy (Yard) Road

Ady Rd.

Inya Lake Hotel

Kamayut Station

Insein Road

Inya Lake

Pyay Road

Station Rd.

KAMAYUT

Kamayut Market

Myanmar Sailing Club

Yangon University

Kanbe Staton

Kaba Aye Pagoda Road

Kanbe Road

Yankin Rd.

SOUTH OKKALAPA

Hledan St.

University Avenue

Woodcarvers

Hanthawaddy Rd.

Weavers

Tsing Tsong Ave

Inya Myaing Rd.

Thanlwin (Windermere) Rd.

Inya Road

East Race Course Rd.

West Race Course Rd.

Saya San (Godlike) Street

Thingangyun Rd.

Bago and Mandalay →

KEMENDINE

Nya Zei Night Market

Hlaing

Kanna Street

(Pyay [Prome] Ferry)

U Wisara Road

LANSDOWNE

Kyauk Htat Gyi Pagoda

Shwegondine Rd.

TAMWE

Kemendine Station

Bargayar Road

Bamboo House

Koe Htat Gyi Pagoda

Hume Rd.

Shinsaw Pu (Windson) Street

Shan Road

Dhamma Zedi (Boundary) Rd.

Komin kochin Rd.

Nga Htat Gyi Pagoda

Ngahtatgyi (Campbell) Rd.)

KANDAWGYI

Nat. Mauk Yeiktha

U Po Sein Rd.

Banyarda Ln

Bo Aune Street

Mahlwagon Station

Arzani (Transport) Rd.

Martyrs Mausoleum

Nat. Mauk Ave.

BOGYOKE AUNG SAN PARK

Royal Lake

Kyaikkasan

U Tun Myat Rd.

Shwedagon Pagoda

Aung San Statue

Kandawgyi Hotel

Karaweik

Lower Kemendine Road

Mission Street

Myayenanda (Mission) Street

Ahlone Road

Manawhari Road

Pyidaungsu

Yekta Rd.

Pyay Road

Budd Rd.

Zoological Garden

Lake Rd.

Factory Rd.

Upper Pazundaung Rd.

Pazundaung Creek

Forest Rd.

Sin Min Rd.

Thantaman (Tank) Street

Myoma School (Godwin) Street

U Wisara Road

State School of Music and Drama

Bo Min Gaung St. (King Edward Ave.)

Signal Pag

Upper Pansodan St.

Horticultural Garden

Lu Oh Yone St.

Myan Ma Gon Yi St.

Pazundaung Station

THAKETA

Khielly St.

Lanthi St.

Lanthi St.

Phonegy St.

Bogyoke

Lan Ma Daw Rd.

Shwedagon Pagoda Road

Latha St.

Shwebontha St.

Sule Pagoda Rd.

9

Aung San

Bo Aung Gyaw St.

Anawrahta

Bandoola

Merchant Street

Theinbyu Rd.

Botataung Pagoda Rd.

Lower Pazundaung Rd.

St.

St.

St.

Yangon Station

Yangon

Maha

U Ohn Khaing St.

Lower Hiedan Street Jetty
Pyay (Prome) Steamer

Strand Road

Twante Canal

Strand Road

Monkey Point Rd.

Pathein Steamer
→ Mawtin

Htinbonseik Jetty
Syriam Steamer

Mandalay Steamer Jetty

YANGON

"Then, a golden mystery upheaved itself on the horizon – a beautiful, winking wonder that blazed in the sun, of a shape that was neither Muslim dome nor Hindu temple spire. It stood upon a green knoll... 'There's the old Shway Dagon,' said my companion... The golden dome said, 'This is Burma, and it will be quite unlike any land you know about.'"

> – Rudyard Kipling,
> *Letters From the East* (1889)

It's been more than 100 years since Kipling sailed up the Yangon (Rangoon) River to the Burmese capital, but the glistening golden stupa of the Shwedagon continues to dominate Yangon's landscape and image as perhaps no other single structure does in any other major city in the world.

The massive pagoda not only is a remarkable architectural achievement, it is also the perfect symbol of a country in which Buddhism pervades every aspect of life. Indeed, it is hard to imagine a more stunning sight than watching the first rays of dawn bounce off the brilliant gold-plated pagoda and reflect in the serene waters of the Royal Lake.

But while the Shwedagon Pagoda may dominate Yangon from its post on Singuttara Hill north of the city centre, it is far from the whole show.

If you look beyond the aging, British colonial architecture of most of Yangon's buildings you will find a cosmopolitan city of 19th-century charm, with quiet, tree-lined avenues and a people that is known to be gracious and fun-loving. Even though the centre around Sule pagoda will soon see some highrise buildings, the facelift that is being conducted by the present government has changed little of the appearance of the city, preserving the city centre in the same state as when the British left in 1948.

Water on three sides: A burgeoning city of 3 million people (the population has more than tripled in three decades), Yangon is surrounded on three sides by water. The Hlaing or Yangon River flows from the Bago (Pegu) Yoma (hills) down Yangon's west and south flanks, then continues another 31 kilometres (20 mi) to the Gulf of Martaban. To the east of the city is Pazundaung Creek, a tributary of the Hlaing. To the north are the foothills of the Bago Yoma; it is here that one finds the Shwedagon and the charming lakes artificially created by the British, now the centres of thriving residential districts.

Sri Lankan chronicles indicate there was a settlement in the region of present-day Yangon about 2,500 years ago. Probably a coastal fishing village or a minor Indian trading colony, Okkala, as the settlement was known, grew in fame following the construction of the Shwedagon Pagoda. For centuries, its history was inextricably bound to that of the great golden pagoda.

The town with the golden pagoda: We first hear of "Dagon, the town with the Golden Pagoda," from European travellers in the 16th century. The English

merchant Ralph Fitch in 1586 described Shwedagon as "the fairest place, as I suppose, that is in the world." But it was the nearby town of Syriam, across the Bago and Hlaing Rivers from Dagon, that was the most important European trading colony and Burma's main port well into the 18th century.

King Alaungpaya essentially founded Yangon and started it on its modern path in 1755 when he captured the village of Dagon from the Mon people. He called the settlement Yangon, or "End of Strife" which the British then converted into Rangoon, a name that was carried for over 150 years.

With the destruction of Syriam the following year, Yangon assumed its commercial functions. After the British conquered the town in 1824 during the First Anglo-Burmese War, its importance as a trade port flourished. But fire devastated the town in 1841. Then,11 years later, it was again almost completely destroyed in the Second Anglo-Burmese War.

Deltas and industrial suburbs: Yangon may have been a coastal village when the Shwedagon was built. But after 2,500 years, a vast delta has been created in Lower Burma by the Ayeyarwady (Irrawaddy) and the Hlaing rivers carrying silt to the sea. Still, Yangon's river is easily navigable to the capital and beyond, and a vast majority of Burma's import and export trade is still handled on Yangon's docks.

Industrial suburbs have recently mushroomed in the eastern and northern sections of the city, providing work for many of the immigrants flocking to the Yangon area. There is a sizable Indian community in the city – a holdover from the time when Burma was still a part of the British India colony – as well as a large number of Chinese and indigenous ethnic minorities.

A stroll through Burma's capital is a unique experience. In what other modern city of more than 3 million people would the tallest structures be golden pagodas? And in what other 20th century capital city would nightlife be virtually nonexistent, save for the hustle

Mogul Street in colonial days.

and bustle of street markets?

However, with tourism and business heralding in a new age, traffic jams and an influx of modern cars have been added to the crowed streets crammed with older jitney-type local buses, trishaws and bicycles.

Exploring Yangon: "Sule Pagoda Road, with its five theaters, was mobbed with people, dressed identically in shirt (*longyi*) and rubber sandals, men and women alike puffing thick green cheroots, and looking (as they waved away the smoke with slender dismissing fingers) like a royal breed, strikingly handsome in this collapsing city, a race of dispossessed princes," wrote Paul Theroux, in his book *The Great Railway Bazaar*.

To stroll the streets of Yangon is to know the "dispossessed princes" of which Theroux writes. In the downtown area, amidst the mildewing grey brick government offices erected by the British colonialists, is the city's commercial centre, its markets and cinemas. And it is here the true colours of Yangon's

diverse population can be seen.

Theroux goes on to write: "I walked aimlessly... slowing down at temples where children – still awake at 11 at night – wove ropes of flowers and laughed before Buddhas. Older people knelt in veneration, or set up displays of fruit, balancing a melon in a hand of bananas on a temple shelf and sticking a red paper flag into the melon. Elderly women leaned against flower stalls, the smoking cheroots in their hands giving them a look of haughtiness and self-possession."

Temples, cinemas and savoury spices: Walking through Yangon like Theroux, you'll notice the pagodas sending their golden spires skyward among an assortment of latter-day Chinese and Hindu temples, Islamic mosques, Anglican cathedrals and a Jewish synagogue. You'll see the movie theatres, where the citizens flock to watch Western, Burmese and Indian films. You'll also be able to spot tiny residences opening directly onto the sidewalks, where vendors have spread a miscellany of spices

Yangon's Indian quarter.

and cheap domestic goods for sale to the highest bidder.

Occasionally, most frequently during the dry season, you'll stumble upon a night festival, featuring colourful shops and cafes lining the streets and a late-night performance of the *pwe*, the Burmese dance drama. And any time of the year, day or night, you'll find loquacious Burmese with their "whickin' white cheroot" of which Kipling once wrote so eloquently.

Sule Pagoda – the heart of the city: If the Shwedagon is the soul of Yangon, then surely, the **Sule Pagoda** is its heart.

For centuries, it has been the focus of much of the social and religious activity of the city. The British established the pagoda as the centre of the urban area when they structured their Victorian grid-street system around it in the mid-19th century.

Today, the 48-metre (157-ft) pagoda remains the tallest building in the town area, and although the street names have been changed to Burmese from English, the thoroughfares in the central city still intersect at right angles with geometrical symmetry.

The origins of the Sule Pagoda are bound up in the mythical pre-history of Burma. Perhaps the most credible tale is that of two monks, Sona and Uttara, who were sent from India as missionaries to Thaton after the Third Buddhist Synod about 230 BC. After some hesitation, the King of Thaton gave them permission to construct a shrine at the ft of Singuttara Hill. In it the monks preserved a hair of the Buddha which they had carried from India.

For centuries, the pagoda was known as Kyaik Athok ("Pagoda containing the hair relic" in the Mon language) or Sura Zedi, after Maha Sura, minister to the King of Thaton who supervised the construction of the pagoda. The name Sule Pagoda comes from a later period and can be linked with the Sule Nat, guardian spirit of Singuttara Hill.

The octagonal structure of the Sule Pagoda, which is consistent up to the bell and inverted bowl, clearly indicates its Brahman-Buddhist heritage. During

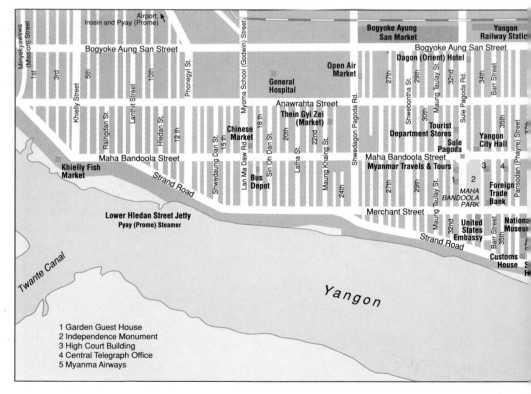

1 Garden Guest House
2 Independence Monument
3 High Court Building
4 Central Telegraph Office
5 Myanma Airways

the first centuries of the Christian era, when the influence of Indian merchants and settlers was especially strong, astrology blended with *nat* worship and Buddhist doctrine to create the unique Burmese brand of Buddhism. Even today, the Sule Pagoda, whose name and shape document this religious development, is a magnetic centre for astrologers and fortune-tellers.

Around the outside of the Sule Pagoda, which in the daytime acts as a tranquil traffic island in the middle of the city's busiest streets, are a number of small shops dealing in various trades. Inside the pagoda are the usual shrines and Buddha images, including four colourful Buddhas with neon halos behind their heads!

Temple festivals and feasts are frequent events held in the evening, and visitors might be lucky enough to catch one after dark. If a special procession is expected, the gates of the Sule Pagoda will be kept open past the usual 10pm closing time.

As with all pagodas, visitors should stroll around in a clockwise direction. The Sule Pagoda's eight sides, like those of the Shwedagon, are dedicated respectively to the days, planets and animals of the eight cardinal points. Its gold coat has worn off over the many years, and generous donations from all of Yangon's sectors have been collected to finance a new gilding.

Colonial remnants and museum relics: On the northeast corner of Sule Pagoda Road and Maha Bandoola Street, facing the pagoda, is the **Yangon City Hall**. Built by the British, it is a massive stone structure worth a glance for its colonial architecture with a Burmese touch. Note especially, the traditional Burmese peacock seal high over the entrance. On the southeast corner of the intersection is **Maha Bandoola Park**, named after a Burmese general of the First Anglo-Burmese War.

In the centre of the park is the **Independence Monument**, a 46-metre (150-ft) obelisk surrounded by five smaller 9-metre (30-ft) pillars. The monument represents Burma's five former semi-

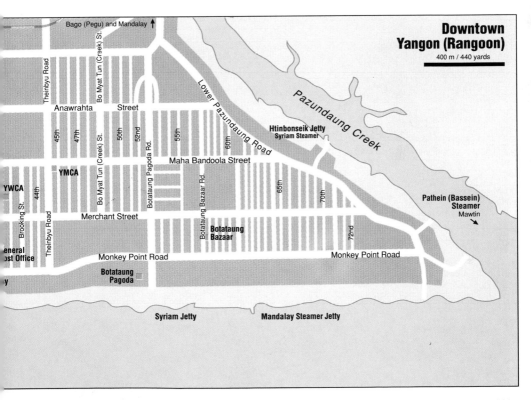

autonomous states – Shan, Kachin, Kayin (Karen), Kayah and Chin – in harmonious union with their larger Bamar (Burman) brother.

Facing the square on the east side stands the British-built **Supreme Court and High Court Building.**

If you travel east one block on Merchant Street, south of the park, and south on Pansodan (Phayre) Street, you'll arrive at the **National Museum** (to be relocated soon). The showpiece of the museum is the Lion's Throne, on which King Thibaw once sat in his hall of audience at Mandalay Palace.

Taken from Mandalay in 1886 after the Third Anglo-Burmese War, the throne and 52 other pieces of royal regalia were carried off by the English. Some items were left behind in the Indian Museum in Calcutta; others were kept in the Victoria and Albert Museum in London. They were returned to Burma as a gesture of goodwill in 1964 after Ne Win's state visit to England.

The throne, made of wood, is 8-metres (27 ft) high and is inlaid with gold and lacquer work. It is a particularly striking example of the Burmese art of wood carving. Among the other Mandalay Regalia, as they are known, are gemstudded arms, swords, jewellery and serving dishes.

Also in the archaeological section of the museum are artefacts from Burma's early history in Beikthano, Sri Ksetra and Bagan (Pagan). There is a 18th-century bronze cannon, a crocodile-shaped harp and many other items. The museum is open from 10am to 3pm, Monday to Friday.

Living in the past: Just around the corner from the National Museum, on Strand Road, is the famous **Strand Hotel**. By stopping over for the night or just simply for a meal, a visitor can get nostalgic over the British colonial era. Before its recent renovation, most of the then mosquito-infested rooms were still cooled by electric paddle fans. Indian waiters, however, still hover attentively over every table and every guest in the high-ceilinged restaurant.

The hotel has received a thorough

The Victorian High Court building.

facelift and rooms are no longer as reasonably priced as they were during the 1980s. Still, it's worth stepping into the teak-furnished lounge where you can have a cup of tea to the accompaniment of Burmese harp music during the afternoon. In the newly furnished bar, instead of the once mandatory Mandalay Beer, you can now also enjoy the usual drink of the colonial tropics – gin and tonic, which just a decade ago was unavailable in the country.

Across the street from the Strand, on the other side of a small park, you can see the muddy Yangon River. Several wharves jut into the river from one end of Yangon to the other, handling the country's maritime trade. Further downstream are jetties for steamers plying the route between Yangon, Pathein, Pyay and Mandalay.

Beholding the Botataung: Heading east on Strand Road for several blocks, you'll come to the **Botataung Pagoda**. It is said that when eight Indian monks carried some relics of the Buddha here more than 2,000 years ago, 1,000 mili-

tary officers (*botataung*) formed a guard of honour at the place where the rebuilt pagoda stands today.

The original Botataung pagoda was destroyed on November 8, 1943, when an Allied bomb scored a direct hit.

During the clean-up work, a golden casket in the shape of a stupa was found – and it contained a hair and two other relics of the Buddha.

In addition, about 700 gold, silver and bronze statues were uncovered, as well as a number of terra-cotta tablets. One of these tablets was of special interest; it was inscribed both in Pali and in the south Indian Brahmi script, from which modern Burmese developed.

Part of the find is displayed in the pagoda today. However, the relics and more valuable objects have been locked away once again for safe-keeping. Among them is the tooth of the Buddha, which Alaungsithu, one of the kings of Bagan, tried unsuccessfully to acquire from Nan-chao (now China's Yunnan province) in 1115. It was presented to the Burmese people by the People's

Republic of China in 1960.

The 40-metre (131-ft) stupa is unusual in that it is hollow, and visitors are able to walk around inside of it. A glass mosaic covers the interior of the room enclosed within the bell-shaped form of the stupa. There are many small alcoves here for private meditation.

Outside the pagoda is a small lake with thousands of turtles; nearby stalls sell food for the turtles, enabling the generous giver to acquire merit for a future existence.

At the end of Botataung Pagoda Road is the Syriam Jetty. Persons intent on making the 45-minute ferry trip across the river to Syriam should be warned, however, that the Syriam ferry leaves not from this jetty, but from the Htinbonseik Jetty on Pazundaung Creek, some distance east on Monkey Point Road (the eastern extension of Strand Road), then north.

On the way, you'll pass near the lively Botataung Bazaar on the left and a teak mill on the right. Though the ferry crossing is a lively experience, there is, for the less adventurous, the new Thanlyin bridge across the Bago River that connects Yangon with Syriam and shortens the travelling time considerably.

The oriental bazaar is still alive: West and north of the Sule Pagoda is Yangon's market district. Before World War II, a large majority of the inhabitants of Yangon were Indian or Chinese. The influence of their particular lifestyles is still reflected in Burmese markets today. The flavour of an oriental bazaar – the supermarket of preindustrial times – pervades, despite the inevitable adaptation to modern needs.

Largest of Yangon's markets and a must for every visitor, is the **Bogyoke Aung San Market** (formerly the Scott Market). At the corner of Sule Pagoda Road and Bogyoke Aung San Street, next to the red-brick Railway Administration Building with its Moorish arches (which is soon to be converted into a first class hotel), you can find under one roof all the consumer goods a Burmese family could possibly need or want. From spices to bicycles, local artefacts to Japanese stereo systems, everything is available here.

One can quite easily find the Western whisky and cigarettes sold to black-marketeers earlier the same day by Western travellers, though, since FEC's have been introduced, it is no more the profitable business it once was.

The days when it was difficult to buy so much as an electric light bulb in Yangon are now long gone. For Yangonians the problem has now become the affordability of the goods available. Since the government has introduced a market economy, those goods that once were smuggled in from Thailand are now imported legally.

Some of the smaller streets around Merchant Street already resemble the streets of Hong Kong, with TV sets, cameras, refrigerators, tape and video recorders piled case upon case. There are, however, no bargains, as prices are quite high, not only for Burmese.

Apart from consumer goods, visitors to Burma will find a wide variety of textiles and craft items in the Bogyoke Market. Woodcarvers, metalworkers,

Colonial elegance within the Strand Hotel

artists and weavers all have their stalls; lacquerware, dolls, musical instruments, printed *longyis*, Shan bags and wickerware are all attractive.

Opposite the Bogyoke Market is the **New Bogyoke Market** which deals mostly in imported textiles, household appliances, medicines etc.

The fabled "1,000 Scents of the Orient": To the south of the Bogyoke Market, off Shwedagon Pagoda Road, are the **open-air market** – especially noted for the delicious Chinese soup sold at many of its stalls – and, on the other side of an interesting **Hindu temple** on Anawrahta Street, the **Thein Gyi Zei** (Indian market). The oft-described "1000 Scents of the Orient" dominate this wholesale fruit and vegetable market. Mounds of red chillies and fragrant cinnamon bark, boxes of tropical fruits like mangosteen and durian, dried fish and seafoods, medicinal herbs and bottled concoctions, indigenous snack treats to tempt the palate, and so much more –it's hard to turn away.

Mushrooms and songbirds: There is,

however an equally fascinating destination when you leave the Indian market. Turn west on Maha Bandoola Street and follow it to Yangon's Chinatown.

Here, at the corner of Lan Ma Daw Road, is the **Chinese Market**. Amidst the flowers, live crabs and dried mushrooms, you'll find caged songbirds, tropical fish for aquariums, hand-made rice paper and knick knacks. As with the Indian market, the earlier you arrive in the morning, the wider the selection. In the evening these streets turn into one large sidewalk restaurant.

Adjoining the Chinese market is an iron bazaar, and a little further along, on the next block south is a colourful **Chinese temple**.

Most visitors will be satisfied to spend hours browsing through the streets between the Chinese Market and the Sule Pagoda, and north to the Bogyoke Market. For this quadrant is the scene of an almost picture-book-like hustle and bustle, especially in the early evening hours. The racial diversity and air of industry for which Yangon was famous in the

The harbour, where old meets new.

British colonial era can still be found, though there are no more betel nut sellers. The government has prohibited selling the ingredients on the street to get rid of the red stains that still mark most lower sections of the house walls.

A half-block north of the Sule Pagoda, on the west side of Sule Pagoda Road, are the **Tourist Department Stores**. Tourists are encouraged to shop here, especially for precious stones, on which the Burmese government has a monopoly. In fact, it is safer to make jewellery purchases from the stores here, as quality is guaranteed. There is a wide selection of other goods available here as well – but all payment must be made in foreign currency.

Close to the Yangon inland port lies the **Nyaung Pin Lay Market** which deals in basic consumer goods. Here you can find beans, rice, salt, pulse and many other staples, as they are shipped directly from the producers.

Along the southern and eastern stairway to the Shwedagon, the typical Buddhist "nibbana goods" are sold. Buddha images in alabaster, ivory and marble; gilded *nat*-images, umbrellas and prayer flags, puppets and rosaries; they are all found in a variety of stalls which offer fragrant jasmine, champak and magnolia flowers as well.

Beyond the Shwedagon, on a hill on Arzarni Road (Transport Road) just to the north, is the **Martyrs Mausoleum**. This patriotic monument contains the tombs of Aung San, (father of Aung San Suu Kyi), the leader of the Burmese independence movement, and six of his ministers who were assassinated during a cabinet meeting on July 19, 1947. Aung San was only 32 at the time. The pre-war prime minister, U Saw, was later found to be the instigator of the plot, and was executed in May 1948 along with the hired assassins.

From the mausoleum, go north to the intersection of Shwegondine Road, then turn east and you will soon reach the **Kyauk Htat Gyi Pagoda**.

Not really a pagoda in the traditional sense, the Kyauk Htat Gyi is actually a *tazaung* (pavilion) housing a 70-metre

A Yangon resident.

(230-ft) long reclining Buddha. The Buddha figure is just a few decades old, and required a total donation of 500,000 kyat (US$ 68,000) to produce.

Before its presence, an older Buddha figure dating from the turn of the 20th century was housed under the pagoda's roof. The newer sculpture is larger than the reclining Buddha of Bago (Pegu), but is not as well-known or venerated.

Elsewhere in the pagoda enclosure is a centre devoted to the study of sacred Buddhist manuscripts. About 600 monks live in the monastery annex and spend their days meditating and studying the old Pali texts.

Travelling southwards, you'll pass the **Nga Htat Gyi** on Campbell Road. Here, a huge sitting Buddha, sometimes called the "five-storey Buddha" because of its size, is housed in the **Ashay Tawya Kyaung** monastery.

Picnics and playgrounds beneath the martyr's gaze: The city of Yangon has more than a dozen parks where Yangonians love to spend the hot hours of the day, preferably beside a lake, in the shade of huge, old trees. They offer also an enjoyable break for visitors who are criss-crossing the city from one sight to the other.

On the north shore of the Royal Lakes is **Bogyoke Aung San Park**, featuring a statue of Burma's most famous martyr. The park stretches beyond the statue into the lake like fingers on a hand. Plants and trees have been labeled for easy identification as in a botanical garden. The children's playgrounds and picnic areas have become favorite attractions for Yangon's citizens, and families can be seen idling away leisure hours beside the lake.

Another memorable view is from the **Karaweik Restaurant** on the lake's eastern shore. This luxurious dining spot, constructed in the early 1970s, was designed after the distinctive *pyi-gyi-mun* barge of Burmese royalty. With its double bow depicting the mythological *karaweik*, a water bird from Indian prehistory, and a multi-tiered pagoda carried on top, the Karaweik restaurant represents the style and workmanship

The Karaweik restaurant on the Royal Lakes.

of traditional Burmese architecture.

Although the restaurant was constructed of brick and concrete (wood was ruled out because of its relatively short lifespan) and anchored to the lake bottom, the interior contains some marvelous lacquer work embellished with mosaic in glass, marble, and mother-of-pearl. You have to pay a small admission charge just to take a look, but once inside, the food is good – and the view of the Shwedagon is stunning. Classical dance performances normally are held here in the evening.

From orchids to apes: On the southern shore of the Royal Lakes are several attractions. The former Natural History Museum has been moved – and its structure remodeled into the joint venture Kandawgyi Hotel – but the flora can be examined in more detail at the **Horticultural Garden** off Lu Oh Yone Street, while the **Zoological Garden** on Bo Min Gaung Street (King Edward Avenue) has a good collection of birds, reptiles, apes and the like.

The main attraction used to be a rare white elephant, the very possession of which was enough to begin wars during the course of Burma's rocky history. Unfortunately, the beast died in 1979. The zoo is open from 6am to 6pm daily, and at 4pm everyday, visitors are permitted to ride the elephants and camels.

The next station northwest of Yangon on the circle line is **Kemendine** where, a short walk away from the station, is the **Koe Htat Gyi Pagoda** on Bargayar Road. There is a 20-metre (65-ft) high sitting Buddha inside the pagoda, and a small casket inside the statue is said to contain relics of the Buddha and some of his disciples. In the area of the pagoda are a great many *kyaung* (monasteries). This is a good place to watch the *pongyi* (monks) as they pour onto the streets early in the morning with their begging bowls. If you happen to come to Kemendine in the evening, the **Night Market (Nya Zei)** is lively.

Continuing northeast through the winding residential streets north of the Shwedagon, past the "Yangon modern" stucco houses built for westerners dur-

Water Festival celebrations in Yangon.

ing the colonial era, you'll reach the huge man-made **Inya Lake**. On the southern shore are the **Yangon Arts and Sciences University**, with over 10,000 students and some of the most modern architecture in the city, and the **Myanmar Sailing Club**, which sponsors regular races on the lake.

There are several artisan shops within the area of the lake, including weavers (No. 113 Thanlwin Street [Windermere Road] is a noted location), woodcarvers (especially near the corner of University Avenue and Kaba Aye Pagoda Road), and glass-blowers (just off Yogi Kyaung Street).

Perhaps the best known structure on the lake is the **Inya Lake Hotel**, built by the Soviet Union in the early 1960s. During the last 30 years most visitors to Yangon had to stay there in spite of its dismal reputation. In a joint venture with a company from Hong Kong, and an investment involving US$ 6.5 million, it has, however, recently been renovated and is now a 4-star hotel that lives up to its status.

U Nu and the legend of the Kaba Aye Pagoda: Just a little way north of Inya Lake is the **Kaba Aye Pagoda**. U Nu, the first prime minister of independent Burma, had this structure built between 1950 and 1952. Although it is a contemporary building, there is already a legend surrounding its origin. An old man dressed in white appeared before the monk Saya Htay while the latter was meditating near the town of Pakokku on the Ayeyarwady, and handed the monk a bamboo pole covered with writing. He requested that Saya Htay pass the pole on to U Nu, and demanded that the prime minister should actively do more for Buddhism.

U Nu, as well versed in religious affairs as in politics, received the bamboo pole – and complied with this miraculous demand. He built the Kaba Aye Pagoda about 12 kilometres (7.5 mi) north of downtown Yangon in preparation for the Sixth Buddhist Synod of 1954 to 1956, and dedicated the pagoda to the cause of world peace.

While lacking some of the aesthetic

Kyauk Htat
yi Pagoda.

appeal of other Yangon pagodas, the Kaba Aye is interesting nonetheless. Circular in shape, its height and diameter are an identical 34 metres (112 ft), and it contains relics of the two most important disciples of the Buddha. These were discovered in 1851 by the English general Cunningham in India, and was given to Burma after many years in the British Museum. Five 2.4-metre (7-ft, 10-inch) high Buddha statues stand opposite each of the five pagoda entrances, and a platform holds another 28 small gold-plated statues, representing the previous Buddhas. In the inner temple is a Buddha figure cast with 500 kg (1,102 lbs) of silver.

A "great cave" built by volunteers: On the grounds of the Kaba Aye Pagoda is the **Maha Pasan Guha**, or "great cave." U Nu had this artificial cave specially built for the Sixth Buddhist Synod. It is supposed to resemble India's Satta Panni Cave, where the First Buddhist Synod took place shortly after the death of Gautama Buddha.

Devout Buddhists worked voluntar-

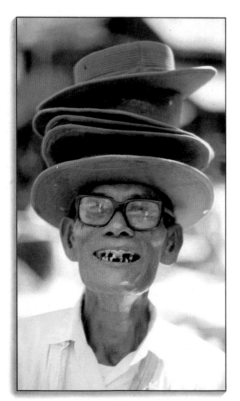

ily, without pay, on the construction of the cave, which measures exactly 139 by 113 metres (456 by 371 ft) and has an assembly hall which can house up to 10,000 people. The cave was completed after 14 months' work on May 14, 1954, three days before the start of the synod.

Upon conclusion of the Sixth Buddhist Synod, an **Institute for Advanced Buddhistic Studies** was founded with headquarters in the Kaba Aye Pagoda compound. Ford Foundation funds helped with the construction of its handsome building, a blend of modern architecture and traditional symbolism. Not far from it is the **Maha Vijaya Pagoda** which was built in 1980 to commemorate the unification of all Theravada orders in Burma.

Further north, near the Yangon Airport in the suburb of Okkalapa, is the **Mai La Mu Pagoda**. It is named after the mother of King Okkalapa, founder of Dagon. Legend maintains that Mai La Mu had this pagoda built to alleviate the suffering she felt upon the death of her young grandson. Her statue can be seen on the southwestern flank of the Shwedagon Pagoda.

This pagoda is of particular interest because it contains many illustrations and figures from the *Jataka* tales – depicting the Buddha in earlier lives – fashioned in a curiously Burmese style. There is also a reclining Buddha.

West of the airport, in Insein township, is the **Ah Lain Nga Sint Pagoda**. This pagoda serves as a centre of worship for the branch of Burmese Buddhism which lays greatest emphasis on the belief in the occult and supernatural phenomena. The grounds contain a five-storey tower, a hall with statues of all kinds of occult figures, and a *kyaung* where monks and believers in the occult live. It is fitting that this pagoda is outside Yangon city itself.

Generally speaking, Yangon residents are not as inclined to worship supernatural deities as are their rural counterparts. But even though few houses in Yangon today have coconuts hung in their corners in tribute to the house *nat*, few urbanites would totally deny the existence of such spirits.

Left, a cheerful hat peddler in Yangon. Right, bathing in the streets of Yangon

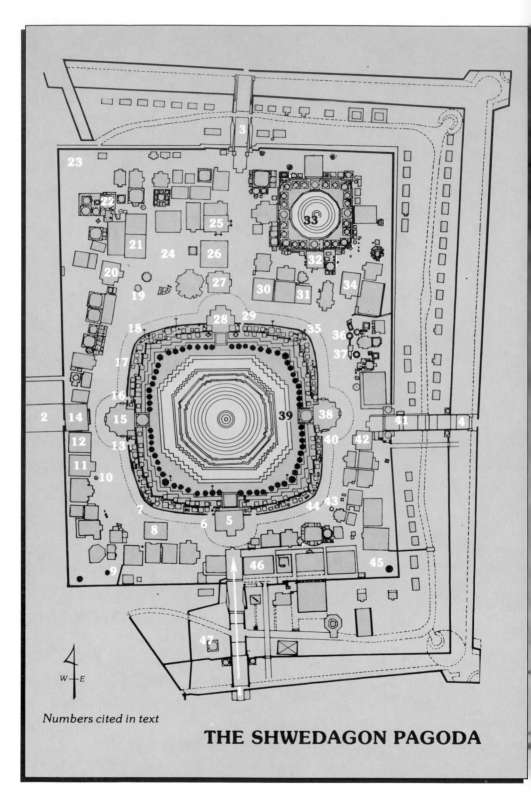

THE SHWEDAGON PAGODA

Numbers cited in text

W—E

124

THE SHWEDAGON PAGODA

"The Shwe Dagon rose superb, glistening with its gold, like a sudden hope in the dark night of the soul of which the mystics write glistening against the fog and smoke of the thriving city."

– W. Somerset Maugham,
The Gentleman in the Parlour (1930)

It has been said there is more gold on the Shwedagon Pagoda than in the vaults of the Bank of England. So even when not seen with mystical eyes, but rationally, Burma possesses a hidden kind of wealth. The massive bell-shaped stupa, which soars nearly 100 metres (326 ft) above its hilltop surroundings, is a treasure-trove inside and out.

Inside, according to legend, are enshrined eight hairs of the last Buddha, as well as relics of three previous Buddhas. Outside, the stupa is plated with 8,688 solid gold slabs, each worth more than US$ 400 today. The tip of the stupa is set with 5,448 diamonds and 2,317 rubies, sapphires and topaz. A huge emerald sits in the middle to catch the first and last rays of the sun. All this is mounted on and above a 10-metre (33-ft) *hti* (umbrella), built upon seven gold-plated bars, decorated with 1,065 golden and 420 silver bells. The golden stupa is surrounded by more than 100 other buildings – smaller stupas, pavilions and administrative halls.

A queen's weight in gold: While the origins of the pagoda are shrouded in legend, it certainly was well-established by the time Bagan (Pagan) dominated Burma in the 11th century. Anawrahta visited the Shwedagon during one of his southern campaigns. In 1372, King Byinnya U of Bago (Pegu) had the pagoda renovated, and 50 years later King Binnyagyan raised the stupa to a height of 90 metres (295 ft).

Binnyagyan's successor, Queen Shinsawbu (ruled 1453–1472), is still revered today for giving the pagoda its present shape and form. She established the terraces and walls around the stupa, and gave her weight in gold (40 kilograms/90 lbs) to be beaten into gold leaf and used to plate the stupa. This act has been repeated by many rulers in the course of the Shwedagon's history, as thin layers of gold cannot withstand the region's heavy seasonal rainfall. Queen Shinsawbu's successor, Dhammazedi, gave four times his weight in gold.

Even today, it is an important event for Burmese families who make a pilgrimage to the pagoda, to be able to buy a packet of gold leaf at one of the pagoda bazaars, and paste their offerings to the Shwedagon or another stupa or a Buddha image at the pagoda.

In 1485, Dhammazedi erected three stones on the Shwedagon's eastern stairway, telling the history of the pagoda from the time of its legendary founding in Burmese, Pali and Mon languages. The inscriptions can still be seen today.

Much of the ensuing history of the Shwedagon is the story told of its bells. A bell weighing approximately 30 tons, which Dhammazedi had donated, was plundered in 1608 by the Portuguese mercenary Philip de Brito y Nicote, who was based in Syriam. De Brito had intended to melt the bell down to make cannons – but as he attempted to ferry it across the Bago River, it fell into the water and was never recovered.

The pagoda's great bells: King Hsinbyushin of the Konbaung dynasty raised the stupa to its current height after a devastating 1768 earthquake brought down the top of the pagoda.

His son, Singu, had a 23-ton bronze bell cast in 1779; known as the Maha Gandha bell, it can be found today on the northwest side of the main pagoda platform. The British pillaged the pagoda during their 1824 to 1826 wartime occupation and tried to carry the bell to Calcutta, but fell victim to the same fate as the Portugese de Brito: this bell, too, sank into the river.

The British failed in several attempts to raise it. The Burmese said they would raise the bell on the condition it would be returned to its original resting place in the pagoda, and the British, thinking nothing would come out of the attempt, agreed. But the Burmese had an ingenious plan. Divers tied countless bamboo poles underneath the bell and floated it to the surface. The undertaking helped to instill the Burmese with nationalism during the years of British occupation.

A third bell weighing over 40 tons was donated by King Tharrawaddy in 1841 along with another 20 kilograms (45 lbs) of gold-plating. This bell, called the Maha Tissada, today sits on the northeast side of the pagoda enclosure.

British control and King Mindon's defiance: The Shwedagon was under British military control for 77 years between 1852 (the Second Anglo-Burmese War) and 1929. But the Burmese still had access to the pagoda.

In 1871, King Mindon of Mandalay sent a new diamond-studded *hti* to the pagoda, leading to a festive procession by more than 100,000 Burmese at the Shwedagon. The British were not pleased by the ruler's open statement of independence, but were powerless to stop the action.

In the 20th century, natural disasters have taken their toll. In 1931, two years after British troops left the pagoda, a serious fire broke out at the bottom of the western stairway and raced up and around the northern flank of the Shwedagon before being halted on the eastern stairway; many ancient monuments were destroyed. A 1930 earthquake caused minor damage, and another quake in 1970 – the ninth sizable tremor since the 16th century – led the government to undertake a special project to strengthen the pagoda's crown.

Despite its roller-coaster history, the Burmese people are convinced no lasting damage can befall the Shwedagon. Whenever the pagoda was endangered, unfailing generosity would restore it to an even greater glory.

The pagoda monsters: The passage most commonly used by visitors to the Shwedagon is the **Southern Stairway** (*zaungdan*) **(1)**, which comes from the direction of the city centre. Its 104 steps lead from Shwedagon Pagoda Road to the main platform.

Running up both sides of the stairs is a bazaar, licensed by pagoda authorities

The Maha Gandha Bell in 1825.

THE LEGEND OF SHWEDAGON

The legend surrounding the ancient Shwedagon pagoda is one of miracles. The story revolves around Okkalapa, king of Suvannabhumi, land of the Talaings. He lived in the region near Singuttara Hill in Lower Burma during the time when Siddhartha Gautama was still a young man in northern India.

Singuttara Hill was, and still is, a holy place, because of the relics of three previous Buddhas enshrined on top of the hill. These were a staff, a water dipper and a piece of garment.

It is said that a new Buddha comes into existence every 5,000 years. Therefore, it was believed that because nearly 5,000 years had passed since the last Buddha had walked the Earth, the hill was soon to lose its blessedness – unless the next Buddha appeared and offered a new gift to be enshrined as a relic for the next five millenia. Due to the urgency of this prophesy, King Okkalapa spent countless hours on top of the hill, meditating and praying so that relics might be obtained soon.

In India, meanwhile, Gautama was close to achieving enlightenment under the Bodhi tree in Bodhgaya. Legend has it that he magically appeared before Okkalapa around that time, promising that the king's wish would be granted.

Gautama Buddha had been meditating under the Bodhi tree for 49 days before he accepted his first gift from his disciples: a honey-cake offered by Tapussa and Bhallika, Burmese merchant brothers who had come from the village of Okkala. To express his sincere gratitude, Gautama plucked eight hairs from his own head and gave them to the brothers in appreciation.

Unfortunately, the merchants' journey back to Burma was beset with problem after problem. On the overland section of the trip, the king of Ajetta robbed the brothers of two of the Buddha's hairs. Then, while crossing the Bay of Bengal, the brothers encountered more misfortune, this time in the form of the seabed-dwelling king of the Nagas, who took another two of Gautama Buddha's holy hairs.

However, despite the brothers' loss, King Okkalapa had prepared a great feast for them when they arrived back home to Okkala. According to the legend, all the native gods and *nat* took part in the festivities, and together they decided on a place to erect a grand stupa to enshrine the relics of Gautama, the latest Buddha.

The story goes that when King Okkalapa opened the casket containing the Buddha's hairs, he discovered that all eight hairs were miraculously in place, despite the robbery of half of them.

As he gazed upon them in amazement, the hairs emitted a brilliant, heavenly light that rose high above the trees, radiating to all corners of the world.

All of a sudden, the blind everywhere found that they could see again; the deaf could hear again, the dumb could speak, and the lame could now walk. While all this happened, the earth quaked, lightning bolts flashed, the trees blossomed and bore ripe fruit, and a shower of colourful, precious stones rained down onto the ground.

Regardless of the truth of the popular legend, a 20-metre (66-ft) high golden pagoda was in fact erected on top of Singuttara Hill, still the present site of the jewel-encrusted golden pagoda.

Burma's holiest pagoda was built over the shrine containing the actual relics. Smaller pagodas made of silver, tin, copper, lead, marble and iron brick were built, one over the other in the golden pagoda, to enshrine the relics. ∎

to sell offerings – flowers and incense – and gilded remembrances to the Buddhist faithful.

The entrance is guarded by two mythological figures – a *chinthe* or leogryph, a half-lion, half-griffin beast; and an ogre, a man-eating monster often depicted as a giant. Their main duty is to make sure each visitor to the pagoda removes his or her shoes and socks before climbing the stairway.

As you climb the steps, you can still see a few older teak beams which survived the April 14, 1852 British assault, although the structure was rebuilt after the Second Anglo-Burmese War.

Half-way up, the stairway crosses the former pagoda moat over a concrete bridge; until 1928, there was a drawbridge here. The richly embellished landing on the terrace was renovated in 1934 by a wealthy Chinese man.

There is a lift at the foot of the south stairs for those who might find the climb too strenuous and need to rest. This is the one entrance foreign visitors have to take, since entering the pagoda is no longer free, and a ticket, paid with cash, has to be presented.

Fire on the stairway: The **Western Stairway (2)**, which leads up from U Wisara Road, was closed for almost 80 years during the British occupation.

Originally erected by Ma May Gale, the wife of King Tharrawaddy, it was damaged during the Second Anglo-Burmese War and kept closed by a British garrison. In 1931, a year after the stairway had been reopened, a stall at the foot of the stairs caught fire and the blaze spread through much of the pagoda area, causing severe damage to the precincts. This is the longest *zaungdan* with 166 steps. The landing on the platform bears the name **"Two Pice Tazaung" (14)** because of the contribution of two *pice* (a small copper coin) given daily by Buddhist businessmen and bazaar stall holders for the stairway's reconstruction.

The **Northern Stairway (3)** was built in 1460 by Queen Shinsawbu, and has 128 steps. The decorative borders to the steps are shaped like crocodiles.

Two water tanks can be seen to the north of the stairway; the one on the right bears the name *thwezekan*, meaning "blood wash tank." According to legend, during King Anawrahta's conquest of the Mon capital Thaton, his commander-in-chief, Kyanzittha, used the tank to clean his bloody weapons.

The **Eastern Stairway (4)** is much like an extension of the Bahan bazaar, which lies between the Royal Lake and the Shwedagon.

Souvenir, flower and book stalls are here, and there are a couple of tea shops on the stairway near the **Dhammazedi Stones (41)**, placed there by the king in 1485. This stairway, 118 steps in length, also suffered heavy damages during the British attack on the pagoda in 1852.

"Fantastic richness": After the stroll up the stairs, you'll undoubtedly be stunned, as was Maugham, by your first glimpse of the upper terrace:

"At last we reached the great terrace. All about, shrines and pagodas were jumbled pell-mell with the confusion with which trees grow in the jungle. They had been built without design or

Father and daughter on the way to worship.

symmetry, but in the darkness, their gold and marble faintly gleaming, they had a fantastic richness. And then, emerging from among them like a great ship surrounded by lighters, rose dim, severe, and splendid, the Shwe Dagon."

The terrace was created in the 15th century when the rulers of Bago (Pegu) levelled off the top of the 58-metre (190-ft) high Singuttara Hill. The terrace measures 275 metres (902 ft) from north to south and 215 metres (705 ft) from east to west. It is 5.6 hectares (14 acres) in area and is supported by a 15-metre (49-ft) high retaining wall.

The main platform is inlaid with marble slabs, which can be very hot under unaccustomed bare feet, so a mat pathway is laid out around the platform. As you walk on, you'll discover various pavilions (*tazaung*) and resting places (*zayat*) with traditional roofs of five, seven or nine tiers.

Eight sides, 64 stupas: At the centre of the platform is the famed gold-covered stupa. Its circumference at platform level is 433 metres (1,421 ft). Its base is octagonal and on each of the eight sides are eight smaller stupas, making 64 in all. (Maugham was wrong; there was method in the madness.) The four stupas opposite the stairways are the largest. At each of the platform's four corners are *manokthiha* (sphinxes), each surrounded by several *chinthes*.

On top of the main platform are three rectangular terraces (*pichayas*). These are topped by octagonal terraces, which in turn are topped by five circular bands. By means of this geometry, the vertical sides of the terraces merge with the swollen shape of the stupa's bell. The terraces account for 24 metres (79 ft) of the stupa's height. The next 22 metres (72 ft) comprise the bell (*khaung laung bon*). This section is 105 metres (344 ft) in diameter with a design of 16 petals on its shoulder.

Above the bell is the 12.5-metre (42-ft) high vaulted turban (*baungyit*), then an inverted bowl (*thabeik*) covered with lotus petals (*kyahlan*), which together measure 9.5 metres (32 ft) in height. The slender, heavily bejeweled part of the stupa begins above this point with a

16-metre (52-ft) banana bud (*hnget pyaw bu*). The whole edifice is crowned with the 10-metre (33-ft) vane capped by a golden orb (*seinbu*), tipped with a single, exquisite 76-carat diamond.

Now that you've savoured the magnificent stupa, it's time to cast your eyes over the rest of the pagoda's treasures. From the top of the southern stairway, begin walking left, or clockwise – the direction always to be taken at all Buddhist monuments.

Straight ahead at the top of the stairs is the **Temple of the Konagamana Buddha (5)**. Renovated in 1947, it is one of four *tazaungs* dedicated to previous Buddhas. In this temple are a great number of Buddha figures, probably among the oldest to be seen at the pagoda. The style and finish of these figures differ quite markedly from those produced today.

To the left and right of the Konagamana Temple is a **Planetary Post for Mercury (6)**. There are eight of these planetary posts around the stupa, and a gilded alabaster Buddha figure is

Resting with the *chinthe*.

to be found beside each one. Offerings of flowers and small flags are made here, and the figures are ritually washed. The planet Mercury is associated with a tusked elephant; its special day is *Bohddahu*, which runs from midnight to noon on Wednesday according to the eight-day Burmese week.

On the southwestern side of the stupa is the **Planetary Post for Saturn (7)** allied with the *naga* (mythological serpent) and Saturday. Opposite this post is the *tazaung* of the **Chinese Community (8)**, a pavilion housing 28 small Buddha figures representing the 28 Buddhas who have so far lived on earth. Near the south-west corner of the platform is a **Commemorative Column (9)** inscribed in Burmese, English, French and Russian, a salute to the 1920 student revolt which sparked Burma's drive for independence from Great Britain. A short distance north, the **Guardian *Nat* of the Shwedagon (10)**, Bo Bo Gyi, is kept behind glass (he's on the right) with the figure of Thagyamin, king of the *nat*.

Entering Nibbana: Continuing down this side of the platform, one next comes to the **Rakhine (Arakan) Tazaung (11)**. Next to this pavilion, built by two Rakhines (Arakanese), is an 8.5-metre (28-ft) reclining Buddha. The Buddha's head is pointing north, indicating that he is in a state of transition into nibbana. At his foot is a figure of Ananda, his favourite pupil, as well as figures of Shin Sariputta and Shin Moggalana, two of the Buddha's apostles who left this world before their teacher. Pictures on the rear wall of the Rakhine Tazaung depict the legend of the founding of the Kyaiktiyo Pagoda near Thaton. The pavilion is inlaid with beautiful, intricate wood carvings, as is the neighbouring **Chinese Merchants' Tazaung (12)**. There are many Buddha images here.

Opposite these two pavilions are **Statues of Mai La Mu and Sakka (13)**. These two legendary figures are said to be the parents of King Okkalapa, the founder of the Shwedagon. They are situated under white umbrellas, the symbol of royalty, on the first terrace on the

Pagoda sweepers earn merit.

130

southwestern side of the stupa. The homeland of Sakka (or Thagyamin), king of the *nat*, is in the heavenly province of Mount Meru, the centre of the universe. Mai La Mu, considered the founder of a pagoda bearing her name in northern Yangon, is said to have been born from the La Mu fruit.

Directly across the platform from the **Two Pice Tazaung (14)** is the **Temple of the Kassapa Buddha (15)**. Originally built by Ma May Gale in 1841, it was destroyed in the great fire of 1931 and later rebuilt. Flanking it is the **Planetary Post for Jupiter (16)**. This planet is allied with the rat and Thursday. Further to the north is a **Statue of King Okkalapa (17)**, situated under a white umbrella on the northwestern side of the stupa. In the northwest corner is the **Planetary Post for Rahu (18)**, the mythical planet allied with the tuskless elephant and Wednesday afternoon.

Sunny days and bath days for the Buddhas.

In an open area to the northwest of the stupa is a small octagonal pagoda known as the **Pagoda of the Eight Weekdays (29)**. On each side is a niche containing a small Buddha image, with an animal above it corresponding to the eight Burmese weekdays.

Behind it is the **Maha Gandha Bell (20)**, the huge bronze bell King Singu had cast in 1779 and which was raised from the Yangon River in 1825 after the British attempted to carry it off. The bell weighs 23 tons, is 2.2 metres (7 ft, 3 in) high and has a diameter of 1.95 metres (6 ft, 5 in) at its mouth. A 12-line inscription in Burmese requests that the donor (Singu) reach nibbana for performing this good deed.

When *Sayadaw* talk, monks listen: Across from the bell pavilion is an **Assembly Hall (21)** containing a nine-metre (30-ft) high Buddha image. Lectures on Buddhist teachings are often held in this *tazaung*. The *sayadaws* (abbots), who often speak here in front of several hundred saffron-clad monks, are among the most respected men in Burmese society. The Buddha figure gives the impression that he is present and watching the proceedings.

There are a number of small stupas in

the northwestern corner of the terrace. In one of these is the **Wonder Working Buddha Image (22)**, virtually always decorated with flowers and surrounded closely by the faithful. The gilded Buddha in the stupa's niche has the reputation of being able to fulfill wishes and work miracles.

In the far northwest corner of the terrace are two **Bodhi Trees (23)** adorned with flowers and small flags. The smaller of the two trees is a cutting from the holy Bodhi tree in Bodhgaya, India, under which the Gautama Buddha gained enlightenment. It was planted by U Nu, first prime minister of Burma. The second tree is slightly older, having been planted in 1903, and its roots have grown to surround several small altars.

Returning to the main part of the pavilion, you'll notice an especially busy location. This is known as the **Wish Fulfilling Place (24)**, where devotees kneel, facing the great Shwedagon stupa, praying in great earnest that their wishes will come true.

In a nearby cluster of pavilions near the north entrance is a **Tazaung With Buddha's Footprint (25)**. Lifesized statues of Indian guards stand in front of this hall, and a dragon stands guard over a representation of the Buddha as prince. In front of the "prince" is a *chidawya*, or footprint of the Buddha. This is actually a copy of the original, but is said to have been made by the Buddha himself from the footprint in the Shwesattaw Pagoda in Upper Burma. The footprint is divided into 108 sections, each of which has a special significance.

The building to the south is the Library of the **Zediyingana Society (26)**. More than 6,000 books, many of them rare texts on religion and Burmese culture, are housed in the library. The Zediyingana Society is one of seven societies responsible for maintaining Burma's pagoda and making necessary improvements.

Between the library and the stupa is the **Sandawdwin Tazaung (27)**, built in 1879 over the spring in which, according to legend, the Buddha's eight hairs were washed before they were **Monks at an open-air university.**

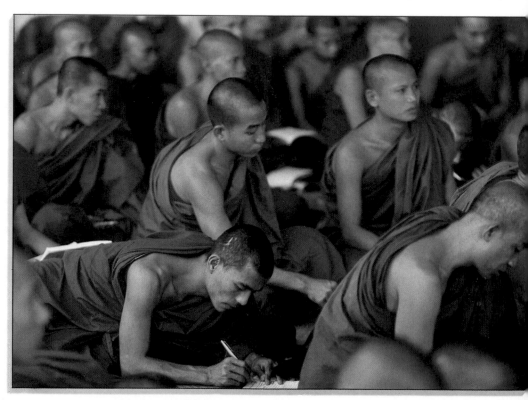

enshrined. The spring is said to be fed by the Ayeyarwady (Irrawaddy) River.

On the north side of the main stupa is the **Temple of the Gautama Buddha (28)**. It is dedicated to the Buddha whose world dominion will last until the 45th century. Beside it is the **Planetary Post for Venus (29)**, especially frequented by persons born on Fridays.

Across the platform is the **Mahabodhi Pagoda (30)**, a replica of the original pagoda of the same name in Bodhgaya, India. It is noticeably different from all other pagodas in the Shwedagon precincts which are built in distinct Bamar (Burman) or Mon styles.

A Burmese oracle: Across from the northeast corner of the stupa is the **Kannaze Tazaung (31)**. Legend says it was here that King Okkalapa prayed for relics of the Gautama Buddha. The Buddha figure in this shrine is therefore called Sudaungbyi, "Buddha grants the prayer of the king." In front of this is the "wish-granting stone," a sort of Delphic oracle. One bows before Sudaungbyi and lifts the stone, saying, "May this stone seem light to me, if my wish is to be fulfilled." If the stone still feels heavy, one has not been successful.

North of this pavilion is the **Shin Itzagona Tazaung (32)**. Inside it is a Buddha statue with large eyes of different sizes. It is said to have been erected by or for Shin Itzagona, a *zawgyi* (alchemist) from Bagan's early period.

According to legend, his obsession with discovering the Philosopher's Stone, the mythical substance said to be able to change base metals to gold or silver, had plunged the country into poverty. When his final experiment was about to end in failure, he poked out both his eyes to satisfy the king. But in his final casting, he produced the Philosopher's Stone. He quickly sent his assistant to the slaughter house to obtain two eyes which would, with the stone's help, allow him to regain his sight. The assistant returned with one eye from a goat and another from a bull; from that time on, Shin Itzagona was known as "Monk Goat-Bull."

Just to the north is the **Naungdawgyi**

Pagodas
dwarf monks
on the
Shwedagon
terrace.

Pagoda (33), situated in the place where the eight hairs of the Buddha carried by the merchants Tapussa and Bhallika were originally kept. The stupa, which looks like a smaller version of the great Shwedagon stupa, was reportedly erected by King Okkalapa and was later enlarged by King Bayinnaung.

Nearby is the **Maha Tissada Bell (34)**, commissioned by King Tharrawaddy in 1841. It weighs almost 42 tons, is 2.55 metres (8 ft, 4 in) high and has a diameter of 2.3 metres (7 ft, 6 in) at its mouth.

The **Planetary Post for the Sun (35)** is at the northeast corner of the great stupa. Its special day, of course, is Sunday; it is associated with the *galon*, the mythical bird (called *garuda* elsewhere in Southeast Asia) which guards one of the terraces of Mount Meru. Across the platform to the east are a **Replica of the *hti* (36)** originally donated by King Hsinbyushin in 1774, and a **Replica of the Apex of the Pagoda (37)**, sent by King Mindon from Mandalay in 1871.

Keep your eye on the hand: Opposite the Eastern Stairway is the Temple of the **Kakusandha Buddha (38)**. It was originally built by the wife of King Tharrawaddy, Ma May Gale, as was the Western Stairway. But the fire of 1931 destroyed it. The temple was rebuilt in its original style in 1940. The Buddha figure in this *tazaung* is renowned for the fact that the palm of its right hand is turned upward – contrary to that of other representations of the Buddha. In front of the niche are four more sitting Buddhas, three of which are depicted in the same unusual posture.

Behind the temple, in a niche on the eastern side of the upper platform, is the **Tawa Gu Buddha (39)**. This statue is said to be able to work miracles. As the upper platform of the pagoda is reserved for men, a five-kyat admission ticket can be purchased by men only at the administration building on the west side of the pagoda. On the upper platform, the visitor will come across devout Buddhists, both monks and novices, deep in meditation.

Beside the Kakusandha temple is the

Lighting candles at a planetary post.

Planetary Post for the Moon (40), which is recognized as one of the eight planets in Burmese astrology. The tiger is its animal and Monday is its day. From this point, one can turn around and descend the Eastern Stairway a short distance to arrive at the **Dhammazedi Stones (41)**.

The *tazaung* which originally housed these stones was one of the last buildings destroyed by the 1931 fire before the blaze was finally brought under control. Because of these inscriptions, King Dhammazedi – himself a *zawgyi* – has gone down in Burmese history as the "master of the runes."

Next to the eastern entrance of the terrace is the **U Nyo Tazaung (42)**, which has wood-carved panels relating events in the life of the Gautama Buddha. Close to the southeast corner of the platform is a **Hamsa Tagundaing (43)** or prayer pillar. Such pillars are said to guarantee the health, prosperity and success of their founders. At the top of the pillars is a *hamsa* or *hintha*, sacred bird of the Bago (Pegu) dynasty. On the southeast side of the great stupa is the **Planetary Post for Mars (44)**. This planet is associated with the lion and its corresponding day is Tuesday.

At the far southeastern corner of the terrace is a **Bodhi Tree (45)** which, like its cousin in the northwest corner, is said to be a cutting of the original at Bodhgaya. On the octagonal base which surrounds it is a huge Buddha statue. A **Curio Museum (46)** is situated to the east of the pagoda's south entrance. It contains a collection of small pagodas, statues and other objects.

Partway down the Southern Stairway is a **Pigeon Feeding Square (47)**. Pagoda pilgrims can buy food here to feed the dozens of pigeons, thereby earning merit for a future existence.

The Shwedagon is open daily from 4am to 9pm (though tickets for foreigners are not available before 6am). This ensures that pre-dawn and post-twilight visitors have plenty of leeway. Buses and taxis make the run from downtown Yangon up Shwedagon Pagoda Road in approximately 15 minutes.

Feeding the birds of peace within the pagoda grounds.

PEACE PRESBYTERIAN CHURCH
7624 CEDAR LAKE ROAD
ST. LOUIS PARK, MINNESOTA

IN
Remembrance

EARL N. DORN
1921-1996

PEACE PRESBYTERIAN CHURCH
7624 CEDAR LAKE ROAD
ST. LOUIS PARK, MINNESOTA

JULY 23, 1996   1:30 P.M.

A SERVICE IN MEMORY OF **MR. EARL N. DORN**

Organ Prelude

Call to Worship

Invocation

*Hymn#280   Amazing Grace

Old Testament - Selected Scripture

Solo   "What A Friend We Have In Jesus"

New Testament - Selected Scripture

In Memoriam   **EARL N. DORN**

A Time For Sharing

"My Psalm"   John Greenleaf Whittier

*Hymn   "The Lord's Prayer"
            (Please refer to the music insert)

The Benediction

*Please stand.

426 The Lord's Prayer

This, then, is how you should pray. Matt. 6:9

Our Fa - ther, which art in heav - en, Hal - low - ed
be Thy name. Thy king - dom come,
Thy will be done on earth as it is in heav -
en. Give us this day our dai - ly bread, And for - give us our

TEXT: Matthew 6:9-13
MUSIC: Albert Hay Malotte; arranged by Donald P. Hustad
Copyright used by permission of G. Schirmer, Inc.

(PLEASE TURN TO OTHER SIDE)

MALOTTE
Irregular meter

Organist . . . . . Merna Knight

Soloist . . . . . Betty Kringlee

Pastor . . . . . The Rev. Mr. John Foss

STEP BY STEP

He does not lead me year by year,
  Not even day by day.
But step by step my path unfolds;
  My Lord directs my way.

Tomorrow's plans I do not know;
  I only know this minute.
But He will say, "This is the Way;
  By faith, now, walk ye in it."

And I am glad that it is so;
  Today is enough to bear.
And when tomorrow comes, His grace
  Shall far exceed its care.

What need to worry, then or fret?
  When God who gave his Son
Holds all my moments in His Hand,
  and gives them one by one.

— Author unknown

The Dorn family invites all in attendance to please
come to the fellowship hall on the lower level of
the church for coffee and refreshments and a chance
to visit with the family and each other.

BAGO, SYRIAM AND SOUTHERN BURMA

Near the small town of Hlegu, high-wheeled ox-carts piled high with golden rice trundle slowly down the road, driven by beaming country youths delivering their just-harvested bounty to government purchase stalls.

In ancient Bago (Pegu), multitudes of reverent Buddhist worshipers offer incense and flowers to the Shwethalyaung Buddha, a 55-metre (180-ft) long reclining Buddha with a smile to make the Mona Lisa envious.

In Syriam, Mawlamyine (Moulmein), Pathein (Bassein) and other cities whose names ring like temple bells from Burma's past, citizens carry on their daily activities as they have for centuries, affected very little by the modern Western influence that has so dramatically altered lifestyles in neighbouring countries of Southeast Asia.

Indeed, once the visitor gets out of Yangon, he will find a different Burma waiting to be explored and savoured. One of the best ways to begin is by making the 80-kilometre (50-mi) day trip to Bago (Pegu).

The many monuments of Bago today stand in solemn witness to the glory that once belonged to this provincial capital. Formerly Burma's greatest seaport – medieval European travellers commented on its magnificence – the city of 50,000 lies northeast of Yangon on the Bago River. The massive Shwemawdaw Pagoda, the famous reclining Buddha and many other reminders of bygone empire are worthy of a visit.

Down the Thanlwin to a "Golden Land": To appreciate a trip to Bago, one must first understand the history of the Talaing (Mon) people in Burma. Like the Pyus (predecessors of the Bamars [Burmans]), they arrived from the north.

The Talaings, however, came a little earlier, and ventured down the Thanlwin River instead of the Ayeyarwady. Their "Golden Land of Suvannabhumi" stretched from present-day Malaysia to the Bay of Bengal, with its capital of Thaton situated on the east side of the Sittoung (Sittang) River.

According to legend, Bago at the time was a tiny island off the coast in the Gulf of Martaban. It was so small that there was room enough on the island for only one *hamsa* (*hintha*), a mythological duck. Indeed, the duck's mate had to perch upon his back and even today, the women of Bago are teased about their "*hamsa*-like" attachment to their men. The legend gave the town the name by which it was known during the years of its greatest power: Hamsawaddy.

From ducks' nest to Talaing seaport: Over the years, the mythological nesting place was joined to the Burma coastline by the accretion of silt deposited by the rivers. A seaport was founded there, allegedly in AD 825 by two brothers from Thaton, who, like other inhabitants of this coastal stretch, were descendants of Talaing and Indian settlers. (Many historians believe the name "Talaing," which until recently referred to the Mon people along the Gulf of Martaban coast, may be descendants of the immigrants from Telingana near Madras, India.)

In 1057, Anawrahta of Bagan (Pagan) conquered Thaton, the Mon capital, and the whole of southern Burma fell under Bamar sovereignty for the next 250 years. Thaton never managed to recover from the conquest.

When Wareru established his own Talaing Empire in 1287 after the downfall of the First Burmese Empire at the hands of the Mongols (led by Kublai Khan), he picked Martaban, near Mawlamyine, as his capital. His successor, Byinnya-U, transferred the capital to Bago (Hamsawaddy) in 1365, beginning a golden era for the city that lasted until 1635 In that year, the capital was transferred by King Thalun's Second Burmese Empire to Innwa (Ava), near Mandalay. By that time, the harbour at Bago had become so shallow as a result of silt deposits, that trading vessels could no longer dock there.

Shinsawbu and Dhammazedi: During its 270-year "golden era," however, Bago's Hamsawaddy dynasty produced rulers who are still loved by the people of Burma today, and who left behind many sacred monuments. They included King Razadarit (1385–1425), Queen Shinsawbu (1453–1472) and King Dhammazedi (1472–1492).

Born in 1394, Shinsawbu was the daughter of King Razadarit. Twice widowed, she was married to the King of Innwa (Ava) when, in her 30s, she began to study ancient Buddhist texts. Two Mon *pongyi* living in Innwa, Dhammazedi and Dhammapala, tried to help her with her studies.

In 1430, unhappy with her life at the Innwa court, she decided to flee to her homeland, assisted by the two monks. Both men were familiar with the science of runes (a branch of alchemy), and using this knowledge to their advantage, they changed daily the colour of the boat in which they were fleeing down the Ayeyarwady.

When Shinsawbu became Queen of Hamsawaddy 23 years later, she sought to find a successor to the throne during her own lifetime and concluded that it must be one of the two monks. One morning she placed a robe, a model of a white (royal) umbrella, a yak's tail, a crown, a sword, and some sandals in one of the begging bowls used by the monks, and hoped the more worthy of the two would take up the bowl. Dhammazedi made the choice. Dhammapala felt he had been unfairly pushed into the background and challenged Dhammazedi to a battle of runes. In the end, Dhammapala lost, his runes too weak to withstand the symbols of Dhammazedi.

Her eyes fixed on the Shwedagon: Shinsawbu devoted her final years to enlarging the Shwedagon Pagoda, and actually settled in the village of Dagon. She lived to be 78 years old, and legend says she cast a final glance at the famous golden stupa as she died.

Dhammazedi ruled for 20 years after Shinsawbu's death, but was to be followed by weaker rulers.

In 1541, Tabinshweti, king of the Toungoo Dynasty and founder of the Second Burmese Empire, peacefully annexed Bago and made it the capital of his empire. His successor, Bayinnaung,

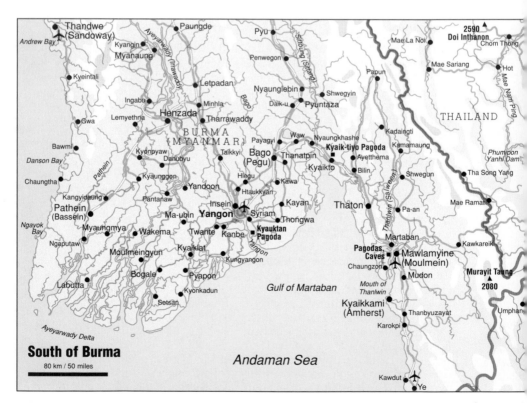

South of Burma

extended the empire's boundaries but drained the treasury with his campaigns. He twice conquered Ayutthia, capital of Siam, but was never in a position to leave a stable government in the subjugated region. Although Bago may have been the most splendid city in Asia during the period, the country itself was reduced to poverty.

In 1599, the finishing touches were applied when Anaukhpetlun, ruler of Toungoo, conquered Lower Burma and razed Bago as well as Syriam. Thus Bayinnaung's magnificent Hamsawaddy, which had in no small measure been built up from the proceeds of his campaign booty, was reduced to ashes within 33 years of his ascendancy.

In 1740, Bago became the capital of a short-lived Mon Empire. After only 17 years, however, the city again had to suffer the agony of total destruction. Alaungpaya, founder of the Konbaung dynasty, was ruthless in suppressing the upstart empire. Bago's Mon inhabitants either fled to Thailand or interbred with the victorious Bamars. King Bodawpaya (1782–1819) attempted to rebuild the city, but with the changing of course of the Bago River, it never again approached its former greatness. Today, only Bago's many monuments serve as reminders of a glorious past.

Travelling to Bago: A trip to Bago is to be highly recommended. Only recently, a hotel, the Shwewartun, has been opened that can also be used by foreigners. This offers the opportunity to stay overnight in this fascinating city. You can also just go on a day trip. Trains depart hourly from Yangon, and overcrowded buses leave every half-hour from the highway bus centre at Hledan Street in Kamayut Township. A taxi is probably the best way to travel, especially if the cost can be split among several people.

An extra bonus in travelling by taxi is the vista across the countryside between the Bago (Pegu) Yoma and the Sittoung River, one of the most intensive rice-cultivating regions of Burma.

During the harvest months of January and February, it is especially rewarding to stop about halfway through the journey in **Hlegu**, where the government operates stalls to accept delivery of the bounty from newly-harvested rice paddies. Watching the country people at work, the visitor gets a clear sense of the easygoing cheerful spirit which, together with Buddhism, has determined the pattern of village life here for centuries.

Before reaching Hlegu, though, the traveller from Yangon comes to a fork in the highway at **Htaukkyan**. The western road heads into Upper Burma via Pyay (once Prome now also called Pyi) and the Ayeyarwady Valley. The eastern road follows the Sittoung (Sittang) Valley and leads to Mandalay via Bago and Toungoo. Taking the eastern fork, you'll discover the **British War Cemetery** shortly after leaving Htaukkyan on the right. Some 27,000 Allied soldiers who fell during the World War II campaign in Burma are buried there. The Imperial War Graves Commission maintains the grounds.

Buddha and the cobra – the Naga cult: A little further along the road, at a military checkpoint, you'll notice to your left a

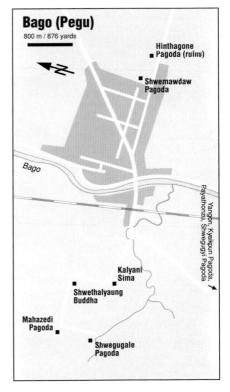

Bago (Pegu)

800 m / 876 yards

Hinthagone Pagoda (ruins)

Shwemawdaw Pagoda

Bago

Yangon, Kyakpun Pagoda, Payathonzu, Shwegugyi Pagoda

Kalyani Sima

Shwethalyaung Buddha

Mahazedi Pagoda

Shwegugale Pagoda

long wall built in Mandalay style. Behind it is a *kyaung* and a huge **Naga-Yone Enclosure**: a Buddha figure sits entwined by a cobra, whose head is bent over the Buddha. The enclosure is surrounded by a moat, and houses the eight astrological guardian animals at its eight cardinal points. An expression of typical Burmese religion, this combination of Buddhism, Brahman astrology and the *naga* cult is a nonetheless fascinating insight into the culture of the Burmese peoples.

The origin of the *naga* cult is still unknown. It left traces of its pure form in China and India, and was worshiped in pre-Buddhist times in Tagaung. But when Buddhist kings assumed power in those areas where the *naga* cult was dominant, the cult was assimilated in folk Buddhism.

According to legend, during the fifth of the seven weeks he spent meditating after achieving enlightenment, the Buddha's life was threatened by a storm which blew up over Lake Mucalinda. A *naga*, or serpent, living nearby observed the peril. The animal coiled its body protectively around the Buddha, covering the Enlightened One's head with its own hooded head, thereby shielding the Buddha from the storm.

This story symbolizes the assimilation of the *naga* cult with Buddhist doctrine, and forms the basis of all *naga-yone* enclosures in Burma. The *naga* itself, half snake and half dragon, is no longer worshipped. But it is still present in the customs of Upper Burma.

For instance, a man who has been a monk will never, if he can avoid it, travel in the opposite direction to that in which the head of the *naga* is pointing. Every three months, the *naga* is said to change the direction of its gaze, and a journey "into the jaws of the *naga*" can only bring disaster, it is said.

Shwemawdaw Pagoda – the pride of Bago: Just as Yangon's glory is reflected in the stupa of the Shwedagon, Bago has its own golden landmark. This is the **Shwemawdaw Pagoda** ("Great Golden God Pagoda"), visible from about 10 kilometres (6 mi) outside the city. At the

A *naga* on the road to Bago.

eastern end of Bago, it has many similarities to the Shwedagon – and is in fact even taller than its more fabled cousin, today standing a full 114 metres (374 ft) in height.

Legend has it that two merchant brothers, Mahasala and Kullasala, returned from India with two hairs personally given to them by Gautama Buddha. They built a small stupa over the relics, a shrine which was enlarged several times over the years, once by the historical founders of Bago, Thamala and Wimala. Sacred teeth were added to the relic collection in 982 and 1385. King Dhammazedi had a bell cast and inscribed it with runes that are still indecipherable today from their post on the pagoda's main platform.

In the 16th century, King Bayinnaung gave the jewels from his crown to make a *hti* for the pagoda, and later, in 1796, King Bodawpaya donated a new umbrella and raised the height of the pagoda to 90 metres (295 ft).

The Shwemawdaw has been hit by three serious earthquakes this century, and was almost completely destroyed by the last one in 1930. After World War II, however, it was rebuilt larger than ever with voluntary donations and unpaid labour. In 1954, it got a new diamond-studded *hti*.

Climbing to the terrace: Like Yangon's Shwedagon, the Shwemawdaw's main terrace is approached from four directions by covered stairways. There are not as many brightly coloured *tazaungs* or *zayats* as at the Shwedagon, but there is a small museum containing some ancient wood and bronze Buddha figures salvaged from the ruins of the 1930 quake. The terrace also contains the eight planetary prayer posts, of course, as well as a number of statues honouring certain *nat*. The latter are especially revered by the people of Bago, as the *nat* are heroes of Bago's history.

The stairways leading to the pagoda are guarded by huge white *chinthe*, each containing a sitting Buddha in its mouth. The stairways themselves are like bazaars, with everything from medicinal herbs to monastic offerings for sale.

Bago's Shwemawdaw Pagoda.

Faded murals along the main entrance steps recall the destruction of the pagoda by the 1930 earthquake and its later reconstruction.

Just behind the Shwemawdaw is **Hinthagone Hill**. The ruins of an ancient pagoda stand on top of the hill; in front of it is a statue of a pair of *hamsa* one mythological duck on top of the other, as in the legend of Bago. Indeed, geologists suspect that this hill was at one time an island in the Gulf of Martaban. A high-roofed platform atop the hill provides a good view of the region surrounding Bago.

As the Shwemawdaw is at the opposite end of Bago from other buildings of tourist interest, the visitor should retrace his steps in the direction of Yangon, crossing the Bago River bridge (behind which lies the interesting market) and the railroad tracks. About 0.5 kilometre (1 mi) west of the station, a short distance to the north of the main road, are a number of sacred structures.

Ceylon and Burmese Buddhism: The first one you'll encounter is the **Kalyani Sima**, or hall of ordination. King Dhammazedi built this *sima* in 1476 for the rejuvenation of the Burmese Sangha. When the unity of Buddhism in Burma was threatened by schisms in the wake of the downfall of the First Burmese Empire, Dhammazedi sent 22 monks to Ceylon (Sri Lanka), then regarded as the stronghold of Theravada Buddhism. The monks were ordained at the island's Mahavihara Monastery, founded in 251 BC on the banks of the Kalyani River. Upon their return to Burma after surviving a shipwreck, Dhammazedi had this building constructed and named it after the Ceylonese river. The Mahavihara *pongyi* performed a unified ordination of Burmese monks early in the 16th century, thus assuring the continuity of Burmese Buddhism. To this day, novices are ordained into the Sangha in this hall.

To the west of the Kalyani Sima are 10 large tablets containing detailed information on the history of Buddhism in Burma, and on the country's 15th century trade with Ceylon and south India.

The great reclining Shwethalyaung Buddha.

Three stones are inscribed in Pali, the other seven in Mon. Although some of the tables are shattered and illegible in places, the complete text has been preserved on palm-leaf copies.

The Kalyani Sima, model for 397 other *sima* built by Dhammazedi, did not escape the ravages of the Mons' war-like history. The Portuguese adventurer de Brito destroyed it first in 1599. Alaungpaya razed the reconstructed hall when he sacked Bago in 1757, and the *sima* suffered the same fate as the Shwemawdaw during the earthquake of 1930.

The *sima* was rebuilt in 1954 and dedicated to its original purpose at a ceremony attended by U Nu. Around the *sima* are lodgings for monks, and the park-like grounds radiate a feeling of peacefulness readily associated with Buddhist *kyaung*.

At present the archaeological department is conducting extensive excavations at Begu which should shed a new light on this period of the country's colourful history. The Palace of Bayinnaung is being reconstructed and should soon give us a good idea of the splendour of Bago's heyday.

The Shwethalyaung Buddha – Gautama enters Nibbana: To the northeast is the **Shwethalyaung Buddha**, revered throughout the country as the most beautiful reclining Buddha. It is said to depict Gautama on the eve of his entering nibbana. Some 55 metres (180 ft) long and 16 metres (52 ft) high, it is not as large as Yangon's Kyauk Htat Gyi Buddha built in the 1960s, but is much better known and loved – a result of its artistry and long history.

Bago's reclining Buddha was built in 994 by King Migadippa I, well before the Mons had been overpowered by the Bamars. It was left to decay for nearly 500 years until it was restored during Dhammazedi's reign. In the centuries that followed, Bago was twice destroyed, and again the Shwethalyaung Buddha was covered by tropical vegetation.

It was not until 1881, when the British were building a railway nearby, that a contractor discovered this lucrative

Bustling market in Bago.

"source of brick and stone" hidden in an earthen mound in the jungle.

In 1906, after the undergrowth had been cleared away, an iron *tazaung* was erected over the Buddha. Although the appearance of the *tazaung* detracts from the statue inside, the pavilion does a sufficient job of protecting the Buddha from tropical downpours. The statue was renovated again in 1948, regilded and given a new coat of paint.

The Mahazedi Pagoda: The road leading from the Shwethalyaung turns north. The tourist – after passing a wall to the left of the road – will come across the Mahazedi Pagoda. *Maha zedi* means "great stupa," and the appropriateness of this name is evident when looking at this impressive structure. Unlike other large stupas in Lower Burma, the Mahazedi has steep stairways winding two-thirds of the way up its exterior. It is reminiscent of some of the most beautiful buildings of Bagan.

Legend of King Bayinnaung: The Mahazedi was built in 1560 by King Bayinnaung to house a tooth of the Buddha. Bayinnaung, whose 11 white elephants (including seven taken from the King of Siam during the conquest of Ayutthia) confirmed his divine reign, was intent on obtaining a tooth to assure his place in history as the greatest king of all time.

As luck would have it, 1560 was the height of Portugal's power in India. Don Constantino de Braganca attacked the Buddhist kingdom of Jaffna in Ceylon and made off with a large booty that included a tooth, inlaid with gold and adorned with precious stones. He thought it was the Tooth of Kandy, the most revered of all Buddhist relics, which had been taken to Jaffna for a religious festival shortly before the Portuguese raid.

The greedy Bayinnaung, upon hearing the news, offered the Portuguese a huge sum of money for the tooth. The governor of Portuguese Goa was willing to deal – but the threat of the Inquisition led him to think twice. He ordered the tooth to be publicly pulverized in a mortar, then strewn into the open sea.

Mandarin oranges at a street stall.

Thus the Portuguese felt they had gotten rid of one more heathen symbol.

"The heavens have looked upon me with favour": The indestructible tooth reappeared soon thereafter in the court of the King of Colombo. Bayinnaung dispatched a delegation to Ceylon to negotiate for the tooth and the king's daughter. The delegation returned to Burma in 1576, their journey a success, and Bayinnaung greeted them at Pathein (Bassein). Medieval documents tell of an enormous welcoming party on what was Bayinnaung's greatest day.

"The heavens have looked upon me with favour," said the king. "Anawrahta could only get a replica of the tooth from Ceylon, Alaungsithu went in vain to China, but this tooth has been granted to me because of my piety and wisdom."

Not long after, Bayinnaung was informed that the Tooth of Kandy had never left Ceylon, and was still to be found there. He apparently chose not to give credence to the report, and locked the tooth away in the Mahazedi Pagoda with a begging bowl that was supposed have strong supernatural powers.

But the tooth of the Buddha remained in the Mahazedi for only 34 years. In 1599, Anaukhpetlun conquered Bago, and he insisted the pagoda's cherished relics be transferred to his capital of Toungoo. This was done in 1610. A short time later, King Thalun transferred the Burmese capital to Innwa (Ava) and built the Kaunghmudaw Pagoda in nearby Sagaing for the relics. The tooth and begging bowl can still be found there today.

The Mahazedi Pagoda was destroyed during Alaungpaya's time, and was leveled again by the 1930 earthquake. With the reconstruction work recently completed, the uppermost walkway around the stupa affords a marvelous view of the surrounding plain, bejeweled with ancient monuments.

Sixty-Four Buddhas in a circle: A short distance west of the Mahazedi stands the **Shwegugale Pagoda**, in which 64 Buddha figures sit in a circle in a gloomy vault around the central stupa.

Four kilometres to the south of Bago

The Ye Le Paya (Kyaukyan) Pagoda near Syriam.

and about 100 metres (330 ft) off the road to Yangon, sits the **Kyaikpun Pagoda**. Built by Dhammazedi in 1476, it consists of four Buddha figures, each 30 metres (98 ft) high, seated back to back against a square pillar facing the four cardinal directions. The figures represent Gautama Buddha (he faces north) and his three Buddha predecessors, Konagamana (south), Kakusandha (east), and Kassapa (west). The latter was largely destroyed by the massive earthquake of 1930.

An old legend holds that four sisters took part in the building of the monument, and it was prophesied that if any of them were to marry, one of the statues would collapse. Believers feel the collapse of the Kassapa Buddha statue points a finger at one of the sisters.

Another kilometre or so toward Yangon lies **Payathonzu**, where there are a number of buildings dating to the time of Dhammazedi. The most important of these is the **Shwegugyi Pagoda**, modeled on India's Bodhgaya Temple. In a circle around the temple are earlier buildings and figures, representing the seven stages through which the Buddha had passed while in the seven-week period of meditation following his enlightenment.

Syriam – oil, beer, and a rich Hindu culture: The Syriam of the 1990s belies the Syriam of the 17th and early 18th centuries. Once the centre of foreign trade for all of Lower Burma, Syriam remains an important industrial town today, well worth a day trip from Yangon. It's a short trip to Syriam, since a new bridge now connects both cities. Its glory, like that of so many other Burmese cities, lies in the past.

At various times prior to Syriam's destruction at the hands of King Alaungpaya in 1756, it was home to trading posts of Portuguese, Dutch, French and British merchants. Its greatest importance was in the early 1600s when the Portuguese adventurer de Brito established his own private kingdom here; the ruined walls of Lusitanian baroque-style buildings can still be seen.

Many of Syriam's 20,000 people to-

A Syriam peasant takes his geese to market.

day are employed by Burma's largest oil refinery or by the "People's Brewery." Others are involved in the rice trade, as Syriam is a centre for Burma's "East Delta" rice-cultivating region.

When the British opened up the Ayeyarwady Delta for rice growing, they imported Indian labour to work the fields. During the height of the British colonial period, an estimated one million Indians lived in Burma, the majority of them in the delta region.

Today, the largest of the hold-over Indian communities – of those that survived both World War II and Ne Win's 1960s nationalization movement – remains in the Syriam region.

Even though Syriam's Indians have Burmese citizenship, their customs and way of life are still very much determined by the Hindu religion. Every February, for example, after the rice harvest has been gathered, the community observes the ritual of penitence known as *Thaipusam*. Devotees repenting past sins or asking future favours, walk trancelike through the streets, car-

rying heavy weights which dangle from sharp hooks thrust through their flesh; others even stroll barefoot across a bed of burning coals in penance.

It is a 45-minute ferry trip from Yangon to Syriam across the Bago River. Boats leave the capital hourly from the Htinbonseik Jetty on Pazundaung Creek.

Upon arriving in Syriam by ferry, there are three modes of transport from which to choose: horse-drawn cabs, buses and jeeps. The jeeps tend to charge exorbitant rates, but Syriam's buses are always crowded and don't leave the dock until the last seat is taken.

Portuguese ruins and a hilltop pagoda: If you're not planning to go far from Syriam, find an English-speaking horse-drawn cab driver to take you to the Portuguese ruins and the **Kyaik Khauk Pagoda**. Like the Shwedagon and the Shwemawdaw, this pagoda is situated at the top of a hill, and its golden stupa is visible for miles across the delta silt. In fact, the Kyaik Khauk matches its two more famous cousins in architecture and atmosphere as well as hilltop

Mahout and **elephant in Mon State**.

location. In front of the pagoda are the graves of two venerated writers, Natshinnaung and Padethayaza.

Isle of giant catfish: A more unusual monument is the **Kyauktan Pagoda**, about 20 kilometres (13 mi) south of Syriam on a tributary of the Yangon River. The journey by jeep or bus takes about 45 minutes from Syriam.

Also called the **Ye Le Paya** ("situated in the middle of the river") Pagoda, the Kyauktan is indeed on an island in the middle of the river. The island, which is completely covered by buildings, can be reached by rowboat from the riverbank. Within the pagoda complex are paintings of all the most important pagodas in Burma, and some in other Theravada countries.

At the boat landing, pilgrims can buy food for the huge catfish (some more than 1 metre [3 ft]) long, whose dorsal fins can be seen piercing the waters on all sides of the island. Feeding these harmless fish is a favourite pastime for many Kyauktan visitors.

Stretching along the riverbank opposite the colourful pagoda buildings is an interesting market.

Further to the south and to the east of the Yangon River estuary, a small seaside resort with a 30-room hotel has been developed at **Letkhokkon,** providing the nearest access to the sea from Yangon. If you'd like to escape the hustle and bustle of city life and don't have enough time to go to Rakhine, it's the only choice you have. The other available resort, though with a better beach, would be at Chaungtha on the coast of the Bay of Bengal.

The land of the Mons: Across the Sittoung (Sittang) starts the land of the Mons. This was Lower Burma's original cradle of civilization, Suvannabhumi, the "golden land". Since a cease fire agreement with the Mon (but not with the Kayin who are also living here) has materialized, certain areas, like the Golden Rock and Mawlamyine (Moulmein) can be visited without problems; for others, approval can be obtained through MT&T.

It was probably **Thaton** to which the

Mawlamyine (Moulmein) Pagoda at the turn of the century.

great Indian King Ashoka sent two missionaries (Sona and Uttara) to spread the gospel of Theravada Buddhism in the 3rd century BC.

In any case, it was Thaton which served as the first great capital of the Mon Empire, and Thaton which posed the greatest threat to Upper Burma. It was only after King Anawrahta of Bagan was victorious over Thaton's King Manuha in 1057 that Anawrahta established the First Burmese Empire.

Although Thaton's influence waned from that point on, visitors to the ancient capital can still see some remains of the medieval fortifications – although modern Thaton was built on top of the old town.

Local legend maintains that the Shwezayan Pagoda, believed to contain four of the Buddha's teeth, dates to the 5th century BC. The **Thagyapaya Pagoda**, situated nearby, has three terraces, the uppermost terrace containing four large recesses with standing Buddha figures. Various terra-cotta glazed tiles, dating from the 11th and 12th centuries, illustrate the *Jataka* tales. Scenes from the 10 best known *Jataka* stories also decorate the **Kalyani Sima**, hall of ordination. Also worth seeing is the **Pitakat Taik**, or library.

"By the Old Moulmein Pagoda": About 70 kilometres (44 mi) south of Thaton lies **Mawlamyine (Moulmein)**, the third largest city in Burma with a population of 220,000. It was British Burma's administrative centre between 1827 and 1852, but is best known today from Kipling's verse: "By the old Moulmein Pagoda, looking lazy at the sea..."

The English writer was probably referring to the Kyaikthanlan Pagoda, whose hilltop location offers breathtaking views over the city and its harbour, a centre for the export of rice and wood (especially teak). Just up the Thanlwin River – navigable for a short distance from Mawlamyine and its sister town, Martaban, across the river – there is a sawmill where the words of Rudyard Kipling again come to life: "Elephants a-pilin' teak..."

Mawlamyine boasts many beautiful

Harvesting rice.

pagodas. Among them is the **Uzina Pagoda**, which houses four life-sized statues of the four images – an old man, a sick man, a dead man and an ascetic – which convinced young Siddhartha Gautama to devote his life to finding a means to ending human suffering.

Also in the vicinity of Mawlamyine are two large caves. The **Cave of Payon** contains many Buddha figures among its stalagmites and stalactites. The **Cave of Kawgaun**, also known as the Cave of the Ten Thousand Buddhas, holds an enormous number of Buddha figures of all shapes and sizes.

A POW cemetery and a colonial resort: About 65 kilometres (40 mi) south of Mawlamyine, near the town of **Thanbyuzayat**, is a large and well-kept war cemetery. Buried here are Allied prisoners-of-war who died constructing the World War II railway to Thailand for the Japanese.

The Burmese government is currently planning a hotel near **Amherst**, a coastal resort some 45 kilometres (28 mi) south of Mawlamyine. During the British co-lonial period, there was a bustling holi-day centre here, the beach at **Setse** being particularly well known. The opening of this area to Western tourists depends, however, on the success of government troops in reducing rebel activity in south-ern Burma in the near future.

Forty-five kilometres (28 mi) north of Thaton is the village of **Ayetthema**. Nearby lies the ruins of an old city wall, which is believed to be the wall of the fort of Taikkala at the original Mon settlement of Suvannabhumi.

Also in the area is the **Kyaikthanlan Pagoda** with inscriptions dating to the time of King Kyanzittha in the 11th century. To the south, standing on an octagonal base, is the conical **Tizaung Pagoda**. Another 1.5 kilometres (1 mi) south of this pagoda are the remains of another wall, this one 2 metres (6.5 ft) high, with beautiful animal scenes chiseled into the rock.

Pilgrimage to Kyaik-tiyo, the famed "golden rock": About halfway between Thaton and Bago lies the town of **Kyaik-tiyo**, famous for its pagoda situated east

Mergui town centre.

of the town at the end of a 10-kilometres (6-mi) long footpath.

This landmark is the **Kyaik-tiyo Pagoda** – the "Golden Rock." The small (5.5-metre, or 18-ft high) shrine is built on a gold-plated boulder atop a cliff, and it gives the viewer the sensation that it is about to crash down into the valley at any moment. Local Burmese will tell you that such a thing could never happen – the fine balance of the boulder is maintained by a hair of the Buddha preserved inside the pagoda.

According to legend, King Tissa, who lived in the 11th century, was the son of a *zawgyi* and a *naga* princess. He was given the Buddha's hair by an old hermit who had preserved it in his own hairknot from centuries earlier when the Buddha had personally visited his cave.

In giving King Tissa the hair, however, the hermit set one condition: the King had to find a rock which closely resembled the hermit's head, and on this rock he must build a pagoda to enshrine the hair relic.

With the help of Thagyamin, king of the *nat*, Tissa located the perfect rock on the bottom of the sea. The rock was transported to the mountaintop by a ship – which subsequently turned to stone.

Today, the ship can be found a few hundred metres (about 1,000 ft) away from the Kyaik-tiyo, and is simply known as the **Kyaukthanban**, the "stone boat pagoda."

Queen Shwe-nan-kyin and the man-eating tiger: During the time that King Tissa was building the remarkable pagoda, he fell in love with the beautiful Shwe-nan-kyin, daughter of a highland chief. Tissa made her his queen, and brought her to his palace.

Some time later, during pregnancy, she became sick, and concluded that only by making offerings to her family *nat* would she recover. Her family had not rejected their traditional beliefs even while absorbing Buddhism, so with King Tissa's permission, her father and brother arrived to escort her home.

About halfway from the palace to the pagoda, a tiger – presumably sent by the offended family *nat* – sprang from the

jungle. Father and brother instantly fled, and poor Shwe-nan-kyin, terrified, watched death approach. Then her eyes fell upon the golden Kyaik-tiyo shrine on the distant cliff-top. With her eyes fixed on the pagoda, she surrendered herself to whatever fate was to be hers. The tiger walked away.

Shwe-nan-kyin continued her journey to the platform of the pagoda. Here she laid down and died peacefully, the truth of the Buddhist Dhamma lodged in her mind. She is now the guardian *nat* of the Kyaik-tiyo Pagoda, a *nat* radiating compassion.

From base camp to pagoda: Until very recently, before the road that leads now most of the way up to the pagoda, only a few non-Burmese have ever made the pilgrimage to the Kyaik-tiyo Pagoda. MT&T, however, realized the tourist potential of the place, they had a hotel built and are now guiding tourists into the hills. Though it is more comfortable to drive up, walking up from Kinpun has its own charm.

It is a fairly arduous walk – five hours from the **Kinpun** base camp near sea level to the pagoda at about 1,200 metres (4,000 ft) elevation. Most pilgrims carry a bedroll and spend the night at the *kyaung* near the pagoda.

Gaining merit and cleansing one's soul: For the Burmese, the climb to Kyaik-tiyo is a sort of soul-cleansing experience. It is a means of gaining merit, of worshiping the *nat* of the region and of being reminded again and again of the Buddhist Dhamma.

The millennium-old path leads through otherwise impenetrable bamboo jungle and along a seemingly interminable mountain ridge.

There is an oasis halfway up the second hill, where a thoughtful businessman has built several bamboo sheds over a clear spring; here journeyers can cool off in the refreshing water before continuing the trek.

At various stages along the way, images have been conspicuously erected. They describe the chapters of the temple legend, integral to the pilgrims' appreciation of the trip.

The town square in Pathein.

156

Once on the ridge, the going gets noticeably easier, and the Golden Rock can be seen in the distance; this seems to immediately relax the walker's strained limbs and reinvigorate his soul, which makes the journey's completion a much-easier task.

As tiring as the climb may be, even the sick and the old are not kept from reaching the golden boulder. Neither, for that matter, are the rich or the idle. Baggage will be carried from Kinpun to the temple for a small charge, and there are palanquins to carry persons unable – or unwilling – to trek on their own two feet. It is quite a sight to see a pair of 15-year-old boys marching up the steep mountain slopes, toting an overweight merchant who mutters, *"Ahmya,"* which means, "Share with me the merit I gain by doing good things."

Finally, there is the Kyaik-tiyo Pagoda itself at the highest point of the mountain ridge. Seemingly perched on the top of the world, one cannot help but be awed by this religious wonder of the world balancing perfectly on a projecting boulder that even a few young boys can rock and move.

Charming isles of the Myeik (Mergui) Archipelago: One of the most scenic and charming island groups in Southeast Asia is the Myeik (Mergui) Archipelago. Comprising more that 800 islands off the south Tanintharyi (Tenasserim) coast, it is home to the Salons, sea gypsies who until recently were notorious for their piracy. Like the Bajaos of the Sulu Sea, they live on their small boats; the countless bays of the archipelago offering shelter from storms and a bountiful supply of food.

The Japanese are currently engaged in the lucrative business of pearl fishing in the Myeik Archipelago. Other unusual products of this island group include sea cucumbers (*beches-de-mer*) and edible birds' nests, popular in soups. These swifts' nests are found in cathedral-like limestone caves, many of them accessible only at low tide.

Due to the insecure situation of the region, it has for long been off-limits for foreigners. This is changing now. By 1995 a 250-room hotel will be ready on **Salon Kyun Island** and can easily be reached from Ranong in Thailand without too many formalities. From there, the southern islands of the archipelago with their crystal-clear waters, unspoilt beaches, limestone cliffs and their sea gypsies can easily be reached.

Onshore capital of the district is the town of **Myeik (Mergui),** a short distance from the mouth of the Tanintharyi River. A small offshore island helps to enclose Mergui's sheltered harbor. On it, seen from the picturesque city's centre, lies Burma's third largest **Shwetalyaung** (reclining Buddha) lazily watching the town whose style of living seems to be inspired by him.

Myeik still holds the charm of an eastern colonial city in the Thirties. Nothing much has changed since then, except that modern goods, smuggled in from across Thailand, fill the stands of the teeming market.

Down at the seafront is the **house of U Nya Aye,** a Burmese of Chinese descent who seems to be blessed by the gods. Sea swallows have chosen his living

room as a nesting place, making him one of the richest man in the city. Harvesting the nests, he earns 400 000 kyat a year without much stress.

Up on the hill, next to the government rest house, is the place where the Mergui massacre took place in the 17th century and Maurice Collis' famed **haunted house on the ridge** stands. Here one of its victims is supposedly still walking its squeaking stairs – with her head in her arms. Some of the inhabitants swear they have seen her.

This harbour – plus the short overland route to the Gulf of Siam – made Myeik (sometimes also called Beik) an important trade settlement for both the Indians and the Arabs long before the Europeans visited this part of the world. In the 19th century, the British considered Mergui as a possible location for the capital of their East Indian empire.

Unfortunately, the vicinity of Myeik is almost inaccessible to outsiders today. It is a major centre of the illegal Burmese-Thailand smuggling trade, and the Yangon government has been forced to take extreme security measures.

The Ayeyarwady delta port of Pathein (Bassein): With a population of about 350,000, Pathein (Bassein) is the biggest town in the Ayeyarwady delta.

Situated 112 kilometres (70 mi) from the Bay of Bengal, it is a port of export for rice and jute (fibre), and is well known for its colourful umbrellas.

Pathein can be reached from Yangon by train in a rather roundabout fashion, but an inland-waterway ship voyage is probably the best way for visitors to get to know the countryside and the people of the delta region.

It is a long 18-hour journey passing the pottery town of **Twante**, but it is well worth it. Pathein is now open for Western visitors, and the flight from Yangon is only 30 minutes.

The British, with the consent of the court of Innwa (Ava), had attempted as early as 1753 to establish a settlement where the Ayeyarwady empties into the sea at Cape Negrais. However, after the conquest of Syriam soon thereafter, King Alaungpaya had the young settlement burned to the ground.

It was not until the annexation of Lower Burma in 1852 that the British were able to install a garrison in Pathein. At the same time, they endeavored to open up large plots of land for rice cultivation.

The name "Bassein" was a European pronunciation of *Pathein*, said to derive from the Burmese word for Muslims: *Pathi*. The town was a sizable settlement centuries ago for Indian merchants, many of whom were Muslims. Today, the inhabitants of Pathein include many Kayin (Karen) and Rakhine, some of whom are Christians.

The town spreads out around the **Shwemokhtaw Pagoda**, which during the full moon in May becomes the goal of pilgrimage for the population of the entire surrounding delta region.

According to legend, a Muslim princess was responsible for the pagoda having been built in ancient times. The princess, Onmadandi, had three lovers – all of whom, presumably, were Buddhists – and she told each of them to build a pagoda. The first man constructed the Shwemokhtaw, the second worked on the **Tazaung Pagoda** at the southern end of Pathein, and the third built the **Thayaunggyaung Pagoda**.

Off the mouth of the Pathein (Ngawun) River, in the Andaman Sea, 110 kilometres (70 mi) from Pathein city, is tiny wooded **Diamond Island**. This islet is important commercially for the hundreds of thousands of turtle eggs laid on its banks each year.

In its vicinity, a deep sea harbour is under construction. It will become what the British already had in mind 150 years ago: the gateway to western and central China. Huge river barges will soon bring the goods from China's industrial core, via Bhamo, along the Ayeyarwady to be transshipped here.

A new beach resort: In the early 1990s, an unspoiled beach resort at **Chaungtha** was opened, about 48 kilometres (30 mi) north of Pathein. The resort consists of a hotel, a guest-house and a dormitory – an ideal spot for those who wish to spend part of their Burma visit swimming and sunbathing on the coast of the Bay of Bengal.

A glimpse of Pathein in Delta pottery

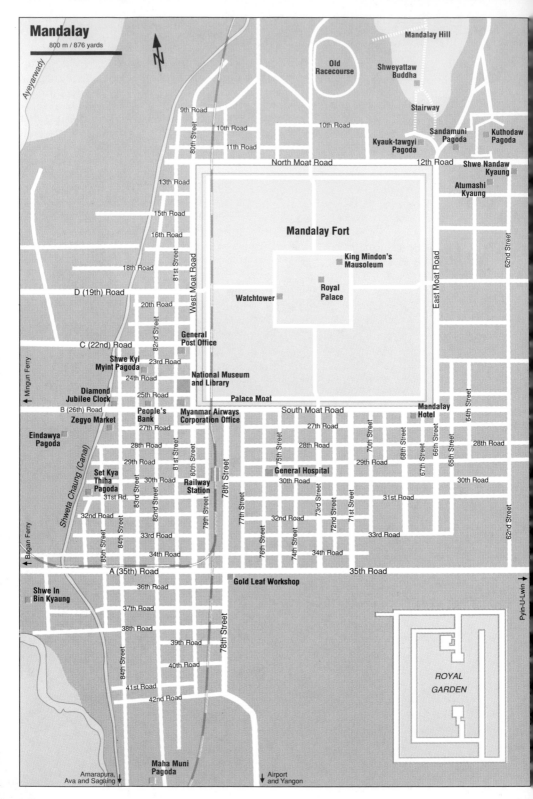

Mandalay

800 m / 876 yards

Mandalay Hill

Old Racecourse

Shweyattaw Buddha

Ayeyarwady

Stairway

9th Road

80th Street

10th Road

10th Road

Sandamuni Pagoda

Kuthodaw Pagoda

11th Road

Kyauk-tawgyi Pagoda

North Moat Road

12th Road

Shwe Nandaw Kyaung

13th Road

Mandalay Fort

Atumashi Kyaung

15th Road

16th Road

62nd Street

West Moat Road

81st Street

18th Road

King Mindon's Mausoleum

East Moat Road

D (19th) Road

20th Road

Watchtower

Royal Palace

82nd Street

C (22nd) Road

General Post Office

Shwe Kyi Myint Pagoda

23rd Road

24th Road

National Museum and Library

Diamond Jubilee Clock

25th Road

Palace Moat

Mandalay Hotel

64th Street

Mingun Ferry

B (26th) Road

People's Bank

Myanmar Airways Corporation Office

South Moat Road

65th Street

66th Street

67th Street

68th Street

70th Street

27th Road

Zegyo Market

27th Road

27th Road

Eindawya Pagoda

28th Road

28th Road

75th Street

28th Road

28th Road

Shweta Chaung (Canal)

81st Street

80th Street

29th Road

29th Road

Set Kya Thiha Pagoda

30th Road

Railway Station

General Hospital

30th Road

30th Road

31st Rd.

83rd Street

82nd Street

78th Street

30th Road

73rd Street

72nd Street

71st Street

31st Road

62nd Street

Bagan Ferry

32nd Road

79th Street

32nd Road

33rd Road

85th Street

84th Street

33rd Road

77th Street

78th Street

74th Street

34th Road

34th Road

33rd Road

A (35th) Road

35th Road

35th Road

Pyin-U-Lwin

Gold Leaf Workshop

36th Road

Shwe In Bin Kyaung

37th Road

38th Road

84th Street

39th Road

78th Street

ROYAL GARDEN

40th Road

41st Road

42nd Road

Maha Muni Pagoda

Amarapura, Ava and Sagaing

Airport and Yangon

162

MANDALAY

"For the wind is in the palm-trees,
an' the temple-bells they say:
'Come you back, you British soldier;
come you back to Mandalay!'"
– Rudyard Kipling,
The Road to Mandalay (1887)

Mandalay, the capital of Upper Burma, is a young city, less than 150 years old. But its lyrical name ignites images as ancient as the languid Ayeyarwady (Irrawaddy) flowing past the city. Nostalgia for Burma's last royal capital, enchantment with the myriad pagodas dotting all corners of the region's landscape, and the warmth and vitality of the native people weave a spell around the visitor that seems impossible to escape.

Sprawling across the dry plains of the upper Ayeyarwady rice-growing district, Mandalay has a population approaching 600,000. It is dusty and often quite hot, lacking the tree-lined neatness and colonial character of Yangon. Trishaws and pony carts are more numerous than motorized vehicles, which more often than not, are World War II-vintage jeeps. However, to the Burmese people, it is Mandalay, not Yangon, which is truly representative of Burma's past and present. And it is Mandalay which is regarded as the centre of Burmese culture and Buddhist learning.

Here in Mandalay, scenic beauty and historical tragedy are inextricably meshed. There is the indestructible Mandalay Hill with its kilometre-long covered stairways and remarkable pagodas; and below it, the ruins of the Royal Palace, King Mindon's "Golden City" of ancient prophecy. In the middle of the city is Zegyo Market, centre of trade for all the people of Upper Burma who can be seen there in their colourful national costumes. Skilled artisans and craftsmen are found here, working their age-old wonders with gold and silver, marble and chisel, thread and loom. The sluggish Ayeyarwady flows by with its bustling wharves and flotilla of rice-laden boats. Mandalay, 620 kilometres

(400 mi) north of Yangon, is only 80 metres (262 ft) above sea level.

Mandalay was founded in 1857 by King Mindon to coincide with an ancient Buddhist prophecy. Tradition has it that Gautama Buddha visited the sacred mount of Mandalay Hill with his disciple Ananda, and proclaimed that on the 2,400th anniversary of his death, a metropolis of Buddhist teaching would be founded at the foot of the hill. Mindon, a deeply religious man, believed he had achieved Buddhist enlightenment; but he also felt that the injustices wrought during his reign could only be set straight by building temple grounds of great magnificence.

The "Golden City" was formally completed in 1859. Mindon shifted his government and an estimated 150,000 people from nearby Amarapura in 1861, dismantling most of the previous palace and taking it with him to help create the new capital.

The dream of Mandalay was short-lived. On November 29, 1885, King Thibaw handed the town over to British General Prendergast and went into exile with his queen. Mandalay soon became just another outpost of British colonialism, albeit one crowned by richly furnished palace buildings, which by now had been renamed Fort Dufferin.

The palace structures were almost universally built of teak, and this was their demise. On March 20, 1945, British troops shelled the stronghold, at the time defended by a handful of Japanese and Burmese soldiers. By the time the siege had ended, the interior of the "Golden City" was in ashes. All that remained intact before part of the palace was reconstructed, were the walls and the moat.

The centre of the world: Mindon had built his **Royal Palace** on the model of Brahman-Buddhist cosmology to represent the centre of the world, the fabled Mount Meru. The palace formed a perfect square, with the outer walls facing the four cardinal directions, and the 12 gates, three on each side are marked with the signs of the zodiac. In the exact centre of the palace was the throne room, called the "Lion's Room". Above it rose a gold-plated, seven-storey, 78-metre (256-ft) high *pyathat* (tower). Through this tower, it was believed, the wisdom of the universe funneled directly upon the king's throne to assist in his decision-making.

Anthropologist Charles Keyes, in his 1977 study, *The Golden Peninsula: Culture and Adaptation in Mainland Southeast Asia*, reported:

"The walls were a mile and one-eighth (almost 2 km) long and were, in turn, surrounded by a moat. The homes of the common people and of 'aliens,' the markets, the workshops of the craftsmen and the shops, were located beyond the walls of the capital city. In contrast to Chinese and medieval European cities, the walls of a traditional Theravadin city were built not so much to serve as barriers against potential invaders as to demarcate a sacred space..."

Today, "Mandalay Fort" serves as the northern headquarters of the national army. To enter the grounds, a permit, and an escort should be obtained and an entrance fee paid at the Myanmar Travels and Tours (MT&T) office.

The Royal Palace with the Lion's Room and the *pyathat* have been rebuilt. Completed, the palace should become one of the main attractions for visitors to the city. A little to the west is a scale model of the ancient palace recreated by archaeologists. The model indicates the location of all main and secondary buildings within the old palace walls, and gives a good idea of the "centre of the world" concept. Also on the palace grounds is a museum and King Mindon's mausoleum.

Mandalay Hill: You should perhaps start your visit to Mandalay by climbing famous Mandalay Hill which rises 236 metres (774 ft) above the surrounding countryside. British and Indian troops suffered heavy casualties here in March 1945, storming the Japanese stronghold which controlled the plains around Mandalay. Today, there remains only the regimental insignia of the British near the hill's summit.

The slopes of Mandalay Hill are clothed in **covered stairways**, which contain small temples at regular intervals. Many of the temples are the work of the late monk U Khanti. Two main stairways ascend from the south, under the glare of the ever-present white *chinthes* demanding the removal of shoes before entering sacred ground. There are 1,729 steps to the top, but the walk is not particularly difficult. The roof, which shades the stairways, keeps the stone steps cool and protects the visitor from the sun while still allowing fresh air to circulate through.

Along the way, astrologers and souvenir peddlers ply their trades while monks and nuns, children and women smoking huge cheroots scale the steps.

About halfway up the hill, you'll encounter the first large temple, which contains three bones of the Buddha.

The Peshawar relics: When Gautama Buddha died at the age of 80 in Kusinara, India, he had left no instructions regarding disposal of his body. The Buddha's followers elected to cremate it, but when only his bones remained, a downpour extinguished the flames. The Mallas of Kusinara took possesion of the remains,

The *chinthes* of Mandalay Hill.

164

and refused to share them with the neighbouring kings until the threat of war arose. Only then did he agree to divide the bones equally among eight monarchs to be enshrined in stupas across the country.

When King Ashoka extended his powerful reign over India some three centuries later, he ordered the relic chambers of the eight stupas opened, and their contents distributed among the 80,000 stupas of South and Southeast Asia. He did so primarily to create more places of worship for Buddhist devotees who were spread throughout the subcontinent.

King Kanishka, the second great Buddhist king of the Kushan dynasty, had several of the Buddhist relics brought to Peshawar, and built a 168-metre-high (550-ft) stupa for them.

The Chinese traveller Hiuen Tsang provided a marvelous description of the stupa in AD 630, but it was apparently destroyed by Muslim conquerors following the Battle of Hund in the 11th century. It remained for the curator of the Peshawar Museum, conducting excavations at the Ganji Gate in 1908, to unearth the fabled Kanishka relic casket. Inside the casket he found a crystal vessel containing the three bones of the Buddha. As these relics were of little importance to the Islamic people of northwest India, the British government presented them to the Burmese Buddhist Society.

It was for these relics that the Burmese built a temple half-way up Mandalay Hill. However, it is surprising that despite the verity of the relics confirmed by the inscription of the Kanishka casket, these relics are accorded relatively little esteem in Burma. Others, including the seemingly countless teeth of the Buddha enshrined in many stupas, are highly venerated.

The legend of Shweyattaw Buddha: About two-thirds of the way to the top of the hill stands a gold-plated statue of the **Shweyattaw Buddha**. His outstretched hand points to the place where the Royal Palace was built. This stance is unique: in all other Buddha images anywhere in the world, Gautama is in a *mudra* posi-

Reading palms on Mandalay Hill.

tion. The statue was erected before King Mindon laid the first stone of his "Golden City," and symbolizes Gautama Buddha's prophecy. On the way up the steps, there is also a statue of a woman kneeling in front of the Buddha, offering to him her two severed breasts.

According to legend, **Sanda Moke Khit** was an ogress – but she was so impressed by the Buddha's teachings that she decided to devote the rest of her life to following the Enlightened One. As a sign of humility, she cut off her breasts. The Buddha smiled as he accepted the gift, and the ogress' brother asked why he did so. He replied that Sanda Moke Khit had collected so many merits that in a future life, she would be reborn as Min Done (Mindon), king of Mandalay.

The view from the summit of Mandalay Hill is phenomenal. To the west lies the Ayeyarwady and beyond that the Sagaing and Mingun hills, themselves encrusted with pagodas and temples. To the north, the Ayeyarwady rice country extends into the distance. The purple

Shan Plateau can be seen in the east; and to the south, in the midst of this vast plain, the city of Mandalay lies with its huge palace fortress. In all directions, the Ayeyarwady plain – from which the hill juts like a huge boulder – is studded with pagodas, erected over the centuries by devout Buddhists seeking merit for future lives.

The world's largest book: At the base of Mandalay Hill's south-east stairway, surrounded by a high wall, is Mindon's **Kuthodaw Pagoda**. Its central structure, the 30-metre (98-ft) high **Maha Lawka Marazein Pagoda**, was erected in 1857, modeled on the Shwezigon Pagoda in Nyaung U, near Bagan (Pagan). Around it are 729 *"pitaka* pagodas," built in 1872 during the Fifth Buddhist Synod to individually house the marble tablets on which, for the first time, the entire *Tipitaka* (Buddhist canon) was recorded in Pali script.

Sometimes called "the world's largest book," it was created by a team of 2,400 monks who required almost six months to recite the text. The canons

Mandalay Palace walls.

were recorded on the marble slabs by devoted Buddhist scholars, and the letters were originally veneered with gold leaf. Close to the Kuthodaw are other important pagodas and monasteries.

The **Sandamuni Pagoda** was built on the site where King Mindon had his provisional palace during construction of the Mandalay Palace. It was erected over the burial place of Mindon's younger brother, Crown Prince Kanaung, who was assassinated in an unsuccessful palace revolution in 1866. Commentaries on the *Tipitaka* have been chiseled onto 1,774 stone tablets housed in the pagoda, a work credited to the monk U Khanti.

Not far from the south staircase is the **Kyauk-tawgyi Pagoda**. Begun in 1853, the original plan was to model this after the Ananda Temple at Bagan, but the 1866 revolt hampered this and other projects. The building was eventually completed in 1878. The main point of interest here is a huge Buddha figure, carved from a single block of marble from the Sagyin quarry. This undertaking was of ancient Egyptian proportions: 10,000 men required 13 days to transport the rock from the Ayeyarwady to the pagoda site. The statue was finally dedicated in 1865, with 20 figures on each side of the image, representing the Buddha's 80 disciples. A painting of King Mindon is also contained within the pagoda.

There are two monasteries located south of the Kuthodaw Pagoda, not far to the east of the palace moat. The **Shwe Nandaw Kyaung**, at one time part of the royal palace, is the only building from Mindon's "Golden City" which has survived the ravages of the last century. It was in this building, then within the palace walls, that Mindon died. Thibaw dismantled it after his father's death and had it re-erected on its present site, where it was able to escape the World War II destruction that burned the teak royal palace to the ground. Thibaw used the building for a time as a private meditation centre, but then gave it to the monks as a monastery. In 1979, the monastery celebrated

"World's largest book" in the Kuthodaw Pagoda.

its 100th anniversary.

Today, the Shwe Nandaw is most famous for its intricate woodcarvings. At one time, Mindon's entire "Golden City" must have had every square metre of space covered with figures or ornamental flowers. Although the monastery was once plated with gold and adorned with glass mosaic both inside and out, today the only gold is layered on the imposing ceiling. Thibaw's couch and a replica of the royal throne are contained within.

Beside the Shwe Nandaw lie the remains of the **Atumashi Kyaung**, which means "Incomparable Monastery." Before it burned down in 1890, taking with it four sets of *Tipitaka* in teak boxes, this was a building of extraordinary splendour. Today, only the foundation walls, heavily embellished with stucco work, and an impressive stairway remain standing. A famous Buddha image, clothed in silk, coated with lacquer, and with an enormous diamond set in its forehead, was once the pride of the *kyaung*, but it was stolen during the British takeover

of Mandalay in 1885. The *kyaung* was described by European visitors as one of the most beautiful buildings in all of Mandalay. (The Burmese archaeological department intends to rebuild this outstanding structure within the next few years.)

The fabled Maha Muni: The most important religious structure in Mandalay is the **Maha Muni ("Great Sage") Pagoda**. It is also called the "Rakhine (Arakan) Pagoda" or "Payagyi Pagoda". Located about 3 kilometres (2 mi) south of the city centre on the road to Amarapura, this pagoda was built in 1784 by King Bodawpaya and was reconstructed after a fire a century later.

The Maha Muni Buddha image within the shrine, taken as booty by Bodawpaya's troops during a Rakhine campaign, is an object of intense devotion to pilgrims from all over the world.

A legend explains why this pagoda is so special. It is said that Gautama Buddha himself went to teach for a week among the people of Dhannavati (now northern Rakhine), stressing the five

A bamboo raft on the Ayeyarwady.

precepts and the Eight-fold Path, and showing the way to salvation.

King Chandra Surya (Candra-suriya) asked Gautama to "leave us the shape of yourself," and the Buddha agreed. He spent an additional week meditating under a Bodhi tree while Sakka, king of the gods, produced a likeness of the Buddha that was so lifelike, it could only have been created by a heavenly being.

The Buddha was pleased. He breathed upon the image and said: "I shall pass into nibbana in my 80th year, but this, with my essence, will live the 5,000 years I have prescribed for the duration of the religion." Gautama then departed, but the Maha Muni took its place upon a diamond-studded throne atop Rakhine's Sirigutta Hill. It was one of only five likenesses of the Buddha said to have been made during his lifetime; according to tradition, two are in India, two are in Paradise.

This is the legend. In fact, archaeologists claim the city of Dhannavati was built in the 1st century AD, about 600 years after the Buddha lived. The Maha Muni Buddha probably was cast during the reign of Chandra Surya, but he did not ascend the throne until AD 146. It was during his reign that Buddhism spread to Rakhine.

King Anawrahta of Bagan conquered the northern part of Rakhine late in the 11th century. During his reign, all non-Buddhist buildings and statues were destroyed. He was unable, however, to carry the Maha Muni to Bagan. Anawrahta's grandson, Alaung-sithu, again raided Rakhine in 1118; his soldiers destroyed all temples, removed the gold from the Maha Muni, and took one of its legs as booty. But the ship transporting the treasure home sank in the Bay of Bengal.

By the late 12th century, when another foray from Bagan was made to Rakhine, jungle had enveloped Sirigutta Hill and the legendary Maha Muni could not be found. The people of Rakhine later succeeded in restoring the Buddha image, only to have it carried off by Bodawpaya's forces in 1784. The king sent his crown prince with a force of 30,000 men to take Rakhine; the troops returned with the Maha Muni in three separate pieces.

It was reassembled at Amarapura, and Bodawpaya had an unusually beautiful seven-story pagoda built about 8 kilometres (5 mi) north of Amarapura to house it. In 1884, the original pagoda was destroyed by fire, and the existing structure is a copy of the first one, although its terraced roof of gilded stucco is unmistakably late-19th century.

Watching the gold grow: The Maha Muni Buddha figure is 3.8 metres (12 ft 7 in) high and is coated with layers of gold leaf several centimetres (1-2 in) thick. Except during the rainy season, when the Buddha's body is cloaked with robes, one can watch Buddhist faithfuls pasting on the thin gold leaf. The statue was originally cast in metal, but the gold leaf has had an unusual effect – the Maha Muni now has an irregular outline.

Carried back from Rakhine with the Maha Muni were six bronze Khmer sculptures. Their story provides a vivid glimpse of Southeast Asia's speckled history. The statues originally stood as

bronze
dvarapala.

guardians of Cambodia's Angkor Wat, and were among 30 statues taken during a Thai raid in 1431.

In 1564, the Mon King Bayinnaung looted Ayutthia and removed the statues to Bago (Pegu). Another 36 years later, in 1600, King Razagyi of Rakhine razed Bago and carried the statues to his capital of Myohaung (Mrauk-U). Bodawpaya's forces took them in 1784.

Only six of the Khmer bronzes have survived the centuries – two *dvarapalas* (warriors or temple guardians), three lions and a three-headed elephant. They are kept in a small building in the Maha Muni Pagoda courtyard. The warriors are a special attraction for pilgrims: it is said they have the power to heal any disease if one touches the corresponding place on their bodies. The gleaming, smooth indentations in the warriors' stomach areas is indicative of the kind of suffering most widespread in Burma.

Near the bronzes is a shed containing a five-ton gong. Also in the courtyard are hundreds of stone slabs with religious inscriptions which Bodawpaya

collected during his many campaigns. A statue of Bodawpaya can be found on the south-western side of the pagoda, in front of a curio museum. The museum displays life-sized statues of King Mindon, King Thibaw and Thibaw's queen, Supyalat all behind glass.

Streets with covered stalls lead up to the Maha Muni Pagoda from all directions, providing the bazaar atmosphere for which Burma was once famous. Along with simple artefacts, one can find precious stones and antiques – whose export is strictly forbidden. On one side of the pagoda is a small pond containing "holy" fish and turtles; feeding them improves one's merit.

The charms of Mandalay: There are four other Buddhist buildings in the vicinity of downtown Mandalay which are definitely worth visiting. The city's grid street plan makes them easy to find.

Heading north from the Maha Muni Pagoda, the visitor first encounters the **Shwe In Bin Kyaung**. This monastery, situated to the south of 35th Road, contains very fine 13st century woodcarv-

Marble polishers at an image maker's workshop.

ings. At 31st Road and 85th Street stands the **Set Kya Thiha Pagoda**, rebuilt after being badly damaged in World War II. The pagoda contains a 5-metre (16-ft) high bronze Buddha, cast at Innwa (Ava) by King Bagyidaw in 1823. A Bodhi tree in front of the entrance was planted by U Nu, the deeply religious first prime minister of Burma.

Proceeding northward, the visitor soon arrives at the **Eindawya Pagoda** at 27th Road and 89th Street. The pagoda houses a Buddha figure made of chalcedony, carried to Burma in 1839 from Bodhgaya, the place in India where Gautama achieved Buddhahood. The pagoda was built in early 1847 by King Pagan Min. Today it has been covered with gold leaf.

The oldest pagoda in the city is the **Shwe Kyi Myint Pagoda** on 24th Road between 82nd and 83rd streets.

Erected in 1167 by Prince Minshinsaw, the exiled son of King Alaungsithu of Bagan, it houses a Buddha image consecrated by the prince himself. It also contains a collection of Buddha figures made of gold and silver and adorned with precious stones. The images were removed from the Royal Palace during the British occupation and previously worshipped by Burmese kings. They are brought out for public veneration on important religious occasions.

A couple of blocks from the Shwe Kyi Myint, at 24th Road and West Moat Road, are the **National Museum and Library**. The museum collection extends across many eras of Burmese history; one of its most interesting pictures shows King Thibaw and Queen Supyalat on the eve of their exile. The library is widely noted for its assemblage of important Buddhist documents.

Market centre of the North: The city of Mandalay is not only the religious and cultural centre of Upper Burma; it is also the economic centre. For the Chins of the west, the Kachins of the north, and the Shans of the east, Mandalay is the primary market for goods. And the Zegyo Market – located on the west side of the city centre, on 84th Street between 26th and 28th roads, is Manda-

U Win Maung, the architect who reconstructed the Mandalay Palace.

lay's most important bazaar.

The Italian Count Caldrari, first secretary of the Mandalay municipal government, had the **Zegyo Market** laid out around the Diamond Jubilee Clock, which had been erected in honor of Queen Victoria's 60-year reign. Today, the market offers visitors, who ordinarily cannot travel far from the beaten track, a fine opportunity to see Burma's ethnic minorities in their national costumes, and at the same time gives an idea of the types of goods in daily use in Burmese homes.

Zegyo Market, which during the past decades was known for its lively night market, and was the one place where you could obtain western-made goods smuggled in from across the Thai border, has recently been rebuilt into a new concrete structure. The newly adopted market economy policy of the government has removed the incentives for the once profitable smuggling business. Nevertheless, today goods obtained through the cross border trade with China are now on display at the markets of Mandalay itself.

With this new turnover point, Chinese money is surging through the Mandalay economy. New hotels and even high-rises appear all over the city and it is not a bad guess if one sees a great future for the region. Being an important trading city on the crossroads between India and China, Mandalay is the centre of Burmese Buddhism and Bamar nationalism, and will soon become again what it once was: the pulsating heart of Burmese culture.

Part of Mandalay's enchantment comes from its location beside the Ayeyarwady River. At the western end of A Road, which follows the railroad tracks north of the Shwe In Bin Kyaung, one finds the jetties where the ships that ply the "Road to Mandalay" are docked. The hustle and bustle of the wharves is fascinating.

But perhaps even more enthralling is the marvelous view across the river to the Sagaing and Mingun hills on the Ayeyarwady's west bank, studded with pagodas and *kyaung* (monasteries). The Pyay (Prome) ferry to Bagan leaves from the piers here; the boat to Mingun departs from a location just a short distance upriver, at the end of B Road.

At the end of C Road is **Buffalo Point**. Here you can see how these powerful animals pull out of the river heavy logs that have been floating down the Shweli and the Ayeyarwady from the north. The whole scene is more than a reminder of bygone days which still live on here at the edge of the river.

The craftsmen's quarters: In the southern part of Mandalay, especially in the precincts of the Maha Muni Pagoda, one finds the artists' and craftsmen's quarters. Buddha figures are hewn from alabaster and marble by stonemasons on a street very near the pagoda.

One can watch as Burmese men, using the same skills and methods as their forefathers, pursue their trade in religious sculpture – Buddha images in all positions, Buddha footprints, lotus-blossom pedestals, or even an occasional Virgin Mary (a reminder of earlier missionary days).

West of the Maha Muni are the makers of pagoda crafts, a booming trade given the Burmese propensity to seek merit through the building and renovation of pagodas. Not far away are the woodcarvers, who create more Buddhas, as well as altars for worship at home and in pagodas. Foundry workers cast replicas of ancient Buddha images, plus musical instruments.

The makers of oiled bamboo paper live on 37th Road, lying between 80th and 81st streets. This kind of paper, which is placed between layers of gold leaf, is produced by means of a remarkable three-year process of soaking, beating flat and drying of bamboo.

Gold leaf is produced in many houses in the southeast section of Mandalay. This craft is extremely old, and the manufacturing process is carried out according to time-honoured tradition.

In the area around Mandalay, visitors should make it a point to see other artisans – the silk and cotton weavers of Amarapura; the silversmiths from the village of Ywataung near Sagaing; and the bronze and brass workers from Kyi Thun Kyat, near Amarapura.

The fabled Maha Muni.

172

CENTRAL AND NORTH BURMA

One of the basic tenets of Buddhism is that nothing is permanent, that everything is in a constant state of change. As one departs Mandalay and roams the surrounding countryside, one can begin to understand how this idea permeates Burmese history. Three ancient capitals – Amarapura, Innwa (Ava) and Sagaing – as well as the medieval town of Mingun lie within a stone's throw of Mandalay. Here, amongst the ruins of palaces, pagodas and *kyaung*, one can find abundant reminders of the political and religious power that belonged to Upper Burma in the 14th through 19th centuries, between the fall of Bagan (Pagan) and the British occupation.

Sagaing was the capital of a Shan-dominated Upper Burma for a brief period beginning in 1315. The seat of government was shifted to Innwa in 1364, and there it remained for almost 400 years. Shwebo (Moksobo) became the royal capital from 1760 to 1764, but the government returned to Innwa, and 19 years later, King Bodawpaya moved the capital to his newly built Amarapura. Kings often moved their headquarters at this time; Innwa was again the capital of Upper Burma from 1823 to 1841, then Amarapura regained the distinction for 20 more years until King Mindon moved his court to Mandalay.

East of Mandalay, in the foothills of the vast Shan Plateau, is the town of Pyin-U-Lwin (Maymyo), a former British hill station. Beyond lies the wild Shan State and the Kachin country of the north, parts of which are still off-limits to tourists because of persistent rebel activity and opium trading.

Immortal Amarapura: Once known as the "city of immortality," Amarapura is now called Taungmyo, "the southern city," by those in Mandalay. It is only 12 kilometres (7.5 mi) south of Burma's second city, and as the metropolitan area burgeons, the two are slowly joining. Centuries ago, King Bodawpaya had a colonnade-flanked road built from his palace in Amarapura to the Maha Muni Pagoda near today's Mandalay.

The youngest of the royal cities near Mandalay, Amarapura was built by Bodawpaya in 1782. It was moved there from Innwa (Ava) on the advice of court astrologers, the Manipurian Brahmans, who were concerned about the circumstances surrounding Bodawpaya's ascendancy to the throne. The power struggle had begun with a massacre and was followed by the horrifying destruction of Paungga village near Sagaing, where the entire population was ordered to be burned. The Brahmans felt the only way to prevent further mishaps was to transfer the capital. In May 1783, all of the inhabitants of Innwa, together with the court, packed their belongings and moved to land allocated to them around the new Amarapura palace.

The Barnabite priest Sangermano witnessed the mass migration, and described in some detail the new city of 200,000 people. Foreigners had their own quarters – Chinese, Indians, Muslims and Manipuris alike – and the smattering of Christians (primarily Portuguese and Armenians) lived in the Chinese quarter. At the centre of the city was Bodawpaya's palace, surrounded by a wall 1.6 kilometres (1 mi) in circumference, with a pagoda standing at each of its four corners. Within the wall were the secular buildings made of wood. Seventy-five years later, they were partly torn down and rebuilt in Mandalay by the Konbaung King Mindon.

Bodawpaya was finished with Innwa. He had the final remains of the city pulled down, the ancient trees felled and the river diverted to flood the city. His actions did not, however, prevent his successor, King Bagyidaw, from rebuilding the city of Innwa and moving the capital back there in 1823. In 1841, King Tharrawaddy resettled in Amarapura, and the capital remained there until Mindon moved the seat of the Konbaung dynasty to Mandalay.

Weavers and Bronze Casters: Amarapura is a city of 10,000 inhabitants whose main livelihood is weaving cotton and silk into Burma's loveliest festive clothing. The *acheithtameins* (ceremonial *longyi*), which can be knotted over the chest or worn as a train on all special occasions, is the most famous product of this city, in which every second house is said to have a loom.

A second noted industry of Amarapura is bronze casting. Cymbals, gongs and Buddha images are made here out of a special alloy of bronze and lead. The famous statue of Bogyoke Aung San at the entrance to Aung San Park in Yangon was cast here.

Nothing remains to be seen of the **Royal Palace**. Some of the wooden buildings were reconstructed in Mandalay by Mindon, and the walls that remained standing were taken by the British as a cheap source of materials for roads and railways. The four pagodas which once marked the corners of the city wall, however, can still be seen. So can two stone buildings – the treasury and the old watchtower. The graves of Bodawpaya and Bagyidaw are also here.

In the southern part of the city sits the well-preserved **Patodawgyi Pagoda**, built by King Bagyidaw in 1820. A bell-shaped stupa, it stands on five terraces which are covered with *Jataka* reliefs. There is an inscription stone nearby which tells the story of the construction of the pagoda.

One of the largest monasteries in Burma is in Amarapura. The presence of up to 1200 monks (during the Buddhist lent) in the Maha Gandha Monastery contributes a great deal to the religious atmosphere of the city. Visitors are welcome and it is quite spectacular to see hundreds of monks line up for their one daily meal every morning at 11 am. Every day the meal is donated by somebody else (at a cost of up to 40,000 kyat). There are always plenty of donators waiting to get the chance to earn merit. To experience the distribution of the food (often by the family of the donator themselves) and the way in which the *pongyi* accept it without a word of thanks, makes you understand the living power behind the concept of merit-making.

To the south of Amarapura is **Lake Taungthaman**, an intermittent body of

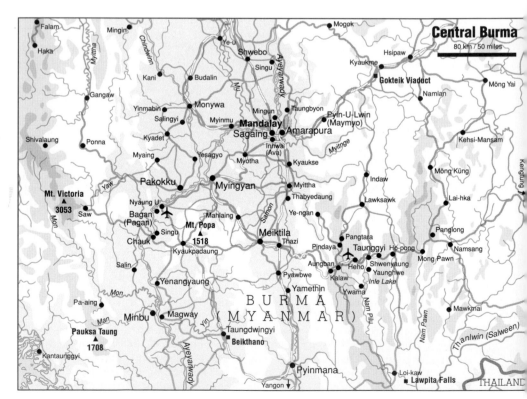

water which dries up in the winter and leaves fertile, arable land in its stead. It is spanned by the 1.2-kilometre (0.7-mi) long **U Bein Bridge**, constructed from the teak planks of Innwa by King Bodawpaya's mayor (U Bein) following the move to Amarapura. This rickety teak bridge stands today just as sturdily as it did two centuries ago. It takes about 15 minutes to cross, and during the hot season one is thankful for the rest-houses which line the bridge, providing shelter from the sun. During the last decade most of the old planks have disappeared; they were used for Buddha statues that are on sale in Bangkok antique shops.

In the middle of a widely scattered village on the east side of the bridge is the **Kyauktawgyi Pagoda**, built by King Pagan in 1847. Like the Kyauk Tawgyi in Mandalay, this pagoda was intended to be a replica of the Ananda Temple in Bagan (Pagan). The exterior is a successful imitation, but the interior arches do not do justice to the original. Instead of the four standing Buddhas found in the Ananda Temple, this pagoda contains an enormous Buddha made of Sagyin marble. The colour resembles that of jade and its height reaches the ceiling of the inner cella.

Within the shrine are 88 statues of the Buddha's disciples, as well as 12 *manusiha*, mythical half-man half-beast beings. The temple's east and west entrances are decorated with murals depicting the daily life of the Burmese at the time of the pagoda's construction. Under careful scrutiny, European faces can be seen among the Burmese in the paintings. A repeated theme of the murals is the good-will of King Pagan toward his people; this is ironic because Pagan was one of the cruelest kings of Burma's Konbaung dynasty. It is said that as many as 3,000 death sentences a year were carried out during his reign.

The area surrounding the Kyauktawgyi Pagoda is full of smaller pagodas in various stages of decay. These temples have been systematically plundered ever since the prices of ancient Burmese artifacts reached astronomical

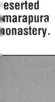

eserted marapura monastery.

levels in the antique shops of Bangkok.

On Amarapura's Ayeyarwady bank, two white pagodas – the **Shwekyetyet Pagoda** and the **Shwekyetkya Pagoda** – remain from the Era of the Temple Builders. They were built by a 12th-century king of Bagan, and can be found about 30 minutes' walk from Amarapura's main street.

A short distance downriver lies the **Thabyedan Fort**, which King Mindon had French and Italian advisors erect in European style. The fort was intended to stop any hostile armies from striking with warships from the Ayeyarwady. Yet when the British invaded Mandalay in 1886 in exactly this way, not a shot was fired – the Burmese, lacking strong armed forces, had already given up.

Ancient Innwa (Ava) – "The city of gems": The No. 8 bus from Mandalay travels right down the main street of Amarapura and continues to Innwa. Near the famed Innwa (Ava) Bridge over the Ayeyarwady (Irrawaddy), a dusty, pot-holed road leads to the Myitnge River ferry; on the river's opposite bank, horse-drawn carriages wait to take travellers on to the ancient capital. During the rainy season, this entire region is flooded, and Innwa can be reached only by boat.

The city's name means "entrance to the lake," a variant of the Shan phrase *in-va*. It is appropriate, as the entire rice trade of the Kyaukse Plain was once controlled from this capital at the junction of the Ayeyarwady and Mytinge rivers. Such economic control was a necessity for the foundation of a sound state and strong dynasty, and it was in this region, around the 11 hamlets of the Kyaukse district, that the nucleus of a new Burmese empire took shape after the fall of Bagan in 1287 to the Mongol army of Kublai Khan.

The city of Innwa was founded in 1364 by King Thadominbya, who built it in the northeast corner of an artificial island created by the Myittha Chaung, a channel dug from the Myitnge to the Ayeyarwady. Even during the 19th century, the entire Burmese Empire was generally known as "Ava" and when the seat of government moved to Amarapura

A farmer goads his animals through the ruins of Amarapura.

and later to Mandalay, the government was still referred to as the "Court of Ava." The classical name by which Innwa is known in Burma, however, is Ratnapura – "the city of gems."

Unlike most other royal cities of Burma, Innwa's city wall is not square, but is shaped like a sitting lion, such as those found in front of large pagodas. Only a part of the wall still stands; the most complete section is at the north gate, known as **Gaung Say Dage**, the gate of the hair-washing ceremony. Every April during the Thingyan Festival, this ritual hair-washing takes place as a purification rite to welcome the king of the *nat*. Today it exists only in homes, but in imperial times, even the king washed his hair at this gate.

Near the north gate are the ruins of the **Nanmyin Watchtower**, the so-called "leaning tower of Innwa." All that remains of Bagyidaw's palace, this erstwhile 27 metre (89-ft) lookout was damaged so heavily by an 1838 earthquake that its upper portion collapsed. Soon, it began leaning because the earth was sinking right beneath it.

Not far from the "leaning tower" is the best preserved of all buildings in Innwa, the **Maha Aungmye Bonzan Monastery**. Also known as the Ok Kyaung, the brick structure was built in 1818 by Nanmadaw Me Nu, wife of King Bagyidaw, for the abbot Sayadaw Nyaunggan, who was rumored to have been her lover. A tall, stucco-decorated building, it was built in the same style as that of more common teak *kyaung*; yet its masonry guaranteed it would survive longer than its wooden cousins.

In the middle of the monastery is a statue of the Buddha, placed on a pedestal trimmed with glass mosaic. Beside the archway at the entrance is an old marble plaque which tells, in English, the story of an American missionary's Burmese wife who was a staunch convert to Christianity until her death during the First Anglo-Burmese War.

Next door to the *kyaung* is a seven-tiered prayer hall. This building suffered heavy damage in the 1838 earthquake, but was repaired in 1873 by

Left, the U Bein Bridge. Right, Innwa's Maha Aungmye Bonzan Monastery.

Hsinbyumashin, the daughter of Nanmadaw Me Nu.

In the vicinity of the monastery is the **Adoniram Judson Memorial**. Judson, an American missionary who compiled the first Anglo-Burmese dictionary, was jailed during the First Anglo-Burmese War and endured severe torture during his imprisonment. He had mistakenly assumed that the Burmese would distinguish between the British colonialists and the American missionaries. The white stone memorial is on the site of the notorious Let Ma Yoon prison.

There are many pagodas in the Innwa region. Among them is the **Htilanishin Pagoda**, built by King Kyanzittha during the Bagan era. Other important shrines include the four-story **Leitutgyi Pagoda** and the **Lawkatharaphy Pagoda**, both in the southern part of the city. Some 1.5 kilometres (1 mi) south of the city stands **Innwa Fort**, which was considered part of the "unconquerable triangle" including Thabyedan and Sagaing forts.

South of the existing city of Innwa is an old brick causeway leading across the canal to the village of **Tada-u**. Within the old city walls are other small villages and paddy fields where the centre of the Burmese Empire once stood.

North of Innwa is the famous **Innwa Bridge**, built by the British in 1934 and still the only bridge across the Ayeyarwady River. It connects Innwa with Sagaing (the crossing can also be made by ferry) some 20 kilometres (12.5 mi) south of Mandalay. There are military posts at each end of the bridge, and a small toll is collected there. Because of its strategic importance, the British blew the bridge up in the face of the Japanese advance in 1942, and not until 1954 was it reopened.

Sagaing – living centre of the faith: Whereas Amarapura and Innwa are ancient capitals left largely at the mercy of the elements, Sagaing remains very much alive. In fact, some consider Sagaing to be the living centre of the Buddhist faith in Burma today.

The city reverberates with the echoes of cymbals, gongs and pagoda bells. Innwa Bridge

Refugees from the hectic pace of urban life retreat here – for a day or a lifetime – to meditate. Devout families bring their young sons to undergo the *shin pyu* ceremony and thereby join the community of the faithful.

In the hills and in the many-fingered valleys of the west bank of the Ayeyarwady are some 600 monasteries, as well as numerous temples, stupas and caves dedicated to the memory of the Gautama Buddha. About 5,000 monks live in this arcadian landscape laced with endless stairways and colonnades. From Sagaing north to Mingun, the slopes are covered with frangipani, bougainvillea, tamarind and mango trees, in whose shadows earthen water bowls await thirsty pilgrims. The monasteries and private houses are hidden in the hills and valleys, but the big temples and pagodas ride the crests of the verdant heights and glitter across the land.

Sagaing is different each hour of the day – in the morning, when the *pongyi* and their students stream out of the *kyaung* with their begging bowls; in the midday heat, when the ringing of the stupa bells and the droning of the monks' prayers rise over all other sounds; in the evening, when the lights of Mandalay illuminate the banks of the Ayeyarwady.

The Burmese view Sagaing as a "foot-hill" of mystical Mount Meru; it is easy to rise above everyday banalities here.

If you've come here on a booked tour, there will be no time for contemplation. The jeep stops briefly at the **Sun U Ponya Shin Pagoda**, the snapshot enthusiast's favourite viewpoint, then rushes on to other sights which can be crammed into a single day's sightseeing. The independent traveller can best savour the inimitable atmosphere of Sagaing by staying over-night in one of the many monasteries (which is officially not permitted), whose abbots are very generous. However, there is now a newly-built hotel in town with a great view and a superb Chinese restaurant.

From Mandalay, Sagaing is reached by collector bus from the corner of 29th Road and 83rd Street. Horse carriages will take the visitor to the monastery-

The hills of Sagaing.

studded hills behind the town, but hiring a jeep is recommended for travelling further afield.

Ancient Shan capital: Sagaing was the capital of an independent Shan kingdom beginning about 1315, after the fall of Bagan (Pagan). The capital was moved to Innwa in 1364, and most of the buildings in the vicinity were constructed during the Innwa period.

Probably the most famous temple in Sagaing is the **Kaunghmudaw Pagoda**. It actually lies 10 kilometres (6 mi) behind the city on the far side of the Sagaing Hills. Built by King Thalun in 1636 to house relics formerly kept in the Mahazedi Pagoda in Bago (Pegu), it is said to contain the Buddha's "Tooth of Kandy" and King Dhammapala's miracle-working begging bowl.

Built in Ceylonese style, this pagoda's rounded shape – a perfect hemisphere – is according to legend, a copy of the perfect breasts of Thalun's favourite wife. The huge egg-shaped dome, 46 metres (151 ft) high and 274 metres (900 ft) in circumference, rises above three rounded terraces. The lowest terrace is decorated with 120 *nat* and *deva*, each of which can be found in a separate niche. A ring of 812 molded stone pillars, each 1.5 metres (five ft) high, surround the dome; each of these posts has a hollowed-out head in which an oil lamp is placed during the Thadingyut Light Festival on the occasion of the October full moon. Burmese Buddhists come to the Kaunghmudaw Pagoda from far and wide to celebrate the end of Buddhist Lent at this annual festival. The history of the pagoda, which is also called the Rajamanicula, is written in Burmese script on a white marble pillar 2.5 metres (8.5 ft) high in a corner of the pagoda grounds.

Two lakes lie behind the Kaunghmudaw Pagoda. One of them was formed when bricks used in the construction of the pagoda were stacked; it is now used for breeding fish. The other lake, called Lake Myitta Kan, is legendary: it is said that no leaf from surrounding trees has ever touched the lake's surface.

There are two interesting attractions

The U Min Kyaukse Pagoda.

on the road between the Kaunghmudaw Pagoda and Sagaing. One is the village of **Ywataung**, home of silversmiths who still work the precious metal in much the same way as their ancestors did. The other is the **Hsinmyashin Pagoda**, also called the Pagoda of Many Elephants. Built in 1429 by King Monhyin, it was destroyed in 1482 by an earthquake. It was restored, but a 1955 quake nearly leveled it, and it has recently been rebuilt again. Two colourful large elephants have also been reconstructed at the long entrance to the pagoda.

The Unfinished Pagoda: The **Htupayon Pagoda** in Sagaing town, built by King Barapati in 1444, is also unfinished. It was destroyed by the 1838 earthquake, and King Pagan – who wanted to have it rebuilt – was dethroned before repairs were completed. The 30-metre (98-ft) high base is standing however, and it represents a rare style of temple architecture in Burma. In a nearby hut is a collection of stone engravings which include the history of the Shan Prince Thonganbwa. The prince wanted to re-

establish the ancient Nan-chao Empire in present-day Yunnan (China), but he was pursued by the Chinese and took refuge in Innwa. King Narapati provided him sanctuary and defeated the Chinese in a battle on the prince's behalf in 1445. A year later, the Chinese returned with a stronger army – and rather than allow himself to be handed over to the Chinese, Prince Thonganbwa committed suicide. His body was found, and Innwa was committed to paying allegiance to the Chinese.

Like the Htupayon, the **Ngadatgyi Pagoda** rests on the western side of Sagaing. There is an enormous seated Buddha image in this temple. The Ngadatgyi was erected in 1657 by King Pindale, the ill-fated successor to King Thalun. Pindale was dethroned by his brother in 1661, and a few weeks later was drowned together with his entire family. (This was a common means of putting royalty to death because there was no blood spilled on the soil.)

The **Aungmyelawka Pagoda**, built by King Bodawpaya in 1783 on the

sayadaw leads a procession of monks.

Ayeyarwady riverfront near the Htupayon Pagoda, is a cylindrical sandstone replica of the Shwezigon Pagoda in Nyaung U. Bodawpaya had it built on the site of the house where he spent the years prior to his coronation. According to the will of Bodawpaya's father, King Alaungpaya, he should have become king upon the death of his brother, Hsinbyushin. But when the latter proclaimed his son Singu to be his successor, Bodawpaya had to stand aside until a short-lived coup by another aspiring ruler gave him the opening he needed in 1782 to claim the throne that was rightfully his. In the interim, Bodawpaya lived in Sagaing. Construction of the Aungmyelawka Pagoda was intended to balance the "necessary cruelties" of his reign and improve his merit for future incarnations. This pagoda is also known as the Eindawya Pagoda.

The **Datpaungzu Pagoda** is of rather recent vintage, having been built only upon the completion of the Myitkyina Railway. It is a repository for the relics of a number of stupas which had to be demolished or relocated in clearing the way for the railway to cross the Innwa Bridge. The relics are much venerated by the people of the region.

On the most easterly point of the two ridges rising above Sagaing stands the **U Min Kyaukse Pagoda**, the architectural style of which is immediately reminiscent of a mosque. Its roof affords a fine view over Mandalay and the Ayeyarwady. The **Shwe Ume Kyaung**, a monastery attached to this pagoda, is a popular *shin pyu* site.

On the western hill stands the **Sun U Ponya Shin Pagoda**, easily reached by car from the Sagaing market. Further back in the western hill chain lies the **U Min Thonze Pagoda**, where 45 Buddha images bask in a soft light, posed in a semi-circle. Mural paintings hundreds of years old can be found in the **Tilawkaguru Cave** as well as in the **Myipaukgyi Pagoda**.

The **Pa Ba Kyaung** is one of the best known monasteries of all Burma. Situated in the floor of the valley between the two ridges, it is enveloped in silence

Htis **for Sagaing's pagodas.**

186

and ideal for the quiet meditation demanded by *pongyi*.

Beyond Sagaing, 160 kilometres (98 mi) from Mandalay is **Monywa,** famous for its **Thambuddhe** shrine. Another 25 kilometres (15 mi) west, after crossing the Chindwinn, you arrive at **Shweba-taung**, **Panga-taung** and **Nwatho-taung**, impressive extinct volcanoes with some 446,444 Buddha images placed in sandstone niches. A new hotel was opened in Monywa recently, paving the way for more tourism.

Mingun – big bell and a mound of bricks: At the northern end of the chain of hills flanking Sagaing, resting on the banks of the Ayeyarwady, is the village of **Mingun**, home of the largest intact bell in the world – as well as an unfinished pagoda sometimes described as the biggest pile of bricks on earth. Sharp eyes can spot it from Mandalay Hill, although it lies more than 10 kilometres (6.5 mi) to the northwest.

Mingun is accessible only by river. Boats leave Mandalay daily at 7.30 and 8.30am bound for the little village; it takes about an hour to make the trip from the end of B Road. Visitors who do not intend to take the Ayeyarwady steamer from Mandalay to Bagan (Pagan) should not miss this short trip, as there is no better way to observe life on Burma's throbbing artery. Ferries, teak and bamboo rafts, paddle steamers, and numerous small boats which always appear to be on the brink of sinking, ply the Ayeyarwady between Myitkyina in the far north and Pathein (Bassein) in the delta. Women can often be seen travelling north from Mandalay, walking along the river bank and towing their boats behind them, as their husbands sit at the tillers to make sure the boats do not strike any hidden obstacles. Parallel rows of well-trodden paths are evidence of the widely varying water levels of the Ayeyarwady: the banks can sometimes be 12 metres (39 ft) above the river during the dry season.

Mingun is a favorite destination for Mandalay residents on day outings. To cater to their tastes, a series of tea shops line the road from the jetty. Where the

Mystic mood
of a monk at
twilight.

row of tea shops ends, there is a convalescent home for homeless Burmese behind the embankment.

Behind and to the left of the home is the famous **Mingun Bell**. It weighs 87 tons, stands 3.7 metres (more than 12 ft) high, and is 5 metres (16.5 ft) wide at its mouth. What's more, it still works. The world's only larger bell is in the Kremlin in Moscow, but that one is cracked and can no longer be used. King Bodawpaya had this bell cast in 1790 to be dedicated to his huge Mingun Pagoda, which was intended to be the world's largest. By imagining how painstaking the molding and casting procedures must have been in the 18th century, one can appreciate what a fine work of art this bell is. Bodawpaya recognized this fact, and to prevent the feat from being repeated, he had the artist executed.

During the 1838 earthquake, the Mingun Bell and its original *tazaung* collapsed. Fortunately, there was no damage. Today the bell is held up by heavy iron rods beneath a shelter. Small Burmese boys who frequent the site are only too willing to show visitors where to strike the bell with a wooden mallet to produce the best sound.

Bodawpaya's pagoda: The **Mingun (Mantara Gyi) Pagoda** stands some 100 metres (328 ft) south of the bell. From a distance, its appearance is that of a large mound, nothing more. Yet it has played a very important role in Burmese history in the last century.

The pagoda was built between 1790 and 1797 by Bodawpaya, fourth son of Alaungpaya, founder of the Konbaung dynasty. Bodawpaya was lord of Tanintharyi (Tenasserim), the Mon lands, and Rakhine, as well as central Burma. He had underscored his invincibility by carrying the Maha Muni from Rakhine to Amarapura, and he had just become the proud owner of a white elephant. He was at the peak of his power and wanted the world to see.

In 1790, a Chinese delegation visited Bodawpaya's court, carrying as gifts, a tooth of the Buddha and three of the Chinese emperor's daughters as wives. Bodawpaya had the pagoda built to

Left, bottled Buddhas. Right, the Mingun Bell.

house the tooth – the same one that both Anawrahta and Alaungpaya coveted but had failed to obtain. Bodawpaya moved his residence to an island in the Ayeyarwady for the next seven years while he supervised the construction work. Bodawpaya intended to make his Mantara Gyi a full 152 metres (499 ft) in height. He imported thousands of slaves from his newly conquered southern territories to work on the pagoda.

Ambitions of a king: The pagoda, however, was not Bodawpaya's only project. At the same time that pagoda construction was commencing, the king had renewed work on the enormous Mektila Dam project, for which he had also "recruited" thousands of workers. In addition, large armies were deployed to help keep his empire under his control. Under great oppression, 50,000 Rakhines (Arakanese) fled to neighbouring Bengal, which was then under British rule, and began a guerrilla war against the Burmese. This later exploded into the First Anglo-Burmese War.

The lack of available labour in central Burma was irritating to Bodawpaya. Worried rumours which had circulated 500 years earlier during construction of the Minglazedi Pagoda had resurfaced, and concerned voices were saying, "When the pagoda is finished, the great country will be ruined." But Bodawpaya, convinced of his destiny as a future Buddha, was not to be dissuaded. He had the pagoda's shrine rooms lined with lead and filled with 1,500 gold figurines, 2,434 silver images, and nearly 37,000 of various other materials. He even included a soda-water machine, just invented in England, according to Hiram Cox, British envoy to Bodawpaya's court. Only then were shrine rooms were then sealed.

The economic ruin which raged at the turn of the 19th century persuaded Bodawpaya to halt construction work on the pagoda. The king died in 1813, aged 75, having ruled for 38 years. He left 122 children and 208 grandchildren – but none of them continued his work on the great pagoda.

Even though it was never completed,

The Hsinbyume Pagoda.

the ruins of the Mingun Pagoda are most impressive. The upper sections of the pagoda collapsed into the hollow shrine rooms during the great 1838 earthquake, but the base of the structure still towers nearly 50 metres (162 ft) over the Ayeyarwady. An enormous pair of griffins, also damaged in the quake, guard the riverfront view. The lowest terrace of the pagoda measures 137 square metres (450 sq ft) in size, and arches project from each of its four sides.

Miniature Monstrosity: In the immediate vicinity is the smaller **Pondawpaya Pagoda**, a small replica of the original Mantara Gyi. Compare it to its large neighbour, and you'll see that King Bodawpaya's monstrosity on the Ayeyarwady reached only one-third of its planned height. After making the comparison, take off your shoes and climb to the platform on the north side of the Mingun Pagoda for the view.

A short distance downstream is the **Settawya Pagoda**. This building is entirely white, and has a stairway leading to its hollow vault from the water's edge. Built by Bodawpaya in 1811, it holds a marble footprint of the Buddha.

At the north end of Mingun, beyond the village, one of the prettiest pagodas in Burma is found. This is the **Hsinbyume** or **Myatheindan Pagoda**, built by Bodawpaya's grandson Bagyidaw in 1816, three years before he ascended the throne, as a memorial to his favorite wife, Princess Hsinbyume. The temple's architecture is founded in Buddhist cosmology, according to which the Sulamani Pagoda stands atop Mount Meru in the centre of the universe. The king of the gods (known variously as Indra, Sakka, or Thagyamin) lives here on top of the mountain, surrounded by seven additional mountain chains. The Myatheindan Pagoda is based on this model: seven concentric terraces with wave-like railings lead to the central stupa, which is guarded by five kinds of mythical monsters placed in niches around the terraces. (Temple robbers have unfortunately decapitated most of the monsters.) In the highest part of the stupa, reachable only by a steep stair-

The Hsinbyume Pagoda is modeled on Mount Meru with its seven ranges of hills.

way, is the cella containing a single Buddha figure. This pagoda suffered severe damage in the 1838 earthquake, but was rebuilt by King Mindon in 1874.

Most visitors to Mingun remain only a half-day, thereby depriving themselves of the magical scenery at the foot of the Mingun hills. As in Sagaing, the mountain-side is covered with *kyaung* and small pagodas woven together by a network of shadowy paths. Those who wish to explore the enchanting hinterland of Mingun must spend the night at one of the monasteries, as the return boat to Mandalay leaves Mingun at 3pm.

Pyin-U-Lwin – British hill station: Those who have a weak spot for the atmosphere of British colonial times, and others just seeking to escape the dusty misery of Mandalay's hot season, must visit **Pyin-U-Lwin (Maymyo),** in the foothills of the Shan Plateau. A two and a half hour drive by jeep from Mandalay takes the traveller to 1,070 metres (3,510 ft) elevation, where there are breathtaking views of the Mandalay plain.

Pyin-U-Lwin (once Maymyo) was named in the colonial era after Colonel May, a British officer in the Bengal Infantry who was stationed at this hill station in 1887 in order to suppress a rebellion which flared after the annexation of Upper Burma to India. The city, called Pyin-U-Lwin by natives, lies at a strategically important point on the road from Mandalay to Hsipaw, a major Shan principality in north Burma.

Pleasant temperatures predominate in Pyin-U-Lwin even during the hot season, and in the cold season there is no frost. It's no wonder the British felt at home here. A number of Indian and Nepali gurkhas whose forebears entered the country with the Indian army have settled here, retaining many of the old colonial traditions in their work as hoteliers, carriage drivers and gardeners.

Pyin-U-Lwin offers a line of former stylish British country houses, rebuilt into small 6 – 8 room hotels. They are jewels of European comfort in Burma's up country and quite inexpensive. To stay there for a prolonged time is a yet untested way of a Burmese vacation. The best known is the former Candacraig, now called Thiri Myaing. This hotel, once a relaxation centre for the Bombay Burma Trading Company, was built in 1905 in the style of an English country home. It still offers many of the niceties which once made the lives of the company's clerk so pleasurable – English food, early-morning tea, and a big fireplace. Pyin-U-Lwin also has a 175-hectare (432-acre) Botanical Garden, an 18-hole golf course, and three waterfalls in the vicinity for swimming and picnics. Horse-drawn carriages are the chief mode of transportation; these closed vehicles with their high doors appear to have been left behind by the 19th century.

27 kilometres (15 mi) to the east are the **Maha Nandamu caves** depicting scenes of Buddha's life in a fairy-tale surrounding. Most of the images have been donated by leaders and family members of the present government to abate for sins committed.

Burma's isolated northern frontier: Beyond Pyin-U-Lwin (Maymyo), Burma's northern and eastern frontiers are accessible to Westerners only with a special government pass, obtainable only in Yangon through MT&T or private travel agencies. The rail line which passes through Pyin-U-Lwin (it is a five-hour train trip from Mandalay) continues as far as the northern Shan administrative centre of Lashio which has recently been opened for tourists.

Paul Theroux's *The Great Railway Bazaar* contains a couple of classic chapters about the joys and hazards of this unusual rail passage. Theroux's tales of vendors carrying fried locusts and skewered sparrows on rice, government soldiers in dented helmets reddening the earth with betel-nut spittle, and cavernous tunnels "smelling of bat shit and sodden plants" are essential advance reading for the would-be back-country Burma traveller.

Going by train you will cross the famous **Gokteik Viaduct**, which traverses a 300-metre (984-ft) deep gorge in the Shan mountains. When it was built in 1903, the viaduct was considered a masterpiece, even by Western standards, because of the technical difficulties and transportation problems that had to be overcome.

Theroux, in his 1973 travels, described the viaduct as "a monster of silver geometry in all the ragged rock and jungle...Its presence there was bizarre, this man-made thing in so remote a place, competing with the grandeur of the enormous gorge and yet seemingly more grand than its surroundings, which were hardly negligible – the water rushing through the girder legs and falling on the tops of trees, the flights of birds through the swirling clouds and the blackness of the tunnels beyond the viaduct."

Beyond the viaduct is the town of **Kyaukme**, where every March the Shan Festival is held. Thousands of Shan tribesmen, representing the second largest ethnic group in Burma, flock to this town from all over the Shan Highlands to participate.

Precious mines of Mogok: As long as the road from Kyaukme is still closed, you will have to take the road from Singu along the Ayeyarwady, opposite

from Kyaukmyaung, that leads to the town of **Mogok**, famous for its ruby mines. Most visitors to Burma are secretly offered rubies from these mines, but only those persons with a real knowledge of stones, and who are willing to risk their illegal export, should consider buying any of them.

Continuing from Kyaukme on the main rail line toward **Lashio**, one passes near **Sakhtana**, where the palace of the *sawbwa* (prince) of the Hsipaw district stands. Finally, the train arrives in Lashio. The city, situated in a very pretty area, is at its best during the winter months, when trees and other plants are in blossom. The market is an important gathering spot for northern Shans, who come here from remote valleys to do their trading. A new hotel for tourists is now open.

From Lashio, the Burma Road – built by the British prior to World War II – leads into the rugged Chinese province of Yunnan and is now the main route for the thriving cross-border trade with China. Shortly before reaching the in-

Morning on the Ayeyarwady south of Bhamo.

ternational border, it intersects with the Ledo Road, which crosses Burma from India. Built by American engineers during the war, it weaves through river valleys and around mountain ridges to Myitkyina, capital of the Kachin State, then on to India's Brahmaputra Valley.

In **Bhamo**, which lies on the road to Myitkyina, there is another colourful market where a real mixture of tribes is found. The Kachins (also called Jinghpaws) can be identified by their black turbans. The Shans are dressed in brown, the Palaungs in multicoloured robes and the Lisus in their blue-and-read-striped national dress.

Not far from the town you'll find the remnants of the ancient city of **Sampanago**, and in the town, a stupa that harks back to the time of King Ashoka. Sampanago is mentioned in many early books and travel documents, and its functions were moved to Bhamo in the 17th century.

Bhamo sits on the Ayeyarwady's east bank, and is the departure point for what is potentially the most impressive river trip in Burma. The Ayeyarwady steamer from Bhamo to Mandalay sails through dense jungle and across three rapids, and (MT&T) plans to make this trip accessible to tourists.

Ancient cities: Going down the Ayeyarwady (see separate chapter) you'll pass **Tagaung**, a city that was thriving before the Buddha was born some 2,500 years ago.

Myitkyina, Burma's northernmost sizable town, lies below the foothills of the great Himalaya Range. Beyond are the nearly inaccessible climes of the remote Kachin State.

The three-day-long **Manao Festival** takes place in Myitkyina every January. For the last decades this festival has only taken place on a village level. Since 1993, however, all the Kachin tribes have been meeting again at **Myitkyina's Manao grounds**.

Since most Kachins have converted to Christianity, this originally animist festival has become a mixture of religion and culture, though it has not lost any of its ancient power.

Next to the grounds on which this festival takes place, is the **ancient spirit house** with all the implements that were used to slaughter the sacrificial animals.

After heading north for another 49 kilometres (27 mi), you will reach one of Burma's most beautiful and important nature spots – the **cradle of the Ayeyarwady**.

Here the **Maikha** and the **Malihka** rivers meet and form the country's main artery. Surrounded by 1400-metre (4500- ft) hills, their confluence occurs in spectacular rapids through which hardy northern tribesman navigate their ramshackle rafts.

Now that Kachin state is peaceful again, the once mine ridden roads, especially those that connect Myitkyina with Bhamo and Putao, have been repaired. Travel however, is at present still restricted. You can fly into **Putao** (the former Fort Hertz) not far from the Assam border where you will be in the centre of the Rawangs' and Lisu's settling area. Sixteen kilometres (10 mi) outside of Putao at **Machembo**, are nice government-owned bungalows with a

A shaman of north Burma.

hilltop resort flair. Once the road is open, (now only a question of time) you should go back by bus or car, stopping at **Sumprabhum**– the trading centre of the northernmost tribes. To the west live the Nagas and to the east a variety of Kachin tribes, their settlements spilling over into India and China.

Alaungpaya's capital: The northern rail line from Mandalay has its terminus in Myitkyina. On the return trip to Mandalay, the traveller passes through **Shwebo**, about 100 kilometres (60 mi) north of Upper Burma's metropolis. Shwebo was an 18th-century capital for Alaungpaya, and it was from here that the reconquest of Burma began after the Mons had seized Innwa in 1752. Alaungpaya's grave is in Shwebo, and his headstone displays an inscription in very fractured English. Otherwise, all trappings of royalty have disappeared.

Eighteen kilometres (11 mi) southeast of Shwebo are the ruins of the old Pyu city of **Halin (Halingyi)**. Legend takes its origins back into pre-history – an Indian dynasty is said to have produced a continuous line of 799 kings until the city one day disappeared under a cloud of ash. Archaeologists, however, place the city's establishment between the 2nd and 6th centuries AD, based upon radiocarbon analyses of the city wall's burnt remains. Remnants of 12 gates in the 3-by-1.5-kilometre wall can still be seen today. In all likelihood, Halin was the northern Pyu capital overrun by the Nan-chao kingdom of the Tai in 832.

To the west, beyond the Chindwinn, connected by air with Mandalay and Yangon, lies **Kalemyo** the gateway to the "skyline road" into the southern Chin hills. To **Falam** and **Haka**. Further to the north, also accessible by air, lies **Hkamti**, the centre of Burma's Naga tribes. Both these destinations will soon be on the agenda of every adventure travel agency.

The Taungbyon Spirit Festival: For eight days before the last full moon every August, the village of Taungbyon, 20 kilometres (13 mi) north of Mandalay, becomes the focus of the Taungbyon Spirit Festival. Tens of thousands of

Burmese attend this annual celebration, held in honour of the Taungbyon Brother Lords. The rites for these two brothers, honoured as *nat*, originated during Anawrahta's 11th-century reign. Wooden figures, representing the brothers, are ceremonially washed and paraded through the crowds as everyone present strains to touch each of the figures at least once.

The brothers are in fact historical figures. They were sons of Byatta, a Muslim warrior from India who used supernatural means to recover the Mons' Buddhist scriptures during Anawrahta's conquest of Thaton. According to legend, Byatta was appointed Anawrahta's flower officer, but he fell in love with Me Wunna, an ogress who lived on the wooded slopes of Mount Popa. She bore Byatta two sons, Shwepyingyi and Shwepyinnge. Byatta spent so much time with his beloved family on Mount Popa that he failed for the third time to provide the king with his daily flowers, and was executed.

Byatta's sons were coerced into accompanying Anawrahta on a campaign in Yunnan. Upon their return, the king's forces paused at the present site of Taungbyon village, where Anawrahta ordered the construction of a pagoda. The brothers, unused to hard work, shirked their assignment of laying bricks in the new Taungbyon pagoda and were condemned to death.

The Burmese mourned the death of the two young men. These two new spirits quickly became so powerful that Anawrahta proclaimed them nat, had a shrine built for them in Taungbyon, and ordered an annual festival be held in their honour.

Perhaps nowhere else is there such an open display of Burmese Buddhism's animistic essence as at the brother's festival in this small village. There are ritual offerings, ceremonial dances, dozens of *pwe*, consultations with shamans, an enormous bazaar, and lots of eating, gambling, and general carousing.

In the words of anthropologist Melford Spiro, it is a "combination, Burmese-style, of an American state fair and a medieval miracle play."

Celebrant at the Taungbyon Festival.

meeting with Shin Arahan, the king was engaged in a cultural and religious campaign against *nat* worship and the Tantric debauchery of the Ari monks of Upper Burma. But inn Shin Arahan's teachings, he found a belief based upon rationalism rather than mysticism.

Now committed to exposing his empire to Theravada doctrines, Anawrahta sent to King Manuha of Thaton a messenger requesting copies of the *Tipitaka* (scriptures).

But Manuha hesitated, repulsed by the thought of sharing sacred writings with "barbarians," and that was his demise. Anawrahta wasted no time in responding to this affront: he massed his armies and invaded Lower Burma, sacking Thaton and bringing back to Bagan everything his elephants and men could carry – 30 sets of the *Tipitaka*, architects, Buddhist monks, even King Manuha himself and the royal family.

Almost immediately upon returning to his capital, Anawrahta embarked on his program of embellishing the countryside with Buddhist monuments. The Shwesandaw Pagoda was the first of these, and many others followed.

As king, Anawrahta was entitled to several wives. He had been given glowing reports by his officials of an Indian princess named Panchakalyani, and sent an envoy to woo her to his court. The princess' father had consented to the match, but on the return journey, the envoy had an affair with the princess. In order to keep this a secret and avoid the King's wrath, the envoy ordered Panchakalyani's escorts to return to her father's court, then informed Anawrahta that the princess' claim to royal descent was highly doubtful because she did not have any escorts.

Anawrahta could not return Panchakalyani to her home because he was by law already married to her. So he banished her to Payeinma on the Chindwinn (Chindwin) River, and it was here that her son Kyanzittha, later to become Bagan's greatest king, was born. The boy was by law the king's son, but was probably the envoy's.

Like father, Like son: Like his biologi-

View of Bagan's pagodas, with the Ayeyarwady in the distance.

200

cal father, perhaps, young Kyanzittha was easily enthralled by a pretty face. Some time after the conquest of Thaton, he was ordered to accompany the daughter of the king of Bago (Pegu) to the court of Bagan, where she was to become Anawrahta's wife. But Kyanzittha fell in love with her, and when Anawrahta caught wind of the affair, he ordered Kyanzittha bound. Anawrahta planned to kill the youth himself.

However, according to legend, on this one occasion, Anawrahta's mythical spear "Areindama" failed him; instead of piercing Kyanzittha's flesh, the blade cut his bonds, and the youth fled and hid near Sagaing with a sympathetic monk.

Anawrahta was killed in 1077 by a wild buffalo. His son Sawlu, who succeeded to the throne, was faced with quelling major rebellions among the Mons to the south, and asked Kyanzittha – a master warrior – for assistance.

There was no love lost between the half-brothers. In one important battle in 1084, Sawlu ignored Kyanzittha's tactical advice and attacked the Mon forces.

His army was soon defeated, and Sawlu was taken prisoner. Kyanzittha stole into the enemy camp one night to attempt to free his king, but Sawlu thought Kyanzittha had come to kill him. Kyanzittha managed to escape, but Sawlu was killed in order to prevent further rescue attempts.

These events put the popular Kyanzittha on the Bagan throne. Shin Arahan, who had been Buddhist primate since Anawrahta's time, crowned him, and Hkin U, the Bago princess whose love had almost cost Kyanzittha's life, became his wife. Under Kyanzittha, Bagan became known as "city of the 4 million pagodas." Thousands of monuments were erected during his 28-year reign. A deeply religious man, Kyanzittha established the Mon Buddhist culture as paramount. It was not difficult to do so; the 30,000 Mon captives who had been brought north after the conquest of Thaton already had significantly altered the lifestyle of the Pyus and Bamars (Burmans).

Kyanzittha's grandson Alaungsithu

European artist's impression of Bagan in 1825.

succeeded him as ruler of Bagan, and held the throne for another 45 years after Kyanzittha's death in 1112. A highly developed system of irrigation canals supported the production of rice by 17 surrounding communities and provided the economic backbone of the empire. But the empire began to weaken in the 13th century under the threat of growing Shan power and the menacing Mongol army of Kublai Khan, which already had overwhelmed China. When King Narathihapate refused to pay a tribute to the Khan, his armies were annihilated on the battlefield, and the Mongols took Bagan.

Bagan was not, as some say, laid waste by the Mongols. Kublai Khan was a Buddhist himself, and never would have permitted his armies to intentionally damage Buddhist shrines. Many of the temples were probably torn down by the Burmese themselves in a last-ditch attempt to build fortifications to slow the Mongol advance. Others became victims of the ages, of the neglect which followed the transfer of power. Only religious monuments were built of brick; royal buildings and other structures were of wood, and they could not have stood un-maintained in Upper Burma for more than 100 years.

The Bagan plain today: Today there are still a number of wooden structures on the Bagan plain – but they're of much more recent vintage. These are the riverside homes where the poor farming families of the district carry out their day-to-day existences, as well as the relocated small guest houses and shops catering to the tourist trade.

The economic centre of the Bagan plain today is at Nyaung U, about 5 kilometres (3 mi) to the north of the walled village of Bagan. There are a few important monuments in the immediate vicinity of Nyaung U, notably the Shwezigon Pagoda, and there are others a few kilometers to the south of Bagan village near Myinkaba. The picturesque Bagan village, once situated around the main temples, was relocated in a controversial military operation in 1990, to clear the principal temple quarter of local habitations. New Bagan, as it is

called, has now been reconstructed some 8 kilometres (5 mi) south of its original site, close to the village, of Thiripyitsaya.

Before that, a massive earthquake jolted the plain of Bagan on July 8, 1975, raising fears throughout the nation and world that the ancient bricks had crumbled and the city left flattened. Thankfully, that was not the case. There was, indeed, serious damage to many of the most important temples; but Burma's Directorate of Archaeology, led by the late U Bokay, immediately began repair work. The reconstruction was finally completed in 1981.

Many of Bagan's temples – especially those containing wall paintings or glazed *Jataka* panels – are closed to protect them from vandalism. Every one of these temples has wardens, however, who are pleased to admit visitors for a small fee.

The best way to get around the ancient city is by horse-drawn cab. Drivers waiting outside the Myanmar Travels and Tours (MT&T) office usually speak passable English and are more than

Decapitated Gawdawpalin Temple undergoing renovation.

happy to work as a guide as well as driver for a small retainer fee. Many of the most interesting monuments are within Bagan's now partially reconstructed city walls.

Ten great Bagan monuments: Many visitors begin their exploration of the ancient ruins at the **Ananda Temple (1)**, just to the east of the old city wall. This impressive whitewashed edifice dominates the view as one enters the village from the north. Considered the masterpiece of Mon architecture, it was completed in 1091.

According to *The Glass Palace Chronicle*, the Ananda Temple was inspired by the visit to Kyanzittha's palace of eight Indian monks, who arrived one morning begging for alms. They told the king they had once lived in the legendary Nandamula cave temple in the Himalaya Mountains. Kyanzittha, always fascinated by Buddhist tales, invited the monks to return to his palace daily during the rainy season to tell him more about this imaginary province.

By virtue of their meditation, the monks were able to make the mythical landscape appear before Kyanzittha's eyes – and the king, overwhelmed, immediately opted to build a replica of this snow-covered cave on the hot, dry plain of central Burma.

When the great temple was completed, Kyanzittha is said to have been so awestruck by its unique style that he personally executed the architect by Brahman ritual to assure that the temple could not be duplicated, thereby sealing its permanence and importance.

The structure of the Ananda Temple is that of a simple corridor temple. Four large vestibules, each opening out symmetrically into entrance halls at the temple's axes, surround the central superstructure, which itself is inlaid with four huge niches. The entire enclosure, 53 metres (174 ft) on a side, is in the shape of a perfect Greek cross.

In the niches facing the four cardinal points are four 9.5-metre (31-ft) tall teak Buddha images which represent the four Buddhas of this world-cycle. Each is dimly lit from the slits in the

A *tonga* waits for visitors at Pahtothamya Temple.

sanctuary roof, giving visitors the impression that they not only are hovering, but are striving upward. Gautama, the most recent Buddha, faces west, Kakusandha faces north, Konagamana east and Kassapa south. The north- and south-facing statues are originals, but those facing east and west are later copies. The originals were destroyed by temple thieves.

The desecration of temples has been, in fact, a serious problem in Bagan. That the Ananda and other temples could have been vandalized as they have, and that the robbers have escaped without sanction, indicate that the rules of Buddhism have not always been followed with the same intensity as they were during the Era of the Temple Builders. Perhaps it is a reflection on the long periods of neglect and anarchy that Burma has gone through.

The true extent of temple desecration in Bagan is particularly evident at some of the less well-known ruins on the plain, at those piles of brick not being renovated by Burma's Directorate of Archaeology. Many Buddha figures here have gaping holes in their stomach areas, and many smaller stupas have at least one side broken open – the legacy of thieves searching for valuable relics in obvious hiding places.

Thohanbwa, a mid-16th century Shan King of Innwa (Ava), gave impetus to the temple robbers when he said: "Burma pagodas have nothing to do with religion. They are simply treasure chambers." It was Thohanbwa in fact, who ordered many of the Bagan pagodas to be plundered in order to fill his own treasure chambers.

The damage at the Ananda, thankfully, has been restored or replaced. Precautions are still taken, however. Access to Ananda's upper terraces, for example, is restricted. Temple authorities will provide a key to keen visitors, who will then be able to climb onto the roof via a narrow staircase.

Terracotta *Jataka*: This roof above the central superstructure consists of five successively diminishing terraces/walkways. There are 389 terra-cotta glazed

The Ananda Temple.

tiles here illustrating the last 10 *Jataka* tales. Together with those inside the temple and at its base, these tiles represent the largest collection of terra-cotta tiles at any Bagan temple.

The temple's beehive-like crown (*sikhara*), capped by a golden stupa which reaches 51 metres (168 ft) above the ground, rises from the tiered roof. Smaller pagodas, copies of the central spire, are at each of the roof's four corners, there bearing witness to a measured Buddhist harmony as well as creating the impression (to the imaginative) of a mountainous Himalayan landscape.

Proof of this temple's purpose as a place of meditation and learning can be found within Ananda's labyrinthian corridors. Each of the four main halls contains the same 16 Buddha images as the other three, enabling four groups of Buddhist students to undergo their instruction simultaneously.

From these halls, facing the vestibules containing the large Buddhas, one can continue into the centre corridor where 80 reliefs illustrate the life of the Bodhisattva from his birth through to his enlightenment. On the west-facing porch are two Buddha footprints, each one is divided into 108 parts as dictated by ancient texts.

Nearby are two statues of particular interest. One represents Kyanzittha, the Ananda Temple's founding father, and the other, Shin Arahan. By the time the Buddhist primate died in 1115 at the age of 81, he had served four kings.

The most important period of the year at the Ananda Temple is during January, when the annual temple festival is held. This is a joyous, colourful spectacle. The corridors and vestibules of the temple, while normally lined with small stalls, are especially lively.

In recent years, the Ananda Temple Festival has become even more exuberant: since the 1975 earthquake, renovation and repair of the Ananda Temple has been financed entirely through Buddhist generosity.

Temple of Omniscience: The centre of Bagan is dominated by the **Thatbyinnyu Temple (2)**, about 500 metres (1,550 ft)

Thatbyinnyu Temple and Tally Pagoda.

to the southwest of the Ananda. Known as the "temple of omniscience," it is the tallest building in Bagan at 61 metres (201 ft). It stands just within the city walls, and is the archetype of the Bamar architectural style.

Built by Alaungsithu in the middle of the 12th century, the Thatbyinnyu is similar in shape to the Ananda, although it does not form a symmetrical cross: the eastern vestibule projects out of the main structure of the building. The construction of this temple introduced the idea of placing a smaller "hollow" cube on top of a larger Bamar-style structure, whereas the previous Mon-style temples were of one story. The centre of the lower cube is solid, serving as a foundation for the upper temple, which houses an eastward-looking Buddha figure.

There are two tiers of windows in each story of the Thatbyinnyu, as well as huge arches inlaid with flamboyant pediments, making the interior bright and allowing a breeze to flow through. The first and second stories of this great temple were once the residence of monks. The third level housed images, and the fourth, a library. At the top was a stupa containing holy relics. The upper storey can be reached by climbing interior stairs to the intermediate terraces, then taking an exterior staircase to the cella. From here a narrow internal stairway leads to the three upper-most terraces, which are crowned by a *sikhara* and a stupa. The view from this platform is marvelous. A half-kilometre away is the Ananda Temple, and beyond that stretches the huge plain where eight centuries ago 500,000 people are said to have lived.

Southwest of the Thatbyinnyu Temple are the remains of two stone pillars which at one time were probably the supporting structures of a huge bell.

To the northwest is a small monument known as the Tally Pagoda. For every 10,000 bricks used in the construction of the Thatbyinnyu, one brick was set aside – as an easy way to keep count; this small pagoda was built with almost unbelievable architectural precision from the "tally-keeping" bricks.

Ywa Haung Gyi Temple.

A short distance north of the Thatbyinnyu is the **Thandawgya Image (3)** – a huge seated Buddha figure. Six metres (19.5 ft) tall, it was erected by Narathi-hapate in 1284. The Buddha's hands are in the bhumisparsa mudra, signifying the moment of enlightenment. The plaster which once gave this image a rounded shape has crumbled away over the centuries, leaving only greenish sandstone blocks which give the statue an entranced, mystical appearance.

Earthquake's epicentre: Back on the road through Bagan village, close to the bank of the Ayeyarwady river, is the 12th-century **Gawdawpalin Temple (4)**. It was built by King Narapatisithu in Bamar style to resemble the Thatbyinnyu Temple.

One of Bagan's most impressive two-storey temples, it was unfortunately at the epicenter of the 1975 earthquake and suffered more damage than any other structure. The *sikhara* and stupa, which previously reached a height of 60 metres (197 ft), collapsed during the quake, and wide crack opened through the middle of the two-storied cube of the central structure.

Because of the breathtaking view this temple affords over the ruins of the Bagan plain, the Directorate of Archaeology was especially intent on its renovation. Now that work is completed, it has become the best-loved "sunset-view" pagoda in Bagan.

Just south of this temple, not far from the **Thiripyitsaya Hotel**, is a **museum** containing displays of Bagan's varied architecture, iconography and religious history. Along the museum verandas are stones collected from the region, bearing inscriptions in various languages – Burmese, Mon, Pyu, Pali, Tamil, Thai and Chinese. The exhibition was moved from a building near the Ananda Temple several years ago.

The oldest of the Bamar-style temples, the **Shwegugyi Temple (5)**, is a short distance up the road toward Nyaung U. King Alaungsithu had it built in 1131. It took just seven months to raise, according to the temple history inscribed on two stone slabs within.

Unlike most Buddhist monuments, which face east, the Shwegugyi stands on a high rectangular platform facing north, where the royal palace was. The hall and inner corridor of this temple are well-lit by large windows and doorways, one of the main features distinguishing Bamar architectural style from the older Mon style.

Alaungsithu died in the Shwegugyi Temple at the age of 81. When the king lay on his deathbed in his palace, his son, Narathu, second in the line of succession after his older brother, Minshinsaw, brought Alaungsithu to the temple and smothered him in his bedclothes. Minshinsaw at that time was away from Bagan, so Narathu immediately proclaimed himself ruler. His short reign (1167–1170) was, however, characterized by brutality.

Atonement for patricide: Despite his brief tenure as king, however, Narathu is remembered as the founder of Bagan's largest shrine, the **Dhammayangyi Temple (6)**.

Deeply concerned about his karma for future lives after having murdered his father, Narathu built the Dhammayangyi to atone for his misdeeds. It is today the best preserved temple in Bagan, with a layout similar to that of the Ananda Temple but lacking the delicate, harmonious touch of its prototype, perhaps reflecting the black cloud that hung over central Burma during Narathu's reign. The masonry, however, is without equal at Bagan.

It is said that Narathu oversaw the construction himself, and he had masons executed if a needle could be pushed between the bricks they had laid.

The building, however, was never completed because Narathu himself was assassinated. Narathu had by law taken his father's wives as his own. He was displeased with the Hindu rituals of one of them – the daughter of the Indian prince of Pateikkaya – and he had her executed. Her vengeful father sent eight officers, disguised as Brahmans, to Bagan, and when Narathu received them in his throne room, they drew swords and killed him. The officers then slew one another, as agreed beforehand, to avoid further bloodshed.

The Dhammayangyi Temple is well over a kilometre to the southeast of the city walls in the direction of Minnanthu. About halfway between the temple and the walled Bagan centre are the **Shwesandaw Pagoda (7)** and the **Shinbintalyaung (8)** which houses a reclining Buddha. One of only three religious structures Anawrahta built in Bagan, the Shwesandaw was erected in 1057 upon his victorious return from Thaton. Its stupa enshrines some hairs of the Buddha sent to Anawrahta by the king of Bago.

The Shwesandaw is sometimes called the Ganesh (or Mahapeine) Temple after the elephant-headed Hindu god whose image once stood at the corners of its five successively diminishing rectangular terraces. The cylindrical stupa stands on an octagonal platform atop these terraces, which originally was adorned with terra-cotta plaques depicting various scenes from the *Jataka*. The chief curiosities on the terraces today, however, are the "antique" objects be-

ing peddled to tourists by young local boys. The pagoda spire collapsed in the 1975 quake, and although it has been replaced, the original *hti* can still be seen lying near the pagoda.

The long flat building within the walls of the Shwesandaw enclosure contains the Shinbintalyaung Reclining Buddha, over 18 metres (60 ft) in length. Created in the 11th century, this Buddha lies with its head facing south and therefore depicts the sleeping Buddha; only the dying Buddha faces north. The walls of the brick building are erected very close around the reclining Buddha, thus making it virtually impossible for the visitor to photograph the statue.

The last Bamar-style temple built in Bagan – the **Htilominlo Temple (9)** – is about 1.5 kilometres (1 mile) northeast of Bagan proper on the road to Nyaung U. King Nantaungmya had this building constructed in 1211 at the place where he was chosen to be king.

According to *The Glass Palace Chronicle*, Nantaungmya was the son of one of King Narapatisithu's concu- **Shwesandaw Pagoda.**

bines and was selected as heir when, as per custom, the white umbrella of the future ruler tilted in his direction. He and his four brothers created the Council of Ministers to determine state policy; the council called itself the *Hluttaw*, the same name that has been given to Burma's parliament.

The Htilominlo Temple is 46 metres (150 ft) high and 43 metres (140 ft) on a side at its base. Four Buddha figures placed on the ground and four more figures on the first floor face the cardinal points. Some of the old murals can still be discerned, as can a number of the friezes. Several old horoscopes, painted to protect the building from damage, can be found on the walls.

A short distance south of walled Bagan is the **Minglazedi Pagoda (10)**, the last of the great stupas that were erected during the Era of the Temple Builders. Narathihapate – the last of the Bagan kings to reign over the entire Burmese empire – had it constructed in 1284. Six years in construction, it represents the pinnacle of Bamar pagoda architecture.

The Minglazedi's stupa rises high above three terraces mounted on a square superstructure. Flights of stairs lead up to the main platform from the middle of each side. Small stupas in the shape of Indian *kalasa* pots stand at the corners of each of the terraces, and at the corners of the uppermost terrace four larger stupas reinforce the heavenward-striving form of the pagoda, giving the proportions of the whole structure a harmonious quality. The terraces are adorned with large terracotta tiles depicting scenes from the *Jataka*.

However, because many of the Minglazedi's tiles have been broken over the years, the door leading to the pagoda grounds is kept locked. Visitors should contact the pagoda warden in Myinkaba village ahead of time if they wish to enter the enclosure.

"Mr Handsome' and Sister 'Golden Face": In addition to those already mentioned, there are a number of other structures within Bagan proper which are worthy of note. Entering the city from Nyaung U, the road passes through the **Sarabha**

agan in the vening.

Gateway (11), the only section of King Pyinbya's 9th-century city wall that is still standing and that has recently been reconstructed. Although the rest of the wall consists of overgrown hillocks strewn with rubble, Bagan's guardian spirits – the **Mahagiri** *Nat* – have their prayer niches in this eastern gateway.

The two *nats*, Nga Tin De, "Mr Handsome," and his sister Shwemyethna, "Golden Face," are called "Lords of the Great Mountain" because it is believed they made their home on sacred Mount Popa. After Thagyamin, king of the *nats*, they are the most important spirit beings in Burma.

One of the few secular buildings in Bagan that has been preserved over the centuries is the **Pitakat Taik (12)**, King Anawrahta's library. Anawrahta had it built not far within the city's east gate to house the 30 elephant loads of scriptures he brought back to Bagan after his conquest of Thaton. From this structure, it is possible to get an idea of what the wooden secular buildings might have looked like during Bagan's golden age.

Its original appearance, however, was altered in 1783, when King Bodawpaya during a renovation had finials – highly reminiscent of the buildings at Innwa (Ava) – added to the corners of the five multiple roofs. Bodawpaya also had a new collection of *pitaka* texts placed in the library.

The library is near the Shwegugyi Temple. Across the main road is the **Mahabodhi Temple (13)**. This temple is an exact replica of a structure of the same name in India's Bihar State, built in AD 500 at the site where the Buddha achieved enlightenment. The pyramid-like shape of the temple tower is a kind that was highly favoured during India's Gupta Period, and is quite different from the standard bell-shaped monuments in the rest of Burma.

Constructed in Bagan during the reign of Nantaungmya (1210–1234), it followed a tradition of fascination with Indian architecture. Kyanzittha more than a century earlier had sent men and materials to India to carry out some renovation work on the Bodhgaya Tem-

Left, Mahagiri *Nat* "Golden Face". Right, "Mr Handsome".

ple, and Alaungsithu in the mid-12th century made the king of Rakhine (Arakan) do the same.

The lower section of Bagan's Mahabodhi is a quadrangular block supporting the pyramidal structure, which in turn is crowned by a small stupa. The pyramid is completely covered with niches containing seated Buddha figures. Apart from a copy which was erected on the terrace of the Shwedagon in Yangon, the Mahabodhi is the only temple of its kind in Burma. It was severely damaged by the 1975 earthquake, but renovation work has been successfully completed.

Of warships and monks: A short distance north of here is the **Pebingyaung Pagoda (14)**, not able for its conical Singhalese-style stupa. The stupa contains relics mounted on top of the bell-shaped main structure in a square-based relic chamber. The construction of this pagoda in the 12th century confirms that close ties existed between Burma and Ceylon (now known as Sri Lanka), a result of the concern shown by King Anawrahta for the propagation of Theravada Buddhism.

Although the Theravada school of thought had been introduced to Thaton by the Singhalese monk Buddhaghosa in AD 403, it was not until 1076, when Anawrahta was in power at Bagan, that the bond between Burma and Ceylon was strengthened.

The Hindu Cholas had invaded Ceylon, and the island's ruler, Vijaya Bahu I, asked his fellow believer Anawrahta for assistance in driving them out. Bagan's king sent his ships laden with war materials, and the added support gave the Ceylonese (Sri Lankans) the boost they needed to reestablish their hold on the island.

But after 50 years of occupation by "non-believers," the Buddhist infrastructure, especially the Sangha, had badly deteriorated. So Anawrahta sent a number of monks to help in the regeneration of Theravada Buddhism in Ceylon. A century later, Narapatisithu sent another group of monks for the same reason. Among them was Sapada,

View of the Bagan moat.

who built a pagoda bearing his name in Nyaung U. Many scholars feel the *Tipitaka* texts which Anawrahta reputedly seized in his conquest of Thaton actually came from Ceylon.

A few steps from the Pebingyaung on the banks of the Ayeyarwady is the **Bupaya Pagoda (15)**.

According to tradition, the pagoda was built by the third king of Bagan, Pyusawti (AD 162–243), who found a way to get rid of a gourd-like climbing plant (*bu*) which infested the riverbanks. He was rewarded by his predecessor, Thamuddarit, the founder of Bagan (AD 108), with the hand of his daughter and the inheritance of the throne. In commemoration of his good luck, Pyusawti had the Bupaya Pagoda built.

As the original Bagan Pagoda, this edifice became the basic model for all pagodas built after it. It has a bulbous shape, similar in some ways to the Tibetan *chorte*, and is built on rows of crenelated walls overlooking the river. Because of the way it stands out on the banks, it is used as a navigation aid by boats. On the pagoda grounds, beneath a pavilion with a nine-gabled roof, is an altar to Mondaing, *nat* of storms.

Wife-stealing at the palace: The **Mimalaung-Kyaung Temple (16)**, near the old city's south gate, was erected in 1174 by Narapatisithu. The small, square temple – characterized by multiple roofs and a tall spiral pagoda stands on a four-metre (13-ft) high plinth intended to protect it from destruction by fire and floods.

The temple's creator, Narapatisithu, is noted in Bagan's history for the manner in which he acceded to the throne in 1173: his brother, King Naratheinka, had stolen his wife and made her queen while Narapatisithu was on a foreign campaign. The wronged sibling returned to Bagan with 80 of his most trusted men, murdered his brother the king, and ensconced himself on the throne. His wife, Veluvati, remained the queen.

Just to the east of this temple is the **Pahtothamya Temple (17)**, which according to tradition dates from before Anawrahta's reign. King Taungthugyi

Walkway to the Shwezigon Pagoda.

(931–964), also known as Nyaung U Sawrahan, is said to have built the temple to look like those at Thaton. No temple ruins have ever been unearthed at Thaton, however, and the architectural style of this temple has been proven to be that of the 11th century.

To the east is the **Nathlaung Kyaung Temple (18)**, a perfect example of the religious tolerance that prevailed in Bagan during the Era of the Temple Builders. It is thought to have been constructed by Taungthugyi in 931 – more than a century before Theravada Buddhism was introduced from Thaton – and was dedicated to the Hindu god Vishnu. The Nathlaung Kyaung remained Bagan's greatest Hindu temple throughout its Golden Age, a time when Theravada and Mahayana Buddhism, *nat* and *naga* worship were followed and the Tantric practices of the Ari monks were tolerated.

The main hall and superstructure of the Nathlaung Kyaung are still standing today, although the entrance hall and outer structures have long since crumbled and disappeared.

The 10 *avatar* (past and future incarnations) of Vishnu once were housed in niches on the outer walls of the main hall. Seven can still be seen today.

Remains of the Nathlaung Kyaung's central relic sanctuary indicate that it once contained a large Vishnu figure, which sat on the mythical *garuda* with spread wings. It is now in the Dahlem Museum in Berlin.

Immediately to the north, the **Ngakywenadaung Pagoda (19)**, is much like the **Pahtothamya Temple** attributed to King Taungthugyi in the 10th century. A bulbous-shaped structure on a circular base, it stands 13 metres (43 ft) high. Examples of the cylindrical form of this stupa are found in ancient Sri Ksetra.

To Nyaung U and beyond: About 1.5 kilometres (1 mile) down the road from Bagan proper to the regional centre of Nyaung U, and almost directly opposite the **Htilominlo Temple**, lies the **Upali Thein (20)**, or hall of ordination. Named after the monk Upali, it was erected in the first half of the 13th century. Al-

though it is of brick construction, it is said to resemble many of the wooden buildings of the Bagan Era which have long since disappeared. The span-roof has two rows of battlements, and a small pagoda at its centre.

The Upali Thein was renovated during the reign of the Konbaung Dynasty in 1794 and 1795, its walls and ceilings were decorated with beautiful frescoes representing the 28 previous Buddhas, as well as scenes from the life of Gautama. Sadly, the plaster came off the walls during the 1975 earthquake, and most of the fresco work was irreparably destroyed.

Near the village of Wetkyi-in are the **Kubyauknge Temple (21)**, notable for the fine stucco work on its exterior walls, and the **Kubyaukgyi Temple (22)** a short distance further east. The Kubyaukgyi dates from the early 13th century, and has a pyramidal spire very similar to that of the Mahabodhi. Inside are some of Bagan's finest frescoes of the *Jataka* tales. Unfortunately, many of these paintings were "collected" in

Kyanzittha Cave.

1899 by the German von Nottling.

A short distance west of Nyaung U village is the **Kyanzittha Cave (23)**, a cave temple which served as a place of lodging for monks. Although its name would seem to indicate that it had been built by Kyanzittha, in all probability it dates from Anawrahta's reign. The long, dark corridors are embellished with frescoes from the 11th, 12th and 13th centuries; some of the later paintings even depict the Mongols who occupied Bagan after 1287.

Visitors are advised to carry their own flashlights when visiting this cave temple, as the attendant family has only dimly burning candles.

Bagan's greatest reliquary: The **Shwezigon Pagoda (24)**, a short walk north of the cave temple, is the prototype for all Burmese stupas built after the rule of Anawrahta. It was built as the most important reliquary shrine in Bagan, a centre of prayer and reflection for the new Theravada faith Anawrahta was establishing in Bagan.

King Anawrahta, convinced that he was a "universal monarch," set about to obtain all possible relics of the Buddha. From Pyay (Prome), he got the Buddha's collarbone and frontal bone; he also acquired a copy of the Tooth of Kandy from Ceylon and an emerald Buddha figure from Yunnan. To determine a location for the pagoda which would be built to house these relics, he set loose a white elephant – the animal which had borne the tooth from Ceylon – and where it rested, the Shwezigon Pagoda was built.

Ironically, only three terraces of the pagoda had been finished when Anawrahta was killed in 1077. King Kyanzittha supervised completion of the structure in 1089.

The bell of the Shwezigon stands upon the three terraces, reached by stairways from the cardinal directions. The pagoda spire, crowned by a *hti*, rises above the bell in a series of concentric moldings. Smaller stupas can be seen at the corners of the terraces, each one decorated with glazed plaques illustrating the *Jataka* tales. Small square tem-

At the Shwezigon, nuns and lay women attend a lecture.

ples on each side of the central stupa contain standing Buddhas of the Gupta style. To the left and right of the eastern entrance are two stone pillars, each inscribed on all four sides, recording the establishment of the pagoda during Kyanzittha's reign.

Buddhist pilgrims from throughout Burma converge on the Shwezigon every year when the Shwezigon Pagoda Festival is held during the second week of the Burmese month of *Nadaw* (November/December).

The festival is one of the nation's most popular, largely because *nat* worship was combined with Buddhism in the pagoda's construction. Anawrahta had the images of the traditional 37 *nat* carved in wood and erected on the lower terraces, believing that "men will not come for the sake of the new faith. Let them come for their old gods and gradually they will be won over." The *nats* are no longer on the terraces, but they are housed in a small hall to the southeast of the pagoda, where they are still being worshipped today.

An example of a stricter adherence to orthodox Theravada Buddhism can be seen at the **Sapada Pagoda (25)**, situated at the southern end of Nyaung U town on the airport road. Built in the 12th century by the monk Sapada, it is similar in form to the Pebingyaung Pagoda, but bears witness to a great schism in the Theravada school.

Sapada was one of the monks sent to Ceylon in the latter part of the 12th century. He returned to Burma in 1190, after 10 years on Ceylon, expounding a very orthodox version of Buddhism. It differed markedly from the Theravada Buddhism, absorbed from the Mons, which predominated in Bagan at the time. And it was distinctly different from the courtly religion of Mahayana Buddhism, as well as the Vishnu and Shiva cults of Hinduism. But Sapada's interpretation was accepted by King Narapatisithu and was readily embraced by Bagan's people.

There are several cave temples to the east of Nyaung U. Just one kilometre to the southeast of the town are the **Thamiwhet** and **Hmyathat Caves (26)**,

formed by the excavation of hillsides during the 12th and 13th centuries. Their purpose was to give monks a cool place to live, a refuge from the scorching heat of central Burma.

About three kilometres (2 mi) upstream from Nyaung U, standing on the ledge of a cliff overlooking the Ayeyarwady, is the **Kyaukku Temple (27)**. The structure could be described as an ideal cave temple – the manner in which it is built into the hill-side gives the impression that a small stupa stands on top of the temple, when it actually rests on a pillar.

A maze of passages leads from the pillar into the caves behind: the stone-and-brick-built temple is in fact an enlargement of the natural cave structure. A large Buddha sits opposite the entrance, and the walls are embellished with stone reliefs.

The Kyaukku's ground story dates from the 11th century; the upper two stories have been ascribed to the reign of Narapatisithu (1174–1211).

Just about a kilometre down the

The guardian *nat* of the arts rides atop his *hintha*.

Ayeyarwady toward Nyaung U are a number of stupas and temples, among them the **Thatkyamuni Temple** and the **Kondawgyi Temple (28)**. In the former are panels of paintings which depict Ashoka, the great Buddhist king who ruled in India during the 3rd century BC, as well as scenes recording the introduction of Buddhism to Sri Lanka. In the Kondawgyi are wall paintings of *Jataka* scenes as well as floral patterns.

Myinkaba and Thiripyitsaya: When King Anawrahta returned to Bagan in 1057 with the Mon royalty in tow, he exiled King Manuha and his family to Myinkaba (Myinpagan), 2 kilometres (1 mi) south of the Bagan city walls. With Manuha present, Myinkaba became the site of the most splendid Mon-style architecture on the Bagan plain. Many of those monuments still stand.

In addition, the village has established a fine lacquerware industry which has become its economic backbone. There are a lacquer school and museum in Bagan which give visitors an opportunity to observe the various stages of lacquer production and to view some outstanding antique pieces of work.

Approaching Myinkaba from the north, a short distance after passing the Minglazedi Pagoda one encounters the **Kubyaukkyi Temple (29)**. Of great importance for its inscriptions, it was built in 1113 by Rajakumar upon the death of his father, Kyanzittha. A very religious man, Rajakumar – whose mother was the niece of the monk with whom Kyanzittha found refuge on his flight from Anawrahta – was the rightful heir to the throne. But Kyanzittha had designated his grandson, Alaungsithu, as heir, and Rajakumar relinquished his right.

Rajakumar's one-storey temple was built in wholly Mon style. In the dark main hall (lit only by perforated stone windows) are nine rows of contemporaneous murals depicting the 547 *Jataka* tales. The east-facing vestibule contains a representation of a 10-armed Bodhisattva typical of Mahayana Buddhism – but not that of Theravada.

The most notable feature of the

A cramped Buddha at the Manuha Temple.

Kubyaukkyi (do not confuse this with the Kubyaukgyi near Nyaung U) is the **Myazedi Stone**. It is sometimes called "Burma's Rosetta Stone," and was inscribed by Rajakumar in four languages of the time – Burman, Mon, Pali and Pyu. It was discovered in 1887, and provided the key to understanding the previously indecipherable Pyu language. The inscription also provided the final word on the dates of the reigns of Bagan's kings beginning with Anawrahta.

On the banks of the Myinkaba River in Myinkaba village is the **Myinkaba Pagoda (30)**, marking the spot where Anawrahta slew his predecessor and half-brother, Sokkate, in a duel for the kingship in 1044. Sokkate and his elder brother Kyiso had wrested the Bagan throne from Anawrahta's father, Kunhsaw Kyaunghpyu, himself a usurper, in 986; but Anawrahta's victory over Sokkate with his mythical spear "Areindama" put an end to over a century of court intrigues.

This shrine's bulbous form and round terraces mark it clearly as predating the establishment of Mon Buddhist influence in Bagan.

The **Manuha Temple (31)** was built by the captive king of Thaton just south of Myinkaba village in 1059. Because he feared he would be made a temple slave, Manuha sought to improve his karma for future incarnations – and so sold some of his jewels in order to have this temple built with the proceeds. One reclining and three seated Buddha images cramped uncomfortably within the narrow confines of the pagoda are said to symbolize the distressed soul of the defeated king.

In contrast to most other Mon-style temples, the Manuha Temple has an upper storey. This collapsed during the 1975 earthquake and buried the Buddhas beneath it, but renovation work on the temple was completed in 1981.

Burmese friezes: A short path leads past two recent statues of King Manuha and his wife, Queen Ningaladevi, to the **Nanpaya Temple (32)**. Said to have once been Manuha's residence, it later was converted into a temple.

Manuha and his Queen.

ANCIENT CITIES OF THE PYUS

The city of **Pyay (Prome or Pyi)** is located just north of the ancient Pyu capital of **Sri Ksetra**. Little remains of Sri Ksetra, or Thayekhittaya as it is known to the Burmese; but at least eight brick pagodas and temples, some dating to the beginning of the Christian era, testify to its greatness.

The Pyu capital's remains are found near the modern-day railway station of **Hmwaza**, about 8 kilometres (5 mi) south of Pyay. The **Shwesandaw Pagoda,** Burma's most venerated structure stands here.

On the eastern bank of the Ayeyarwady is the Shwesandaw – a prominent landmark for navigators and one of the most beautiful spots in the country, if not the region. Every November, the pagoda-celebrating Tazaungdaing Festival is held here.

Another 7 kilometres (4.5 mi) south is the **Shwenattaung Pagoda**, which has a history going back to the establishment of Sri Ksetra perhaps 2,000 years ago.

Unlike other pagodas in Burma, the Sri Ksetra pagodas were built as conical or

cylindrical stupas based on Indian archetypes. The **Bawbawgi Pagoda's** cylindrical form gives the impression of being hollow inside, while in fact, it is solid.

The **Payagyi** and **Payama pagodas** north of the old city walls are conically-styled, and were built about the same time as the **Bebe Temple**, between the 5th and 7th centuries. The Bebe is a cylindrical stupa lying on a hollow pedestal in which a statue of the Buddha, flanked by two of his followers, stands against a back wall. The **East Zegu** and **Lemyethna temples** are similar in form, the latter having a central support pillar, atypical for a Burmese temple.

Sri Ksetra is the most popular site for archaeological research in Burma. Except for the period during World War II, scientists have been in the field here practically every year since 1907. Artefacts uncovered at Sri Ksetra show conclusively that Theravada Buddhism was common in central Burma before Anawrahta's time.

The historic origin of Sri Ksetra is shrouded in legend. King Duttabaung (whose name later became a reverential address for monarchs) is credited with founding the city. According to the legend, Sri Ksetra was built by Sakka, king of the *nat*. Sakka delineated the city's boundaries by grabbing the tail of Naga, a dragon, and swinging him a full circle. Then he named the city "as beautiful as Sakka's home on Mount Meru", and appointed Duttabaung king.

Sri Ksetra endured until the 9th century AD, finally collapsing because of continual conflict between the many tribes who had moved there. When King Anawrahta of Bagan (Pagan) passed by after his conquest of Thaton, he had the city's walls pulled down and all relics removed from the temples to add to his own. He wanted to ensure that the "true religion" could have no other home than Bagan.

The devotee of ancient history should not miss a visit to **Beikthano**, about 135 kilometres (85 mi) further north. The ruins of this large Pyu town, which predated Sri Ksetra by several centuries, can be found near the modern-day town of **Taungdwingyi** in Magway (Magwe) state.

No Buddha image is found here, indicating that the city existed before the 1st century AD. Little remains of the ruins, as many of the bricks and stones were used in recent centuries for roads and railways.

Despite Beikthano's great age, ruins of even more ancient civilizations exist in Burma, located north of Mandalay – in **Tagaung** and **Halin**. ■

The Nanpaya is square in plan, with a porch. Its interior design is outstanding evidence of the strong Brahman influence affecting the Theravadin Mon kings. Four pillars are decorated with friezes and bas-reliefs.

The relief of the god Brahma is particularly striking. Three faces can be discerned, and all have typically Mon facial features – leading one to assume they are representations of King Manuha. The relief is in a position of veneration, facing four Buddha images which might once have stood back-to-back in the centre of the chamber – but have long since disappeared. On the outside of the temple are friezes of the mythological *hamsa* bird – which, besides being the heraldic crest of Mon royalty, was also the vehicle on which Brahma was usually depicted riding.

A short distance south of here is the **Abeyadana Temple (33)**. It bears the name of Kyanzittha's first wife, whom he married as a young warrior, and is situated at the place where she waited for him during his flight from Anawrahta. Abeyadana was probably a follower of Mahayana Buddhism: the frescoes on the outer walls of the corridor represent Bodhisattvas, or future Buddhas, and on the inner walls are images of Brahma, Vishnu, Shiva and Indra, the gods of Indian mythology.

The **Nagayon Temple (34)**, where Kyanzittha is said to have hidden during that flight from Anawrahta, is a few steps away. Legend has it that a *naga* offered him protection here, much as the Naga Mucalinda shielded the meditating Buddha from a storm. Like all temples built by Kyanzittha, this one has a characteristic Mon style. It is very similar to temples in India's Orissa region; the main difference is that the Nagayon has a number of receding roofs which are topped by *sikhara* and stupa, whereas the Orissa temples' *sikhara* tower directly from the central structures. In the interior of the Nagayon are stone reliefs depicting scenes from the life of the Buddha. A standing Buddha, flanked by two smaller seated Buddhas, is housed within the shrine.

Farming in modern Sri Ksetra.

A rare brick monastery: Almost half-way between Myinkaba and the village of Thiripyitsaya is the **Somingyi Monastery (35)**, one of the few brick-built *kyaung* on the Bagan plain. It is an example of the myriad monasteries which once dotted this plain; most of them, then as now, were built of wood and, over the intervening centuries, have left no trace of their existence. The raised platform of the *kyaung* is surrounded by a lobby on the east, monks' cells on the north and south, and a two-storey chapel which houses an image of the Buddha, In the west, the platform is crowned with a stupa.

The Seinnyet Ama Temple and the **Seinnyet Nyima Pagoda (36)** are a short distance down the road. Tradition attributes these sanctuaries to Queen Seinnyet, who lived during the 11th century, although their architectural style is more typical of the 13th century. The pagoda in particular is notable for its design, incorporating seated Buddhas in niches at each of the cardinal points on the bell-shaped dome, and lions

guarding miniature stupas in the corners of the second terrace.

Five kilometres (3 mi) south of Bagan's walls is tiny Thiripyitsaya, where King Thinlikyaung's 4th century palace was situated. During Bagan's Golden Era, there was a mooring place here where foreign ships – plying the Ayeyarwady from lands as far away as Sri Lanka – dropped anchor.

Today the chief attractions are a trio of well preserved pagodas. Two of them, known as the **Eastern and Western Petleik Pagodas (37)**, were built in the 11th century, but collapsed in 1905. The terracotta plaques originally housed in the vaulted corridors now are preserved under replicas of the original roofs.

The numbered plaques depict 550 *Jataka* tales; they are the only representations of three of the stories, as only 547 are officially recognized.

At the south end of Thiripyitsaya is the **Lokananda Pagoda (38)**, raised in 1059 as one of only three pagodas known to have been built by Anawrahta in the Bagan area. (The other two are the Shwesandaw and the Myinkaba.) The Lokananda has a cylindrical bell, and is very reminiscent of a Pyu stupa. It stands on three octagonal terraces, the lower two having stairways on each side.

The Minnanthu temples: The village of Minnanthu is located about 5 kilometres (3 mi) southeast of Bagan proper. There are a large number of temple ruins in the vicinity, but few of major significance. One of the largest is the **Sulamani Temple (39)**, not actually in Minnanthu itself but about halfway between the village and Bagan. Considered one of Bagan's great two-storied monuments, it resembles the Thatbyinnyu in plan, and was built by Narapatisithu in 1183. The Sulamani is named after the legendary palace of the god Indra, crowning the peak of Mount Meru high above the plane on which ordinary people live.

A paragon of the fully-developed Bamar architectural style, the Sulamani Temple's upper storey rests on a huge central pillar which itself fills out the middle of the ground storey. The lower floor has seated Buddha images on all

Wallpainting at the Kubyaukkyi Temple.

four sides. There are porches facing the four cardinal points on each story, with those facing east larger than the others. The remains of some 18th century murals can be seen inside the temple.

Immediately to the north of the Minnanthu village is the **Lemyethna Temple (40)**. The structure was built by Ananthasuriya, Naratheinhka's minister-in-chief, bearing in mind a poem written by his predecessor and namesake, Ananthathurya. Sentenced to death by King Narapatisithu, this man scribed a poem still regarded as one of Burma's literary treasures. "If ... I were to be released and freed from execution I would not escape Death," he wrote. "Inseparable am I from Karma." The king was moved, but the minister had already been executed.

The Payathonzu Temple (41), a short distance north, actually consists of three buildings. Joined by narrow vaulted passages, each building is crowned with a *sikhara*. Three empty pedestals stand inside, their Buddha images long since disappeared.

This temple is of particular interest because of its Mahayanist and Tantric frescoes: as the Payathonzu was erected in the late 13th century, it can be deduced that Mahayana Buddhism was practised in Bagan throughout the Era of the Temple Builders.

Also known for its Mahayana Buddhist frescoes is the **Nandamannya Temple (42)**, nearby. The erotic murals contained within would not be expected in a Theravada Buddhist structure; but there they are, the daughters of Mara attempting to seduce the Buddha painted on the temple's southern wall. Originally called Ananta Panna ("endless wisdom"), the temple's name was changed to Nandamannya to avoid confusion with the Ananda Temple.

The Journey to Bagan: The easiest way to reach Bagan is by plane. There are daily flights that connect both Yangon and Mandalay with the airport, located a short distance south of Nyaung U.

Travelling to Bagan by train is not recommended, because the journey requires a full day to complete. Coming from either Yangon or Mandalay, one must disembark in the town of Thazi and catch a bus for the remainder of the trip. There is also a "whistle-stop" line to Kyaukpadaung, branching off the main north-south route at Pyinmana, but it is even slower than traveling via bus from Thazi.

Since mid-1995 a comfortable bus line connects Yangon with Bagan. The bus leaves Yangon at 4pm and arrives in Bagan at 5am (US$ 10 for foreigners, 500 kyat for Burmese), it runs via Pyay and Kyaukpadaung.

An alternative for the adventurous is to travel to Bagan by boat. The southbound Pyay (Prome) Ferry, which docks in Mandalay at the end of "A" Road, heads down the Ayeyarwady several times a week, it leaves at 5am. It's an all-day voyage – more if the river is low and the boat gets wedged on a sandbank – but travellers not overly concerned with comfort will find it a fascinating experience. The *Road to Mandalay*, the rebuilt Rhine-steamer, offers that trip in all the splendour of a bygone era. That trip, however, has to be pre-arranged.

The Ananda's hovering Buddha.

MOUNT POPA

In 442 BC, a great earthquake roared through central Burma – and from out of the barren Myingyan plains rose Mount Popa. Volcanic ash on the mountain slopes gradually became fertile soil, and the peak blossomed with flowers of many colours. (*Popa* is the Sanskrit word for "flower".) For the inhabitants of the surrounding regions, the peak became known as the home of the gods, the Mount Olympus of Burma. Alchemists and occultists made their home on the mountain slopes, and others were convinced mythical beings lived in its woods and flowers.

Mount Popa, 1,518 metres (4,981 ft) high, is located about 50 kilometres (31 mi) southeast of Bagan. Part of it has recently become a national park that should attract visitors interested in the fauna and flora of Central Burma. One can go by jeep from Bagan village, or take a bus trip requiring transfers in Nyaung U and Kyaukpadaung. Overnight visitors can stay at the ancient Popa monastery at the foot of the peak. During the month of *Nayon* (May/June), the annual Festival of the Spir-

its is held here, and it is said that at that time, the abbot of the Popa monastery runs what becomes Burma's largest hotel.

While the volcanic cone can be climbed by means of a path beginning at the monastery, it should be attempted only by the physically fit. On clear days, however, the view from the top across the vast dry plain is the most beautiful panorama that can be seen in central Burma.

The goal of a trip to Mount Popa should be to see the shrine of the Mahagiri *Nat*, situated about halfway up the mountain. For seven centuries preceding the reign of Anawrahta, all kings of central Burma were required to make a pilgrimage here to consult with the two *nat* about their reign.

The legend of the Mahagiri *Nat* begins with a young blacksmith and his beautiful sister. They lived outside the northern city of Tagaung in the mid-4th century, when King Thinlikyaung of Thiripyitsaya ruled in the Bagan (Bagan) area. The blacksmith, Nga Tin De, was popular and good-looking.

With such attributes, Nga Tin De was a potential threat to the king of Tagaung – and was hounded by the latter's henchmen. But Nga Tin De was warned in time, and fled into the woods.

The king was enchanted by the blacksmith's sister, Shwemyethna ("Golden Face") and married her. Soon, he asked her to call her brother back from the forest. Now that they were related through marriage, he convinced her, Nga Tin De was no longer his rival. But when Nga Tin De emerged, he was seized by the king's guards, tied to a tree and set aflame. As the fire lapped up her brother's body, Shwemyethna broke free from her escorts and threw herself into the blaze. Their physical bodies gone, the siblings became mischievous *nat* living in the *saga* tree. To stop them from causing harm, the king had the tree chopped down and thrown into the Ayeyarwady.

The story of their tragic deaths spread rapidly throughout Burma. King Thinlikyaung, who had wanted to unite the country in *nat* worship, discovered the *saga* tree floating downstream through his kingdom. He ordered the drifting tree fished out of the river and had two figures carved from it. The *nat* images were then carried to the top of Mount Popa and given a shrine where they reside to this day.

Every king coronated in Bagan between the 4th and 11th centuries made a pilgrimage to the brother and sister *nat*, who would supposedly appear before the ruler to counsel him in affairs of state. ■

223

THE SHAN PLATEAU

Mystical. Magical. Outrageously picturesque. These and many other words have been used in attempts to describe the fairy-tale land of Inle Lake and the amazing Inthas who populate its shores and its surface.

This minority tribe has adapted so perfectly to its lake environment that its homes are built over water on stilts, its vegetable fields float on the lake's surface, and its fishermen stroll their long, narrow boats with a unique leg-rowing motion that has gained them much fame.

An oasis surrounded by the southern Shan Plateau, Inle Lake may be the area's main attraction for visitors, but it should not be the only one. About 550 metres (1,800 ft) and 27 kilometres (17 mi) by road uphill from the lake is **Taunggyi**, a former British hill station. Despite its lingering colonial air, Taunggyi is today the administrative capital of the Shan State, a centre of Shan culture and a major marketplace. In the vicinity are pine forests, colourful bazaars, and – some 110 kilometres (69 mi) to the northwest – is the fabulous **Pindaya Cave** with its thousands of carved Buddha images.

The Shan State is by far Burma's largest, extending east from Taunggyi for 350 kilometres (220 mi) to Laos and the notorious Golden Triangle of opium trade; nearly as far north to the Ledo Road and the Chinese border; and south a lesser distance to the tribal states of the Kayah and Kayin (Karen). This is largely a region of high, roadless peaks, of rugged river gorges, of fiercely independent tribes-people, and of endless anti-government rebel activity. As long as Khun Sa's Mong Tai Army controls the region along the Thai border, the Shan Plateau beyond Taunggyi will remain off-limits to tourists.

A snarl of silt and water hyacinths: The visitor to this region will probably arrive by plane at the Heho airport. From there, it's a 35-kilometre (22-mi) trip by collective bus or Jeep-taxi to **Yaunghwe**, the major town on Inle Lake, or a 40-

kilometre (25-mi) trip to Taunggyi, both via the rail terminus of **Shwenyaung**.

At Yaunghwe, the surprising elements of the Inthas first begin to come to life. The town – the oldest of about 200 Intha settlements around the shallow, 158-square-kilometre (61-sq-mi) lake – is built on the fringe of the 5-kilometre (3-mi) wide belt of silt and tangled water hyacinths that girds the lake and conceals its true dimensions.

This snarl of silt and weed, left to its own devices, takes about 50 years to produce a metre-thick humus-like layer. The state sells 100-metre by 2-metre (328-ft by 6.5-ft) sections of this land to Intha villagers, who tow the floating gardens across the lake to their homes.

Not everyone buys their garden. Many Inthas make their own, collecting the omnipresent, hollow-stemmed, floating weeds and lashing and weaving them together to form a light, deep trough. Others do the same with dried reeds and grasses matted into strips. Whatever the method, the garden is anchored to the bed of the lake with bamboo poles, then

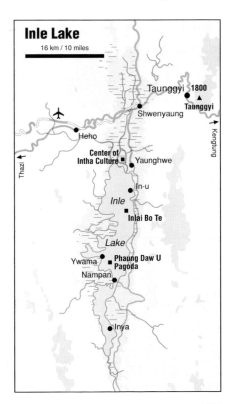

Inle Lake
16 km / 10 miles

Taunggyi 1800
Taunggyi
Shwenyaung
Heho
Thazi
Kengtung
Center of
Intha Culture Yaunghwe
In-u
Inle
Inlai Bo Te
Lake
Ywama Phaung Daw U
Pagoda
Nampan
Inya

filled with mud scooped from the lake bottom with ladles.

These gardens, called *kyunpaw*, are cultivated from boats – usually by women, who use both sides of the fertile strip to plant and harvest crops year-round. Cauliflower, tomatoes, cucumbers, cabbage, peas, beans and eggplant all flourish in the moist conditions.

The Intha people like to say they live off the lake. That cliché refers not only to their gardens, but to their remarkable fishermen, whose fame is due to their unusual technique of propelling their slender craft through the water. Perching precariously on the boat's stern with one foot, the fisherman adroitly twists his other leg around a single long oar – and thus manoeuvres through the shallow lake water, keeping his eyes open to avert clumps of the tangled weeds floating just beneath the surface.

The fishermen's trick: Nearly as curious is the unique method of fishing. Carrying a tall conical trap containing a gill net, the fisherman looks for indications of movement on the water's surface. Where he sees them, he thrusts the trap to the lake bottom (it is 3 metres [10 ft] at its deepest point), releasing a ring that holds the net up. As the meshwork drops, any fish within its limited range – a metre-long Inle carp, a catfish, or perhaps an eel – becomes a meal for the fisherman's entire family.

There are an estimated 70,000 Inthas living on the lake or near its shores. An immigrant tribe from Dawei (Tavoy), Tanintharyi (Tenasserim), they left their former homeland in the 18th century to escape the perpetual conflicts between the Burmese and Thais. They settled on Inle Lake and adopted their name, which means, "sons of the lake".

Here on the Shan Plateau, they have developed an amazing culture, as their farming and fishing skills attest. Their additional talents as metalworkers, carpenters and weavers – have helped to make them one of the wealthiest tribes in all Burma. The famous Shan shoulder bags and *longyi*, sold throughout the country, are manufactured here on the Inthas' looms.

A Shan buffalo cow, led by its young master.

Until a short time ago, Yaunghwe provided the lake's only formal lodging at the modest Inle Inn but now there is also the Inlay Khaung Daing Hotel. Yaunghwe is not the primary destination for Inle's visitors; that honour is reserved for the village of **Ywama**, about 12 kilometres (7.5 mi) away on the lake's south-western shore. Narrow boats outfitted with motors ply the route between the two communities, carrying 10 passengers each across the lake.

A floating market and five balls of gold: Ywama is the site of a daily "floating market" which, unlike its distant cousin in Bangkok, has thus far managed to retain its authentic flavour far from the madness of over-tourism. It is also the location of the **Phaung Daw U Pagoda**, which enshrines five Buddha images carried back to Burma by the widely travelled 12th-century King Alaungsithu upon his return from the Malay Peninsula. The images were deposited in a cave near the lake, and were not rediscovered until centuries later. Since their relocation to this pagoda, however, they have been covered with so much goldleaf that they look more like balls of gold than Buddha figures.

The pagoda is the focal point for the **Phaung Daw U Festival**, an annual celebration which takes place during two weeks in September (*Tawthalin*). The golden images are transported to Inle's 10 largest settlements aboard a recreated royal barge with a huge gilded *karaweik* bird upon its prow. The procession is a reminder of the pomp that once marked the Buddhist courts.

The Phaung Daw U Festival draws celebrants from throughout Burma, not only for the "royal" procession, but also for the famed leg-rowing competitions, pitting crews of Inle Lake oarsmen in sprints through the lake. Anyone who has not booked a room months ahead must settle for floor space in a monastery or pagoda during festival time.

As the Intha civilization lives by the water, it may also die by the water. Inle Lake has been condemned to become a natural landfill. More and more silt is carried into the lake each year by the

Balu Chaung – the canal which feeds the lake from the south – and by mountain streams; the uncontrolled growth of the water hyacinth complicates matters. Whether modern water conservation can be applied in time, or whether the Inthas will again have to demonstrate their adaptability, remains to be seen.

Government tourist authorities, at least, seem unconcerned. A hotel at Inle Lake's western shore, near a sulphur spring,seems to be the first step towards creating a spa resort that will bind the region irrevocably to the nation's tourist network, regardless of Inle Lake's uncertain future.

The "big mountain": Inle Lake lies at an altitude of 878 metres (2,880 ft) above sea level. Overlooking the watery basin in which it lies are numerous lofty peaks – among them Taunggyi, or "big mountain." The wooded height offers a lovely view of Inle Lake from its summit elevation of about 1,800 metres (nearly 6,000 ft). Two paths lead to the top.

At the mountain's foot is the Shan capital Taunggyi. The seat of the Shan Parliament during the British colonial period, three dozen *sawbwa* – hereditary Shan princes – met here on a regularly to make decisions for their people.

Taunggyi was founded by Sir James George Scott, one of the most highly respected colonial officers in the history of British Burma. A devoted student of Burmese history and culture, Scott, under the pseudonym Shway Yoe, wrote the book *The Burman, His Life and Notions* – generally regarded as the 19th century's finest work on Burma. It remains a frequently-consulted source.

Today, the **Taunggyi Hotel** still radiates vestiges of colonial charm. Instead of the British, however, it houses a Burmese government tourist office, at which visitors can arrange for bus or jeep transport to Inle Lake, the Heho airport and other places of interest. Once called the Taunggyi Strand, the hotel is situated a short distance east of the town centre in a pine and eucalyptus grove. Nearby, on the mountain's lower slopes, is a villa where the British superintendent of the Shan states once lived. Today however,

Inle Lake cheroot maker.

it is strictly reserved for state guests .

A major attraction of Taunggyi is its **market**. Every fifth day, markets are held alternately in Taunggyi and the towns of Yaunghwe, Shwenyaung, Heho and Kalaw. The market in Taunggyi is perhaps the best known: colourfully dressed members of the region's hill tribes flock here in a pageantry matched only by native bazaars in isolated parts of Africa or South America. Since nearly all western goods are now available in Burma, the once famous night market has lost some of its former attraction.

In the city centre, close by a monument to Bogyoke Aung San, is the **Taunggyi Museum**. It is small, but is highly recommended to visitors interested in regional ethnology: indigenous costumes of the 30-plus tribes of the Shan Plateau region are displayed within, and a large map indicates their locations. There is also a very rare stuffed two-headed calf on display.

The road leading east from Taunggyi is controlled by Shan rebel troops a short distance east of the town. Should you choose to continue the journey, you would eventually reach Kengtung, capital of the Golden Triangle and gateway to northwestern Thailand. **Kengtung** can, however, be visited from the Thai side at Mae Sai, and many tourists to Thailand are taking this chance to visit Shan State. Also on the Thai border, in the vicinity of Mae Hong Son, those famous "**giraffe women**" can be seen. They cross the border from Kayah State to earn money by being photographed.

On a hill 3 kilometres (2 mi) south of Taunggyi is a temple known as the **Wish Granting Pagoda**. It is a popular pilgrimage destination for Shans and other Buddhists of the region who believe a visit to the shrine will do as the name implies – grant their wishes. The temple's architectural style is distinctly different from the Mon and Bamar (Burman)-style stupas of Bagan (Pagan) and other lowland locales. From its base there is a wonderful view available of the Shan countryside and Inle Lake.

Mission schools and Mandalay rum: Perhaps because of the British influence,

there are many Christians in the Taunggyi area. Until 1968, in fact, a mission school operated here, educating the children of the area's ruling class. Another remnant of British culture is the drinking law, which permits public taverns to exist.

About 70 kilometres (44 mi) west of Taunggyi, well beyond the Heho airport, is the town of **Kalaw**. Perched on the western rim of the Shan Plateau, it was once a favourite hill station retreat for British officials and their families during the hot season. Now a peaceful town surrounded by pine woods, it is an ideal starting point for visits to Palaung villages and the Pindaya Cave.

About 60,000 Palaungs inhabit the plateau near Kalaw. This tribe, which belongs to the Mon-Khmer language family, is easily recognized by the striking costumes worn by its women. Characteristic dress is a blue jacket with a red collar, and a skirt with a crinoline effect given by bamboo. Palaung villages such as **Ta Yaw** and **Shwe Min Phone** welcome visitors; if there is no time for a day's excursion, the alternative is to observe the tribespeople at the highland market held in Kalaw every fifth day.

Several kilometres east of Kalaw, a short distance before the main road passes through the village of Aungban, there is a turnoff to the north. This route leads to the village of **Pindaya**, 41 kilometres (26 mi) from the junction.

The road takes one through a region of such great scenic beauty that it has become known as "Burma's Switzerland." Villages of the Pa-o and Danu minorities dot the mountainsides to the left and right. In Pindaya village itself is the Taungyo tribe, a Burmese-speaking group with houses climbing the hills above a small lake.

From this lake, a covered stairway leads to the **Pindaya Cave**. No one seems to know why the countless Buddha images within the cave were kept here. Thousands of them are many hundreds of years old. But it is certain that new statues have been erected there over the years, as several different sculptural periods are represented in the work.

Near the lake is the gilded **Shwe Ohn Hmin Pagoda** where the hillside is dotted with more white pagodas.

Near the village of Ye-ngan, northwest of Pindaya, are the **Padah-Lin Caves**. These caverns are Burma's most important neolithic excavation site. Countless chips created in the chipping-away of stone axes have been found here, leading archaeologists to believe the caves were a site of tool and weapon-making in prehistoric times. In one of the caves, traces of early wall paintings can still be discerned. A human hand, a bison, part of an elephant, a huge fish, and a sunset (as seen through the cave entrance) are clearly visible.

Routes to the Plateau: As previously noted, the best way for visitors to reach the southern Shan Plateau is by plane to Heho from Yangon or Mandalay. There are, however, other routes for the leisurely traveller. One can disembark from the main north-south railroad trunk line at Thazi and catch a time-consuming freight line to Shwenyaung, midway between Taunggyi and Inle Lake.

One can also travel by road. There are bus services from Bagan (Pagan) and Mandalay. Both take about 12 hours and, though very tiring, offer an unusual glimpse of central Burma. The Taunggyi Mann leaves Mandalay every morning between 4 and 5 o'clock from the 27th Street terminus. The vehicle from Bagan departs at the same time from near the Myanmar Travels & Tours office. In addition, buses leave hourly from Thazi.

Whereas arriving in the Shan State by rail or bus can be relatively easy for those long on patience, the departure can be a little more complicated.

Visitors who hope to resume their northbound or southbound rail journey after disembarking at Thazi invariably have difficulty boarding the express train, because tickets are nearly always booked in advance from Mandalay or Yangon. The only way around this obstacle is to buy an advance ticket for the complete Yangon-Mandalay journey, and only use the portion from Thazi.

The bus journey to Taunggyi is especially recommended to those travelling from Bagan, as even the flight via Mandalay can take most part of a day.

A Pa-o woman of Taunggyi.

RAKHINE

High on a rocky plateau in western Burma rest the remains of what was once among the most spectacular royal cities of Asia. Today, jungle vines creep over its stupas, and myriad priceless Buddha images peer out from the undergrowth. Myohaung (Mrauk-U during medieval times) is the youngest of eight ancient capitals whose bricks crumble under the dense vegetation of inland Rakhine (Arakan).

Rivers like the Kaladan and Lemro have carved deep indentations in the Rakhine littoral. Jungle river boats that ply these waters are the only dependable means of transportation along this isolated coast. The starting point for many of these launches is Sittwe (Akyab), the Muslim-flavoured capital of this unusual Burmese state. Further down the seaboard, 240 kilometres (150 mi) or so toward the Ayeyarwady (Irrawaddy) Delta, is the beach resort of Thandwe (Sandoway), where a beautiful stretch of tranquil sand stretches 11 kilometres (7 mi) along a palm-fringed coastline.

Rakhine. That fabled name has meant mystery and surprise to all who have stumbled upon the state for millennia; even today, it is one of Burma's best-guarded secrets. Only for a few years haveWesterners been granted government permission to travel to Sittwe and Myohaung, and Sandoway's beaches are still seldom visited.

"Wild, uncivilized people": Rakhine is the land where the Mongol and Aryan races, the Brahmanist and Buddhist religions, had their closest encounters. Called *Argyre*, "the silver land," by Ptolemy in the 2nd century AD, its modern appellation came from the name given it by the early inhabitants – *Rakhaing-pyi*. The Indian Aryans used the term *Rakhaing* in pre-Buddhist times, referring to Mongols and Dravidians as "wild, uncivilized people."

It is generally agreed that Buddhism did not become established here until the reign of King Chandra Surya, which began in AD 146. It was during his time that the famous Maha Muni Buddha was cast. The Maha Muni and the Yattara Bell, with its astrological ciphers, became symbols of an independent Rakhine. From their home atop Sirigutta Hill, they were the protectors – the palladia of the small nation. When the Maha Muni was removed by King Bodawpaya in 1784 and carried away to Amarapura, Rakhine's fate was sealed. Even today, the Rakhines (Arakanese) equate the loss of their independence with that of the Maha Muni.

Until AD 957, when Rakhine was overrun by the Pyus, the land was dominated by Indian culture. Ten centuries of blending the Pyu and Indian races have produced the people now known as the Rakhines. When their cultures clashed in the 10th century, the Indians, who had already fused Brahmanism with Buddhism, merged their beliefs with the animism of the Pyus to form a unique mystical union.

At the time of the dominance of the First Burmese Empire, Rakhine was

forced to pay tribute to the rulers of Bagan (Pagan). Because of its geographical isolation, however, the land was able to retain its autonomy. King Anawrahta attacked Rakhine and intended to take the Maha Muni for his capital, but the project was abandoned because of the transportation problems it would have entailed.

A more immediate threat to Rakhine was Mohammedan Bengal, which borders it on the northwest. The Islamic world had been pushing its frontiers east from Arabia for centuries – yet could make no inroads upon the bulwark of Buddhism and Brahmanism put up by the Rakhines. By the late 13th century, Islam had bypassed mainland Southeast Asia entirely, instead establishing an initial foothold on the island of Sumatra.

Islam didn't entirely fail in Rakhine. Many of the state's people today are, in fact, Muslims. In medieval times, Bengal was a strong supporter of Rakhine: when Rakhine was incorporated into the Shan kingdom of Ava for a short time in the 15th century, it was with Bengal's assistance that it was able to break away. After that time, all of Rakhine's kings, even though Buddhist, bore an Islamic title.

Mrauk-U was founded in 1433 by King Minsawmun, and until the decline of the Rakhine empire three and a half centuries later, remained the region's capital and cultural center. The city had thrived for nearly a century by the time the first Europeans – Portuguese pirates – appeared in the Bay of Bengal in 1517. These seafarers based themselves on the Rakhine coast at Dianga, 20 kilometres (12.5 mi) south of Chittagong in present-day Bangladesh. Their coastal raids were far more successful than a miscalculated siege on the impregnable citadel of Mrauk-U; it wasn't long after that failure that the Portuguese put their ships and cannons at the disposal of the Rakhine kings.

The early 17th century was Rakhine's Golden Age. In 1599, King Razagyi returned from a campaign in Bago (Pegu) – then Burma's most powerful kingdom

A mosque in Sittwe.

– with a white elephant, regarded as one of the seven symbols of the "universal monarch." It remained with his successors.

Elixir of immortality: Razagyi's grandson, Thiri-thu-dhamma (ruled 1622–1638), was the most respected king in Rakhine's history. He saw himself as a future "universal monarch" and sought immortality. According to detailed accounts by the Augustan Father Manrique – who came to Mrauk-U in 1629 as the ambassador from Portuguese Goa – Thiri-thu-dhamma had a famed Mohammedan doctor brew him an "immortality elixir" containing the essence of the hearts of 2,000 white doves, 4,000 white cows and 6,000 humans. It didn't work, of course, and he was eventually poisoned by another elixir concocted by enemies in his court.

After Thiri-thu-dhamma's death, the situation in Rakhine got worse. The Portuguese in Dianga switched allegiance, supported the Mogul chief Aurangzeb, and broke Rakhine's dominance at sea. In the court at Mrauk-U,

Afghan and Turkish archers, who had been serving as legionnaires, assumed power. In the first half of the 18th century, there was much turmoil in the government over the fact that the rulers each held power for no longer than two and a half years.

In 1761 and 1762, Rakhine was struck by a pair of exceptionally strong earthquakes. The epicentres of both were near Mrauk-U. The city survived, but along the coast, sections of land rose by as much as 7 metres (23 feet). Buddhists, of course, saw the quakes as an indication of major changes to come.

And come they did. In 1784, King Bodawpaya, on a campaign from central Burma, used Rakhine's confused political situation to annex the territory to his empire. It wasn't a military conquest; he took Mrauk-U by betrayal, with support from a Rakhine populace tired of perpetual civil war. Not satisfied with the popular acclaim, however, Bodawpaya assured his success by making off with the Maha Muni – thus making its fabled magic powers his.

alms
urround a
uddhist
hrine in
ittwe.

Today, more than two centuries after Bodawpaya, Rakhine remains a part of greater Burma. But many of its people still see themselves as a separate entity. In particular, the Muslim minority, the Rohingyas, along the border of Bangladesh. More than 200 000 Rakhines of Bengali descend did recently flee across the Naaf river and are now slowly returning. It is this continuing conflict that is the major reason for Burma's reluctance to allow tourists into northern Rakhine, though visits to Myohaung are now possible.

Rakhine's capital: Sittwe (Akyab) is the capital of Rakhine. It was founded in 1826 by the English general Morrisson, who moved his troops from Mrauk-U to the Kaladan River mouth to escape the inland humidity during the First Anglo-Burmese War.

There is today not much of interest to visitors. A road to Central Burma is under construction and will soon end Northern Rakhine's seclusion. A seemingly endless stretch of beach north of the city, is a minor attraction.

By jungle boat to Myohaung: Of far greater interest, and a "must see" tourist destination, is **Myohaung**. (The name means "old city," a label that was given when the British relocated Rakhine's administrative headquarters from Mrauk-U to the coast.)

Rakhine's medieval capital lies 80 kilometres (50 mi) inland from the Kaladan's mouth, occupying a rocky plateau between the Kaladan and the Lemro river. It's a six- or seven-hour voyage from Sittwe, aboard a boat reminiscent of Bogart's *African Queen*. The craft travels first up the Kaladan, then along several small creeks until the settlement of **Aungdet** is reached. From there, it's a short saunter to Myohaung, built atop and amidst what was once Mrauk-U.

King Minsawmun constructed Mrauk-U to replace the "unlucky" royal city of Launggyet, and thereby placate his citizenry. The king's Brahman astrologers warned him, however, that he would die within the year if he moved his capital from Launggyet; and it wasn't

A 1920s map of Myohaung environs, still usable today.

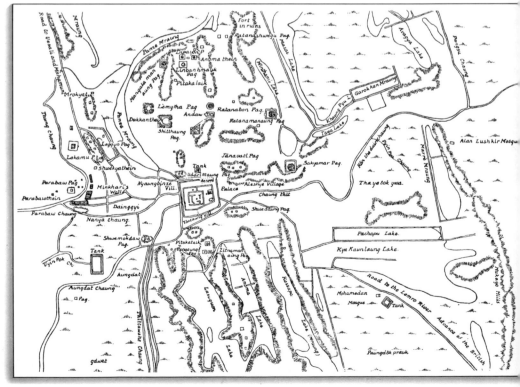

long after the move was made that the prophecy was fulfilled.

It was an ideal capital city though; natural barriers, walls and artificial lakes – the dams of which could be opened to repulse the enemy – helped make the town virtually invincible. Bengalis, Manipurians, Portuguese and Bamars (Burmans) all tried at one time or another to capture the city, and all went down to defeat.

Father Manrique, in the 17th century, left a vivid description of the city's formidable appearance. Surrounded on all sides by high rocky mountains, its thoroughfares were waterways navigable by large and small vessels alike.

"The greater number of houses in the city are made of bamboo," Manrique wrote. "The houses are built in accordance with the rank and position of the builder, and the amount he wishes to spend. Much ingenuity and labour are spent on making for the houses mats of the finest material and of many colors, which are very neat and handsome.

"Even the buildings of the Royal Pal-

ace are made of these...materials, and they have great wooden pillars of such length and symmetry that one is astonished that trees so lofty and straight can exist. Such palace buildings also contain rooms made of fragrant woods such as white and red sandalwood, which thus please the sense of smell by their own natural fragrance."

Manrique's description of Mrauk-U's market at the time of King Thiri-thu-dhamma's coronation is a portrait of a true metropolis:

"So numerous were the different classes of dress and language, such the varied customs at that capital, that the eye was kept busy trying to distinguish different nationalities by their apparel.

"In the shops were being sold in abundance, diamonds, rubies, sapphires, emeralds, topazes, gold and silver in plates and bars, tin and zinc. Besides these articles, there was much copper, fine brass ambergris, musk, civetscent, fragrant resin, essence of almonds, incense, camphor, red lead, indigo, borax, quicksilver, saltpeter, opium, tobacco

A dhow-like sailing boat on the Lemro River.

and lac...". The list goes on.

Mrauk-U, indeed, was a major city, and a cosmopolitan one at that. The remnants of a 30-kilometres (19-mi) long fortification which surrounded the settlement can still be found today. In the centre of the city was the **Royal Palace**, looming high over the surrounding area like an Asian Acropolis. Three layers of square-shaped stonework are all that remains. Where the king of Rakhine once had his private chambers and reception rooms, now there is only a platform from which to view the hilly landscape that surrounds the city.

North of the palace site, hidden behind low hills, are the most important religious shrines of medieval Mrauk-U. But within Mrauk-U's city wall – in every field, and upon each and every hill – stand Buddha images, temples or pagodas. Some of these structures on the hilltops are in active use even today, whitewashed by their devotees to keep them sparkling. Others are in various stages of decay, shrouded in the jungle's dense vegetation and crumbling at the mercy of the green vines.

Temple of 80,000 Buddhas: The visitor must walk for at least 8 kilometres (5 mi) over the hills and through overgrown fields to reach some of the more important edifices. Unlike buildings elsewhere in Burma, these sacred structures were intended to be fortifications as well as shrines. Among the most beautiful is the **Shitthaung Temple**, located atop a small hill. Erected in the 16th century after the unsuccessful Portuguese attack on the city, it is known as "the temple of 80,000 Buddhas." This may be an allusion to the number of statements found in the Buddha's speeches to his followers. But one is left wondering if it isn't the actual number of Buddha images and reliefs enshrined here, many of them gracing the temple's courtyard and outside wall. Other figures out of Buddhist and Brahman mythology are also represented here.

Not far distant is the **Htukkan-thein**, an ordination hall. It has a bell-shaped stupa, and the entire structure is built upon a series of high terraces. In its

On the way to the rice mill in Myohaung.

courtyard are several images which exhibit clothing that was popular in the 16th century.

Numerous sitting Buddha figures can also be found in the **Andaw Temple**. One of the Buddha's teeth, reported to have come from Ceylon, is in the Andaw sanctuary. King Minbin, who built this shrine, also is believed to have founded the **Lemyethna Temple** and the **Shwedaung Pagoda**; both contain frescoes which give visitors a detailed pictorial account of daily life in the Mrauk-U court.

Virtually all of Mrauk-U temples have carved reliefs. There are several thousand in all, depicting Hindu and Mahayana Buddhist religious scenes as well as glimpses of 17th-century royal life. Armed with a strong flashlight, the visitor can stroll for hours through the dimly lit corridors and be surprised by new stories, new gods and new mythological animals.

Between these temple corridors, standing back-to-back in the light arches, are hundreds of Buddha figures. Buddha images, in fact, are to Myohaung as trees are to a forest. They are everywhere, in all sizes, all shapes and all materials. Very often they are broken, a legacy of times when Rakhine had no stable government and the citizen's morale was low. Strewn about as if worthless, these Buddhas could doubtlessly fetch hundreds of dollars apiece on the antique markets of the world. But here at Mrauk-U, they are too commonplace to arouse curiosity.

South of the old royal palace, still within the old city walls, are the three large artificial reservoirs once used to flush out approaching enemies. Today, they are an inviting place for the tired, dust-covered visitor to take a swim.

Despite its former cosmopolitan nature and its great historical importance, Mrauk-U today is a quiet destination. Today's visitor will find himself flanked only by his guide, maybe the chairman of the township council and a half-dozen curious Mrohaungians for whom visitors are still a rarity.

Other ancient capitals: Although it is

Mrauk-U's Shitthaung Temple.

5.5 centuries old, Myohaung is the youngest of all the cities between the Lemro and Kaladan rivers. Near the "old city" are **Launggyet** – the capital before Mrauk-U – and **Vesali**, which dates to the 4th century AD. These cities have fewer visible remains than those of Mrauk-U, but their hills, too, are studded with pagodas and Buddha images.

At Vesali, wherever topsoil is removed, the ground consists of red tiles. The peasants who reside here have innumerable ancient images of all kinds in their bamboo huts. These images once adorned the walls and walkways of a palace which today is buried beneath the huts; the figures are now regarded as the guardians of trees and springs. The government's archaeological department cannot take them away because of the peasants' strong religious attachment to them.

Several other former royal cities – Hkrit, Parein, Pyinsa and Thabeiktaung among them – await excavation. The same is true of **Dhannavati**, some 30 kilometres (19 mi) north of Myohaung

near present-day Thayettbin. The capital of Rakhine between the 6th century BC and AD 350, it was here that the famed Maha Muni image is believed to have been cast in the 2nd century AD.

To reach this site, one must return to Sittwe and take another boat, this time traveling up the Kaladan as far as **Kyauktaw**, about 5 kilometres (3 mi) from Dhannavati and Sirigutta Hill.

If one climbs **Sirigutta Hill** with the knowledge that it was once the center of Buddhist devotion for all of Rakhine, there is a certain sadness in finding it as it is today. While still the most venerated site in the entire Myohaung area, it is but a shadow of its former self. The pagoda on the hill was rebuilt in Bagan (Pagan) style after being destroyed by the Pyus in 957. Three walls enclose a series of courtyards around the structure. In the outer courtyard are a library and a well; in the middle one are statues of 12 Hindu gods who served as guardian spirits of the Maha Muni, and who therefore symbolize the Brahman deities' submission to Buddhist thought. The pagoda itself stands in the inner courtyard, flanked by the legendary **Yattara Bell**.

Signs of Superstition: The bell – a duplicate of the original – is covered by astrological signs and runes of great importance to the superstitious Rakhines of medieval times. Their alchemists wove a magic spell that is difficult to understand even to this day. But an inscription gives the 20th-century observer an insight into the thought processes of people from earlier times:

"To prevent the inroads of the enemies from foreign towns and villages, let offerings of flowers, parched corn and lamps be made day and night at the...pagodas.

"To cause the rulers of the towns and the village in the four cardinal directions to be panic stricken, let a pagoda provided with four archways be constructed...

And let the Yattara Bell be hung and struck at the eastern archway, and the enemies of the east will be panic stricken and quit by flight...Let also the Yattara *bidauk* drum be struck at the relic cham-

Hindu love scene in the Htukkanthein.

244

bers of Buddha. By these means foreign invaders will be seized by fear and take to flight."

Modern observers might be skeptical of the claim that these methods could singlehandedly, as it were, fend off enemy attacks. But the fact remains that as long as the Maha Muni stood beside the Yattara Bell on Sirigutta Hill, Rakhine remained an independent land.

Sturdy travellers with a special permission can go by boat further north along the Kaladan into the southern Chin hills to **Paletwa** and **Kaletwa**, a region of exceptional natural beauty and a people that still live far away from modern amenities.

The beach at Thandwe (Sandoway): Visitors to Burma are usually drawn here by the country's cultural and historic attractions. Few are aware however, of the fact that one of Southeast Asia's most beautiful beaches is located along the southern Rakhine coast – and is open to tourism.

Thandwe, as Sandoway is now called again, is the central community of this beach district, and can be reached from Yangon by air. Formerly just one of several Burmese beaches popular among British colonial officials, it is today one of three seaside resorts with suitable tourist accommodation. Because the beach is very popular among Burmese, advance hotel bookings are advised. Recommended for visitors is the Ngapali Beach Hotel which has a golf course.

In ancient times, Thandwe was an important port of call for Indian merchants and seafarers on the Malay Peninsula. It was then known as Dvaravati, a name taken from a city of *Jataka* myth: when attacked by enemies, it could rise into the sky and hover until the siege had ended.

The Buddha is said to have lived three of his 547 previous lives in Sandoway. Local pagodas enshrine the evidence: the tooth of a cobra in the **Andaw Pagoda**, the rib of a partridge in the **Nandaw Pagoda**, and a yak hair in the **Sandaw Pagoda**. Tradition says Gautama lived these incarnations along the path to enlightenment.

Myohaung villagers and ox cart.

CRUISING THE AYEYARWADY

Two rivers form the Ayeyarwady – the Meikha and the Malihka. Their headwaters delineate the country's northern border, and both have their source on the slopes of the Hkakabo Razi, which at 5,887 metres (19,314 ft), is Burma's highest mountain. This region, at the triangle where India, China and Burma meet, is so rugged and impenetrable that few men have ever gone up there. Little is known of the region, not only to foreigners, but also to Burmese.

Further on the two rivers gather strength while flowing south through deep valleys; rivulets, brooks and creeks join from both sides; and the surrounding hilltops are inhabited by *taungya* agriculturists.

Only two cities of mentionable size are found north of Myitkyina, both in the vicinity of the Malihka. **Putao**, formerly known as Hkamti Long, at the northern end of the Hukawng valley is the centre of the far north. It can be reached by air and is supposed to become the future hub of mountaineering and skiing in Burma.

Further down, **Somprabhum** is the marketplace for the Shans and Kachins of the region. The road running along the Malihka is still in very bad condition and is at present only used by the sturdy Kachins who do not mind if this 160 kilometres (100 mi) journey takes them sometimes up to five days. But with peace settling over Kachin State this too will soon change.

To reach the cradle of the river, one has to go north from Myitkyina. The road to the junction of the Meikha and Malihka has only recently been opened to foreigners. Even today few government cars pass through on their way up to Putao and except very few adventurers, foreigners have not seen the region since the beginning of the sixties.

After leaving the Ayeyarwady plain north of Myitkyina, the road climbs into the hills. It becomes very rough and you'll be happier travelling by a four wheel drive. After some 40 kilometres (27 mi) you'll reach the confluence, a place of exceptional natural beauty and serenity. It has a mystic quality, a place amidst jungle-covered mountains that captures not only your senses but also your mind. When the water is low, you might see huge bamboo rafts drifting through the mingling rivers that form a rapid where they meet. One of them, the Malihka, is quiet and peaceful, the other rushing and foaming. Like at the cradle of the Amazon, where the Rio Negro and the Rio Salmoes meet, you can see for quite some distance how the differently coloured waters mix. Beyond the basin of the confluence, the newly born Ayeyarwady meanders peacefully along sand banks and huge rocks through the jungle towards Myitkyina.

Besides its scenic beauty, this place has also an emotional quality for Burmese and even foreigners. It is here where, with the birth of the Ayeyarwady, the birth of the nation also takes place. Like the merger of rivers from different geographical regions, so is the unity of

different peoples that make up the Burmese nation.

Many different peoples of Burma have come along these Himalaya-born rivers from far-off China, migrating along their banks and settling in the hills beyond. Here the destiny of a nation took shape, and here, the cradle of a nation can be revisited in a dramatic natural setting. This place, with an almost religious quality, has the power to make people understand Burma's urge for national identity and unity.

Since this area will be permanently open to outsiders, the government plans to construct a hotel on the hillock overlooking the junction. The jungle and surrounding hills here are ideal for trekking, and this will be one of the places people have to visit while in Burma.

For the people of the area, this would be a godsend opportunity to earn some income. The poverty in this region is clearly a monetary one. They do not go hungry, but most of their implements are still rudimentary and handmade. Though everything is available on the markets of Myitkyina, little is affordable since their own products have little monetary value.

North of Myitkyina, the Ayeyarwady is negotiable only by rafts. Halfway between the confluence and Myitkyina there is a scenic point with a small restaurant that is also a preferred picnic spot for Myitkyinites. Out in the shallow river young men have set up their gold washing camps, and though the bottom of the river seems to sparkle with small specks of gold, it take hours of hard work, immersed to the hip in the cold water of the still young river, to turn it into a profitable endeavour.

It was after the Yangon-Mandalay-Myitkyina rail link had been completed in 1898 that **Myitkyina** became the commercial hub of the north. The city was levelled during the Second World war, when some of the fiercest fighting between the Allies and the Japanese took place, and the city changed hands several times. Today, an old, overgrown Allied landing strip is still recognizeable at the city limits – place of pilgrimage

The far Kachin Hills.

250

for the few surviving British "Marauders" and "Chindits".

Since the 1993 cease-fire agreement between the SLORC and the KIO, ending more than half a century of civil war, Kachins, Shans, Bamars and Chinese live peacefully together again in a city where Christian churches, Buddhist *kyaung* and Chinese joss-stick houses cater for their different religious needs. Due to the proximity of the jade mines, there is an influx of Chinese money that helps to modernize the city. The first hotel for foreigners, the Popa Hotel at the train station, opened in early 1994. In the first year of operation, more than 100 foreigners have used its admittedly simple facilities.

The Manao: Every year in January, the once famous **Myitkyina Manao Festival** takes place on the ancient Manao grounds. Because of the civil war, this festival was, for several decades, toned down to a small village affair.Today however, this ancient animistic gathering is organized by predominantly Christian Kachins, and since peace has once again been restored, thousands of Kachins, members of all tribes, meet to ascertain their cultural identity.

This festival is a one of a kind occurrence, in which the participants dance for three days around four huge totem poles. The rhythm and sound of their drums, their chants, file-dances and stomping resemble the gatherings of American Indians.

The first defile: Up here the Ayeyarwady is still very shallow and cannot be reached by the big boats that ply between Mandalay and Bhamo. If permitted, you'd have to take a small country boat down to Bhamo. If that's impossible, there is the bus on the newly opened road to Bhamo from where the Ayeyarwady cruise starts. Should the road be closed again, there is a once-a-week flight from Myitkyina to Bhamo. However, going down by country boat from Myitkyina is the highlight of the trip, since 54 kilometres (30 mi) before reaching Bhamo, the boat enters the first and narrowest defile of the river. Before that, it flows through a fertile

Flowered Lisus at the Manao Festival.

plain at the confluence with the Mogaung river that turns into a huge lake after the snow has melted in the mountains.

When the water is high, the first defile is not navigable. The water level rises 12 metres (40 ft) and there is an untold number of rocks either submerged or prominently sticking out at mid-river that produce dangerous whirlpools.

An ancient trading post: Bhamo has been a trading town since times immemorial. Being the point closest to China that can be reached by large boats from the coast, it was one of the main reasons for the British occupation of the country. As an easy point of entry to western and central China, it has inspired western colonialists since the 16th century.

As early as the 15th century, the ancient trading city of **Sampanago** was already mentioned by Nicolo Conti. Not far from the city, remnants, including ruined pagodas and an overgrown city wall, testify to its former greatness.

The **Eikkhawtaw** and the **Shwekyaynar stupas** are ancient structures that tell a legend of a Shan boy who solved a riddle during a Chinese invasion, and thus became the king's son-in-law. Chinese intrusions in internal politics, from Kublai Khan to the aid that the Burmese Communist Party (BCP) received from Beijing, have made the Burmese cautious in their dealings with their mighty neighbour.

Not long ago the city was destroyed by a huge fire, but its centre has now been rebuilt with a spacious marketplace that caters to the peasants of the surrounding hills. The **Thein Maha Chedi**, which contains a tooth relic and is supposed to have been built by King Ashoka in the 3rd century BC, recently received a new invaluable *Seinbu,* covered with rubies from Mogok.

The actual downriver journey starts here. There are three express boats and two slowboats a week that connect Bhamo with Mandalay. The express boat stops six times, at Shwegu, Katha, Tigyaing, Tagaung, Thabeikkyin and Kyaukmyaung; the slowboats stop at any of the 47 mooring places along the river where there is cargo and where

Debilitated Bhamo guest house.

passengers want to embark or disembark. Due to the rising and falling level of the water, the boat has to be moored at different elevations along the steep (up to 20 metres/60 ft high) embankments. Very often, young boys jump overboard with the mooring line in their hands and swim to the shore to anchor it. Downriver, the boats run at 20 kilometres per hour (13 mi/h) and upriver, their speed is 12.5 kilometres per hour (7 mi/h); but that means little since the actual running time depends on the time spent loading and unloading the cargo.

Except for the hundred plus passengers, it is mostly Chinese goods, sugar molasses, salted fish, rattan, beans and peanuts that are shipped to Mandalay. Upriver, cooking oil, rice, chillies, salt and building materials are the main cargo, and petrol that comes by train to Katha is then shipped on to Bhamo.

The express boat that leaves in the morning takes 2 days to Mandalay, stopping overnight at Tigyaing. The slowboat takes up to twice as long.

The second defile. After leaving Bhamo the boat crosses a fertile plain and reaches the second defile after 54 kilometres (30 mi) at **Sinkan**, a small town with several ramshackled monasteries. The 13.5-kilometre (7.5-mi) long defile is the most scenic along the entire length of the river. During the rainy season, the water's depth can reach an amazing 61 metres (180 ft), while when the water is low, elephants pull huge teak logs from the jungle to the river's shore.

Where the hills become the narrowest is a 300-metre (985-ft) cliff, the **Nat-Myet-Hna-Taung** (Face of the Nat Mountain). Also called the Welatha cliff, it adds siginificantly to the sense of grandeur of the place. Not far away is the famous **Parrot's Beak,** a painted rock that acts as a marker. If the water reaches the red beak, the force of the river becomes too strong for boats to pass through the defile. Because the river is so narrow here, most boats here have steel-plated lounges and a military escort. It was also at this point that the Kachin rebels fired their shots during the civil war.

Parrots's Beak.

Leaving the defile, the boat docks at **Shwegu**, a gateway to the Shan hills. Today, wild elephants still roam the jungle in the mountains behind this town. Opposite Shwegu lies the island of **Kyundaw.** It is covered with more than 2700 ancient pagodas; although they are smaller, the stupas here outnumber those in Bagan. This island is also the venue for one of the Shan's most important annual festivals, and every March, Shans from the hills to the east gather here to celebrate.

Before it turns south again, the river turns west and crosses a wide and fertile plain. At Katha, it reaches a side track of the Mandalay-Myitkyina railway.It is on this line that the goods destined for Bhamo are transhipped.

The charms of **Katha** are its raintrees, probably planted a hundred years ago. Today, the trees have converted the town into a shadowy park city; their huge branches stretch across the roofs, protecting houses against rain and sun in a charming, colonial style .

In this beautiful and peaceful place,

people live simple but fulfilled lives. It is the great river, and the link the railway offers to the outside world that make this place different from those to the north in Kachin State.

Slow boat into the past: Four times a week, there is a slowboat to Mandalay that is supposed to dock at every village along the way that has cargo to be transported. It has 12 cabins, a lounge in the bow and a kind of sundeck in front of the second-storey rudder house. Some, but not all of these boats, are tidy, clean and well kept, though still far from conventional western standards. On a cool, sunny day, this trip is quite pleasurable: the landscape of Upper Burma moves through your field of vision, while the hum of the engine is barely audible. In the lounge, lunch and dinner is served by a smiling and friendly steward.

Wherever the boat docks during the harvesting season, huge drums of sugar molasses and sacks filled with sesame are brought on board. If there is a lot of cargo, the trip might take longer than expected, but that doesn't mean much in a country of few or no schedules. In fact, a four or five-hour delay means that they are still on time.

The cramped but cozy decklife: While cargo is being loaded, many saleswomen enter the deck where they try to sell fruits, cookies, *shashlik* and a variety of other local snacks. This boat is the lifeline to the outside world for the people of the Upper Ayeyarwady, since land routes are much too bothersome and, in many areas, still unsafe or even nonexistent. Thus, everything is transported on the two decks. The upper one has square spaces marked by numbers; each one of these spaces can be rented as a three-in-one area for storage of commodities, sleeping, and eating.

Those who travel downriver carry the products of the land to be traded in Mandalay, and those travelling back to their villages carry those goods that can only be purchased with money.

Walking across the deck one finds the whole spectrum of commodities this country produces: fruits, beans, tomatoes and onions show the basic diet of this secluded people. Flowers, *cheroots*, **Sharpening knives at Katha.**

candles, tobacco leaves, sweets, Mandalay Beer, rum and soft drinks are their luxuries. The betelnut seller who has his stand on the lower deck is responsible for all the red stains that mark the floor, and in tiny foodstalls fresh fish is fried on small stoves.

The overcrowded deck is stacked with petrol canisters, charcoal and firewood, sometimes even cars and bicycles. The vendors line their space with their wares – towers of woven cane hats, baskets, hand-woven blankets and live chickens in cane cages. Some of the men bring their Carromme tables along, and hour after hour, with a snap of their fingers, they shoot the discs into the appropriate holes. The players are always surrounded by a crowd of other men who offer zealous advice.

Every morning the womenfolk are busy pasting their faces with *thanaka*. They pound the *thanaka* bark in small mortars, then mix the powder with water and apply the paste in circles onto their cheeks. All this is done with the same ritual concentration as western woman when applying their make-up.

There is even a stall for cheap second hand romance books, sold for a small fee whenever the boat docks at a remote village. Monks have their own platform on which they reside in their common lotus position, puffing one cheroot after another while running their prayer chains through their fingers. In the rear of the upper deck is the kitchen where, on an open fire tea, coffee and a variety of foods are prepared.

Some of the saleswomen have rented up to three of the narrow deck spaces and have set up their stores. Their customers are the passengers on board and the villagers who rush aboard the boat at every stop. These traders sell commodities that are not usually available so far upriver – all the small items for daily use that make life easier, but at little cost. Some of these saleswomen ply the river constantly, having the same stalls and a standard variety of goods. They can take orders and will bring unusual goods on request on the next trip. This form of trade has a long tradition; during the

days of the Irrawaddy Steamship Company, this was the way supplies were distributed to the most remote of villages. Weekly bazaar boats plied the whole river, as they are now doing once again, running between Yangon and Mandalay.

Old-world atmosphere: The sunsets on the Ayeyarwady are glorious, and are best seen from the bridge in front of the wheel house. Often during the night, the boat docks somewhere along the high, sandy embankment. The air is then filled with the shouting of the villagers who carry barrel after barrel of heavy goods on board. Most of the hundred plus passengers on the two decks are awake at this time; and many stand at the railing, watching the young boys straining under heavy loads which they carry on beams across their shoulders.

This aspect of the Ayeyarwady river has yet to be recognized by thrill-seeking travellers. The extraordinary mood on deck, with its multiracial passengers who seem to live in an other century, and the silent cruising, remind one more of sailing than motoring. The landscape, lined by distant jungle-covered mountains in front of which endless paddy fields stretch towards the embankment, is like an ointment, soothing a city dweller's eyes.

South of Katha the boat passes the estuary of the Shweli, a main tributary of the Ayeyarwady. The Shweli enters Burma from China and while crossing the jungles of the Northern Shan State, it turns into Burma's main logging river. It also brings along a lot of silt which has built up into a sandbar at the confluence at **Inywa** and prohibits larger boats entry from the main river.

Due to the heavy silting in this section of the river the boat has to anchor in mid-river abeam of Inywa, since even the local pilot who knows every metre of the river's contours cannot steer the boat safely through the shifting sandbars at night. These pilots enter the ship at different points along the river's course, navigating the boat through the ever-changing channels between the shoals. The ripples on the surface and the speed

Horse-cart drivers.

of the water tells them the depths.

Leaving the Shweli sandbars, the boat calls next at **Myadaung**, a city opposite the southern end of the Mangain Taung, the densely forested jungle ridge that stretches south from Myitkyina. It has a mystical quality when the white pagodas on the hilltop above Myadaung appear slowly through the early morning fog. Such scenes must have inspired the authors of Burma's countless fairy-tales.

In January, after the crops are brought in, everyone is visibly busy preparing for the harvest festival. In front of every house are huge pots and pans on open fires in which a variety of foods are cooked. Tables and chairs are set up to first serve the monks of the *kyaung* and later the rest of the villagers. This scene happens throughout Burma since feeding monks and making offerings is an integral part of Burmese life.

Wide landscapes and high river banks form the typical setting of the fertile Upper Burma plain that stretches all the way to Putao. Each of the docking stations is similar to the last one, with

colourful folks embarking and disembarking while balancing huge sacks, cartons and baskets on their heads.

From Myadaung the boat crosses the river to dock at **Tigyaing**, an equally enchanting town with an old pagoda on its hilltop. Both the pagodas at Myadaung and Tigyaing are said to have been built by King Alaungsithu back in the 12th century– more outposts of the Bagan kingdom.

Strolling through this little community of Tigyaing is a true encounter with Upper Burma life. Small stalls and tea shops line the narrow lanes. Life is calm and peaceful. Only when the Ayeyarwady boat comes does the whole town seem to turn into a frenzy of activity. Regardless of the time of day, even at 3am, the town's entire population assemble on the steep shore, joined by those from far off regions for whom Tigyaing is the vital gateway to the rest of the world.

The top of the Tigyaing pagoda provides a breathtaking view to the north along the river's broad sand banks, criss-

Communal cooking in Myadaung.

crossed during the dry season by a multitude of channels.

Remnants of a Sakya kingdom: The boat later reaches **Tagaung**, one of the highlights of the trip, though at first sight it seems rather uninspiring. However, here lies the origin of the Burmese nation. The first kingdom on Burmese soil was founded in pre-Christian times by immigrants from India. According to the chronicles, it was a prince from the Sakya tribe at Kapilavastu, Gautama's home town, who founded this first kingdom which most probably was a city state. Until last century, all the kings of Burma had traced their ancestry from this dynasty.

In actual fact, the ruins of two lost cities are found here: Tagaung and **Old Bagan**; but most of it has been buried underneath the shifting riverbed or lies beneath the huts, shacks and houses of today's settlement.

At the centre of the village, after passing the market, you'll find the shrine of the **Tagaung Nat,** a huge golden *nat*-head which is said to represent the founder of the ancient city.

If you find your way through the sleepy village on the shore, head past the crumbling and overgrown ancient city walls to a shack where the villagers have placed the beautiful old alabaster Buddha images they had found in the ground. In the late afternoon, the Buddha images glow in the sun's last light which penetrates their delicate bodies.

Behind the shack, amidst a few debilitated stupas at the corner of a field, is a small hill. However, on closer inspection, the "hill" reveals itself as a knoll consisting of broken Buddha images and votive tablets. Taking some as souvenirs might seem irresistable, but the law concerning religious artefacts is quite strict in Burma.

On leaving Tagaung, the calmness of the river at night produces a mesmerizing, peaceful atmosphere. Occasionally, a village drifts past that still has a fire burning; but otherwise, there are only the distant moonlit mountains, the silhouette of the raintrees and palm trees, interspersed by the *hti* of pagodas seem **Morning fog on the river.**

to perch on every prominent outcrop.

Although the boat reaches a region settled predominantly by Bamars, the passengers are still a good mix of Kachin, Shan, Chinese and Bamars. In former times, there were three ferry crossings between here and Mandalay: at **Male**, **Thabeikkyin** and **Kyaukmyaung;** and roads, coming from the Shan hills, lead to the Mu valley in the west and across the jungles of Upper Burma to the Chindwinn. At present, only the one crossing at Kyaukmyaung ferries cars across the river.

Most of the roads in the north have to be rebuilt in the near future – a task the country cannot cope with without foreign assistance. The present system is that every village which will profit from better communication and transport has to supply building materials and labour free of charge. It is the same system that was universally applied in pre-colonial times – a far cry from the system of tax-funded infrastructure.

River of gold: Here, the river runs in a straight north-south direction and en-

ters the third defile 30 miles before it reaches Kyaukmyaung. During the low water season, hundreds of boats can be seen washing gold from the river's sand at **Kabwet,** in the middle of the defile. This is the gold that colours the stupas across the country, giving Burma its name of "Golden Land".

As with the rafts that come downriver, these boats must also carry a red flag to show that they are government-approved. Until November, when the flood waters subside, this stretch of the Ayeyarwady is a rushing channel (with the water level rising 8.6 metres [28 ft]); but during the months before the snow in the Himalaya begins to melt, what is seen is as calm as a quiet mountain lake.

29 kilometres (18 mi) west of Kyaukmyaung lies **Shwebo**, the city from which Alaungpaya, the founder of the Third Burmese Kingdom came. Today, it is seen as the cradle of modern Burmese nationhood. Not far away are the ruins of **Halin**, the last capital of the Pyu people that was destroyed in AD 832. Across the river in **Singu,** you can

join the road that leads to **Mogok**, the main ruby mine of Burma. A little further downriver, also on the eastern side, lies **Sagyin**, the marble mountain that provides the raw material for the typical Burmese Buddha images.

Arriving in **Mandalay** by boat from the north is a memorable moment. When you pass **Mingun** and its broken stupa, Mandalay Hill becomes visible in the distance, and though this trip is something very special, the prospect of spending a night in a comfortable hotel bed adds to the feeling of well-being.

If the boat is carrying too much cargo, it cannot dock at the usual Inland Waterways' dock. Instead, it will continue to a muddy anchoring place a quarter of a mile further on where everyone disembarks, as usual in the north, by walking across narrow planks onto the steep shore. Jeeps and tongas will bring you downtown from this point on.

Here the journey from the north ends, and you'll have to take another boat down to Pyay. While you are changing boats, so the landscape changes as well.

You will be leaving the hilly and fertile northern region to enter into the dry central belt that divides the monsoon-swept delta region from the northern jungles and plains.

A fairy-tale landscape: The boat from Mandalay leaves early, around 5am, but before you can reach the only bridge that spans the Ayeyarwady between Innwa and Sagaing, the sun has already come up, lighting the white stupas like candles. If peace and calm can be perceived visually, then you will see it here, in the Sagaing hills in the early morning light.

Watching this scene, one can begin to understand why the capitals of Burma's kingdoms since the 14th century were built here, a place where the earth seems to radiate an air saturated with Buddhism's inherent serenity.

This 36-kilometre (20-mi) stretch after leaving Mandalay passes through one of the most cultured places on earth. Modern civilisation has largely bypassed this region, where the spiritual wealth is felt in the *kyaungs* of the Sagaing val-

Gold-washing camp at the 3rd defile.

leys, preserved over centuries.

Treacherous shoals: The river now flows for a short while towards the west but soon turns south again. The **Ava (Innwa) bridge**, across which a road and the railway line to Myitkyina runs, was destroyed in 1943 and only rebuilt in 1954. At present, it is the only bridge crossing the Ayeyarwady along its entire 2170-kilometre (1350-mi) length. Two new bridges are under construction, one at Myitkyina and one at Pyay, greatly helping to unite the country.

Shortly after navigating the treacherous shoals in this region, the boat passes the confluence with the Mu river that drains from the Sagaing province. The boat passes **Yandabo,** where in 1825, the treaty that ceded Assam, Rakhine and Thanintaryi to the British was signed. It then carries on for many miles along the confluence with the Chindwinn and its many shifting sandbanks.

Take care not to get stuck: Here, when the water is low, the boat has the most chance of running aground, and it may take hours before the boat is refloated. Luckily, most of the refitted P Class boats (built in 1948 and 1956) that run on the Ayeyarwady now have 150 and 250 hp diesel engines and steerable propeller shafts that can free themselves once they are stuck.

Since 1995, a variety of modern boats cater to hard to hard-to-please visitors between Bagan and Mandalay. One boat, *The Road to Mandalay*, operated by the same company that runs the Eastern & Oriental Express train between Bangkok and Singapore, is designed to transport the passenger into colonial splendour. The boat itself is a refitted Rhine steamer that offers 138 passengers air-conditioned cabins, a swimming pool, bar, restaurant and different lounges – the same luxury travellers are used to in other Southeast Asian destinations.

Once the boat has turned south again, the heartland of the Bamar people lies to the left. This land south of Mandalay, irrigated for over 2,000 years, was the breadbasket that fed the different Burmese kingdoms. Its surplus permitted the development of the advanced civilization that started with the First Bur-

mese Empire in the 11th century.

Passing **Myingyan** during the dry season one can feel the dust and heat that bakes this part of the country where rain is scarce. Late in the afternoon, the boat reaches **Pakokku** – the gateway to western Burma. From here you can reach Mt Victoria, at 3053 metres (10,000 ft), the highest peak of the Rakhine Yoma; but it is an arduous journey, and not for the faint hearted.

If the boat can runs its course without much delay, it will reach **Nyaung U** by nightfall where it will stay until next morning. Here, most tourists disembark and travel by bus to Bagan, just a few miles away.

Passing the silhouette of **Bagan** in the early morning hours is like sailing along the skyline of a perished civilization. The domes, spires and temple structures appear like paper-cutouts against the rising sun; markers of the renaissance of Buddhist thought long after it had vanished from India. Further to the east, the peak of Mt Popa, home of the Mahagiri *nat*, tops the otherwise flat land.

A monk in the shade.

Oil wells in a parched land: South of Bagan, the boat crosses the oil drilling district of Burma. The river's banks are covered with oil storage tanks and at **Chauk**, there is a refinery. Later at **Sale**, there is a Japanese built fertilizer factory and for miles on there are countless oil rigs and rusty derricks to the left and right of the river.

Yenangyaung is the centre of this oil producing region. Here, the river is broad and split up by many channels. During the high water season most of the islands in mid-river are submerged and navigating becomes difficult.

In the evening, the boat reaches **Magway** but due to a huge sandbar in front of the town, the boat can only dock there at high water. Between November and April, it docks opposite of the city at **Minbu**. From Magway, a road leads to **Taungdwingyi** and the ruins of **Beikthano**, the second oldest Pyu city in Burma after Tagaung. Magway itself, centre of the province with the same name, has a beautiful old pagoda, the **Mya Thulun Pagoda** overlooking the entire city and the stretch of the river.

Remnants of colonial times: At **Minhla**, the boat passes the fort where the decisive battle during the 1885 Third Anglo-Burman War took place. After the fort was carried, there was only minor resistance on the way to Mandalay.

Shortly after Minhla is the fourth defile which is only recognizable during high water. The remains of another fort at **Myedé**, (until a short while ago still called **Allanmyo** in honour of Major Allan, the British officer who demarcated the frontier after the occupation of Lower Burma) a city that goes back to about 100 AD. Six miles north of Myedé, there is a tower on the western shore that was the flagstaff marking the British sphere until 1886.

Thayetmyo is the centre of this region. It has a large military establishment north of the town and was founded in 1306 by the son of Bagan's last king.

Downtown Thayetmyo has quite a number of interesting pagodas. The **Shwemoktaw** is said to be another one of the 80,000 pagodas with relics of

Navigating in the early-morning hours.

Gautama Buddha, built by King Ashoka in the 3rd century BC to spread Buddhism around the world.

The **Shwethethlut** is one of the few hollow pagodas in Burma and was built in 1373 by a king who was captured by the Rhakines but was later freed. Thayetmyo still has the atmosphere as described in Orwell's *Burmese Days;* there are the dilapidated colonial administrative buildings, a market that provides a glimpse into the harsh living conditions of the people, and also some charming tree-covered lanes with typical Burmese city dwellings.

On the way down to Pyay, at **Sisayan**, beneath an array of white-washed pagodas, the boat enters the fifth defile. However, like the fourth, it is no hindrance during the low water season. **Pyay,** until recently known as Prome, is the terminus of the Mandalay-Pyay route.

Pyay is an ancient city, and in times long past, before the alluvial delta appeared, it was on the seashore. It was here that the ships from India and Sri Lanka docked, bringing the first Buddhist and Brahman traders to these shores. Close by, at **Hmwaza,** lies **Sri Ksetra,** the erstwhile Pyu capital with its ancient stupas that are built in a style totally different from those in the rest of the country.

The main attractions sit on a hill overlooking the town and the river – the serene **Shwesandaw Pagoda** and a huge standing Buddha. A short trip south to **Shwedaung** brings you to the **Shwemyetmhan Pagoda** which holds a charming spectacled Buddha image.

Going by boat even further down to **Tombo**, you can visit the cliff of the 1000 images put there by sailors who had to wait at the windbreaker cliff for favourable winds to continue their journey upriver.

If you intend to visit the delta region, you can go from Pyay to **Henzada**, then from there by train to **Pathein** and again by boat to Yangon. The shorter route is by boat directly to Yangon or via **Maubin** and **Twante**. If you have seen enough of the river, there is also a night train to Yangon that takes about 8 hours.

The water falls 12 metres.

INSIGHT GUIDES
Travel Tips

FOR THOSE
WITH MORE THAN
A PASSING INTEREST
IN TIME...

Before you put your name down for a Patek Philippe watch *fig. 1*, there are a few basic things you might like to know, without knowing exactly whom to ask. In addressing such issues as accuracy, reliability and value for money, we would like to demonstrate why the watch we will make for you will be quite unlike any other watch currently produced.

"Punctuality", Louis XVIII was fond of saying, "is the politeness of kings."

We believe that in the matter of punctuality, we can rise to the occasion by making you a mechanical timepiece that will keep its rendezvous with the Gregorian calendar at the end of every century, omitting the leap-years in 2100, 2200 and 2300 and recording them in 2000 and 2400 *fig. 2*. Nevertheless, such a watch does need the occasional adjustment. Every 3333 years and 122 days you should remember to set it forward one day to the true time of the celestial clock. We suspect, however, that you are simply content to observe the politeness of kings. Be assured, therefore, that when you order your watch, we will be exploring for you the physical—if not the metaphysical—limits of precision.

Does everything have to depend on how much?

Consider, if you will, the motives of collectors who set record prices at auction to acquire a Patek Philippe. They may be paying for rarity, for looks or for micromechanical ingenuity. But we believe that behind each $500,000-plus

bid is the conviction that a Patek Philippe, even if 50 years old or older, can be expected to work perfectly for future generations.

In case your ambitions to own a Patek Philippe are somewhat discouraged by the scale of the sacrifice involved, may we hasten to point out that the watch we will make for you today will certainly be a technical improvement on the Pateks bought at auction? In keeping with our tradition of inventing new mechanical solutions for greater reliability and better time-keeping, we will bring to your watch innovations *fig. 3* inconceivable to our watchmakers who created the supreme wristwatches of 50 years ago *fig. 4*. At the same time, we will of course do our utmost to avoid placing undue strain on your financial resources.

Can it really be mine?

May we turn your thoughts to the day you take delivery of your watch? Sealed within its case is your watchmaker's tribute to the mysterious process of time. He has decorated each wheel with a chamfer carved into its hub and polished into a shining circle. Delicate ribbing flows over the plates and bridges of gold and rare alloys. Millimetric surfaces are bevelled and burnished to exactitudes measured in microns. Rubies are transformed into jewels that triumph over friction. And after many months—or even years—of work, your watchmaker stamps a small badge into the mainbridge of your watch. The Geneva Seal—the highest possible attestation of fine watchmaking *fig. 5*.

Looks that speak of inner grace *fig. 6*.

When you order your watch, you will no doubt like its outward appearance to reflect the harmony and elegance of the movement within. You may therefore find it helpful to know that we are uniquely able to cater for any special decorative needs you might like to express. For example, our engravers will delight in conjuring a subtle play of light and shadow on the gold case-back of one of our rare pocket-watches *fig. 7*. If you bring us your favourite picture, our enamellers will reproduce it in a brilliant miniature of hair-breadth detail *fig. 8*. The perfect execution of a double hobnail pattern on the bezel of a wristwatch is the pride of our casemakers and the satisfaction of our designers, while our chainsmiths will weave for you a rich brocade in gold *figs. 9 & 10*. May we also recommend the artistry of our goldsmiths and the experience of our lapidaries in the selection and setting of the finest gemstones? *figs. 11 & 12*.

How to enjoy your watch before you own it.

As you will appreciate, the very nature of our watches imposes a limit on the number we can make available. (The four Calibre 89 time-pieces we are now making will take up to nine years to complete). We cannot therefore promise instant gratification, but while you look forward to the day on which you take delivery of your Patek Philippe *fig. 13*, you will have the pleasure of reflecting that time is a universal and everlasting commodity, freely available to be enjoyed by all.

Should you require information on any particular Patek Philippe watch, or even on watchmaking in general, we would be delighted to reply to your letter of enquiry. And if you send

fig. 1: The classic face of Patek Philippe.

fig. 4: Complicated wristwatches circa 1930 (left) and 1990. The golden age of watchmaking will always be with us.

fig. 6: Your pleasure in owning a Patek Philippe is the purpose of those who made it for you.

fig. 9: Harmony of design is executed in a work of simplicity and perfection in a lady's Calatrava wristwatch.

fig. 2: One of the 33 complications of the Calibre 89 astronomical clock-watch is a satellite wheel that completes one revolution every 400 years.

fig. 5: The Geneva Seal is awarded only to watches which achieve the standards of horological purity laid down in the laws of Geneva. These rules define the supreme quality of watchmaking.

fig. 7: Arabesques come to life on a gold case-back.

fig. 10: The chainsmith's hands impart strength and delicacy to a tracery of gold.

fig. 11: Circles in gold: symbols of perfection in the making.

fig. 3: Recognized as the most advanced mechanical regulating device to date, Patek Philippe's Gyromax balance wheel demonstrates the equivalence of simplicity and precision.

fig. 8: An artist working six hours a day takes about four months to complete a miniature in enamel on the case of a pocket-watch.

fig. 12: The test of a master lapidary is his ability to express the splendour of precious gemstones.

PATEK PHILIPPE
GENEVE
fig. 13: The discreet sign of those who value their time.

Reality check. Call home.

—— *AT&T USADirect® and World Connect®. The fast, easy way to call most anywhere.* ——

Take out AT&T Calling Card or your local calling card.** Lift phone. Dial AT&T Access Number for country you're calling from. Connect to English-speaking operator or voice prompt. Reach the States or over 200 countries. Talk. Say goodbye. Hang up. Resume vacation.

American Samoa	633 2-USA	Korea	009-11	Taiwan*	0080-10288-0
Australia	1800-881-011	Macao ∎	0800-111	Thailand♦	0019-991-1111
Cambodia ∎	1800-881-001	Malaysia*	800-0011		
China, PRC♦♦♦	10811	Micronesia ∎	288		
Cook Islands ∎	09-111	New Zealand	000-911		
Fiji ∎	004-890-1001	Palau ∎	02288		
Guam	018-872	Philippines*	105-11		
Hong Kong	800-1111	Saipan†	235-2872		
India♦	000-117	Singapore	800-0111-111		
Indonesia†	001-801-10	South Africa	0-800-99-0123		
Japan*∎	0039-111	Sri Lanka	430-430		

AT&T
Your True Choice

For a free wallet sized card of all AT&T Access Numbers, call: 1-800-241-5555.

TRAVEL TIPS

Getting Acquainted

Time Zones

Burma Standard Time is 6 hours, 30 minutes ahead of Greenwich Meridian Time. If you come from Bangkok, you would have to set your watch back half an hour upon arrival in Yangon. International time differences are staggered as follows:

Burma	noon today
Bangkok	12.30pm today
Bonn	6.30am today
Hawaii	7.30pm yesterday
Hong Kong	1.30pm today
London	5.30am today
New Delhi	11am today
New York	12.30am today
Paris	6.30am today
San Francisco	9.30pm yesterday
Sydney	3.30pm today
Tokyo	2.30pm today

Climate

Like all countries in South and Southeast Asia's monsoonal region, Burma's year is divided into three seasons. The rains begin in May, and are most intense between June and August. This is a time of high humidity – especially intense in the coastal and delta regions – and of daily afternoon/evening showers, as monsoonal winds carry the moisture in off the Indian Ocean. The central inland is drier than other parts of the country, but is subject to much rain during this time.

In October, the rains let up. The ensuing winter "cool season" (November through February) is the most pleasant time to visit Burma. The average mean temperature along the Ayeyarwady plain, from Yangon to Mandalay, is between 21°C and 28°C (70°F and 82°F), although in the mountains on the north and east, the temperature can drop below freezing and snow can fall.

During the months of March and April, Burma has its "dry season." Temperatures in the central Burma plain, particularly around Bagan (Pagan), can climb to 45°C (113°F).

Annual rainfall along the rainshadow coasts of Rakhine (Arakan) and Tanintharyi (Tenasserim) range from 300 to 500 centimetres (120 to 200 in). The Ayeyarwady Delta gets about 150 to 200 centimetres (60 to 100 in), while the central Burma region, between Mandalay and Bagan and the surrounding areas, averages 50 to 100 centimetres (20 to 40 in) of rain each year. In the far north, the melting snows of the Himalayan foothills keep rivers fed with water.

The People

Burma has seven minority-dominated states: Rakhine (Arakan), Chin, Kachin, Kayin (Kawthule), Kayah, Mon and Shan. There are seven divisions populated mainly by Bamars (Burmans): Ayeyarwady (Irrawaddy), Magway (Magwe), Mandalay, Bago (Pegu), Yangon (Rangoon), Sagaing and Tanintharyi.

Burma has a population of 43.1 million (1994 estimate), of whom 80 percent are rural dwellers and 20 percent urban. Population density is 46.9 per square kilometres (123 per sq mi). Annual population growth rate is 1.89 percent (the population is expected to grow to 68.5 million by the year 2020). Life expectancy is 57 years (male), 61 years (female); infant mortality rate is 99 per 1,000 (1989).

Burmese Names

Unlike Western culture, there are no family names in Burmese usage. Men and women, parents and children, married couples and single people cannot be differentiated by their names. Women keep their maiden names upon marriage, and a child can have a name which bears no relation whatsoever to his parents' names.

A Burmese has a name of one, two or three syllables, given to him (or her) shortly after birth at a naming ceremony. Parents consult an authority in astrology and supernatural knowledge – perhaps a monk, a soothsayer or a spiritual medium – in selecting the name. While this practice does not follow Buddhist doctrine, it is customary throughout the country.

In contrast to Western tradition, a Burmese can change his name as often as he likes. If he feels he can bring success to a new enterprise or change his fortune by doing so, he will change his name. Small children are often given unpleasant names to ward off illness and evil; when they have grown up, they change their names to something more pleasant. Only through mode of address can one tell the sex or social status of a Burmese.

For example, a Burmese named Kau Reng, if a man, might be addressed as "U Kau Reng," "Ko Kau Reng" or "Maung Kau Reng." The title "U" says that the person being addressed is a superior in social or official position in age. "Ko" is commonly used among men of similar standing in addressing each other. "Maung" generally is used toward persons who are younger or of an inferior status; it also is commonly used among children and teen-aged boys. Sometimes the dual title "Ko Maung" is used if the Burmese has a monosyllabic name.

A woman named Kau Reng would be addressed either as "Daw Kau Reng" or "Ma Kau Reng." "Daw" implies social status or greater age; it can suggest that the woman is married, although this is not necessarily so. "Ma" is applicable to Burmese women regardless of social status, and is the most commonly used female title, even for married women. It is very discourteous to address any woman in Burma without the use of one of these titles.

Within the family circle, there are several other titles with finer shades of meaning. Wives often address their husbands as "Eing Ga Lu" or "Ein Thar," meaning "Good man of the house." An elder brother is called "Ko Ko." An uncle is "U Lay," "U Gyi" or "Ba Gyi." Similar terms of affection are directed towards women. "Ma Ma" and "A Ma Gyi" refer to an elder sister, while "Daw Daw" is for aunt.

Superiors are often addressed "Ah Ko Gyi," "Ko Gyi" or "Saya" (teacher). "Saya" is also used in reference to medical doctors. Monks are called "Sayadaw" ("Venerable"), "Ashin" ("Reverend") or "Kodaw" ("Your Reverence"), the latter used most frequently by a layman addressing a monk. Military officers are addressed as "Bo."

It is particularly difficult for a Burmese to address a Westerner only by his Christian name, even when they

THOMAS COOK
MASTERCARD
TRAVELLERS CHEQUES...

...HOLIDAY ESSENTIALS

Travel money from the travel experts

THOMAS COOK MASTERCARD TRAVELLERS CHEQUES ARE
WIDELY AVAILABLE THROUGHOUT THE WORLD.

Sail away on a holiday that's smooth as silk.

Crystal clear waters of shimmering turquoise.

Beaches the colour of crushed pearls.

The exquisite beauty of Southern Thailand will literally take your breath away.

And, search the whole world over, you won't find a tropical holiday setting that's as fascinating, or with such a delightfully diverse range of things to see and do.

Snooze on pristine beaches, or set sail among the fantastic limestone out-

crops that rise like nature's chessme from the waters of Phang Nga Bay.

There are ancient towns and vi ages to explore, and coral reefs teemi with fish. Wander through butterf gardens, or tuck into some of the worl finest seafood.

To help plan your holiday in Southern Thailand pick up free copies of our Royal Orchid Holidays 'Thailand – Asia Pacific' and 'Active Thailand' brochures from your travel agent or nearest Thai International office.

In them you'll find every holiday imaginable in this exotic and exciting land. And, naturally, the best way to start your Royal Orchid Holiday is flying to Thailand on Thai, the airline that's smooth as silk.

INSIGHT GUIDES

COLORSET NUMBERS

North America
160	Alaska
173	American Southwest
184I	Atlanta
227	Boston
275	California
180	California, Northern
161	California, Southern
237	Canada
184C	Chicago
184	Crossing America
243	Florida
240	Hawaii
275A	Los Angeles
243A	Miami
237B	Montreal
184G	National Parks of America: East
184H	National Parks of America: West
269	Native America
100	New England
184E	New Orleans
184F	New York City
133	New York State
147	Pacific Northwest
184B	Philadelphia
172	Rockies
275B	San Francisco
184D	Seattle
	Southern States of America
186	Texas
237A	Vancouver
184C	Washington DC

Latin America and The Caribbean
150	Amazon Wildlife
260	Argentina
188	Bahamas
292	Barbados
251	Belize
217	Bermuda
127	Brazil
260A	Buenos Aires
162	Caribbean
151	Chile
281	Costa Rica
282	Cuba
118	Ecuador
213	Jamaica
285	Mexico
285A	Mexico City
249	Peru
156	Puerto Rico
127A	Rio de Janeiro
116	South America
139	Trinidad & Tobago
198	Venezuela

Europe
155	Alsace
158A	Amsterdam
167A	Athens
263	Austria
107	Baltic States
219B	Barcelona
1187	Bay of Naples
109	Belgium
135A	Berlin
178	Brittany
109A	Brussels
144A	Budapest
213	Burgundy
122	Catalonia
141	Channel Islands
135E	Cologne
119	Continental Europe
189	Corsica
291	Côte d'Azur
165	Crete
226	Cyprus
114	Czech/Slovak Reps
238	Denmark
135B	Dresden
142B	Dublin
135F	Düsseldorf
149	Eastern Europe
148A	Edinburgh
123	Finland
209B	Florence
154	France
135C	Frankfurt
135	Germany
148B	Glasgow
279	Gran Canaria
124	Great Britain
167	Greece
166	Greek Islands
135G	Hamburg
144	Hungary
256	Iceland
142	Ireland
209	Italy
202A	Lisbon
258	Loire Valley
124A	London
201	Madeira
219A	Madrid
157	Mallorca & Ibiza
117	Malta
101A	Moscow
135D	Munich
158	Netherlands
111	Normandy
120	Norway
124B	Oxford
154A	Paris
115	Poland
202	Portugal
114A	Prague
153	Provence
177	Rhine
209A	Rome
101	Russia
130	Sardinia
148	Scotland
261	Sicily
264	South Tyrol
219	Spain
220	Spain, Southern
101B	St. Petersburg
170	Sweden
232	Switzerland

112	Tenerife
210	Tuscany
174	Umbria
209C	Venice
263A	Vienna
267	Wales
183	Waterways of Europe

Middle East and Africa
268A	Cairo
204	East African Wildlife
268	Egypt
208	Gambia & Senegal
252	Israel
236A	Istanbul
252A	Jerusalem-Tel Aviv
214	Jordan
270	Kenya
235	Morocco
259	Namibia
265	Nile, The
257	South Africa
113	Tunisia
236	Turkey
171	Turkish Coast
215	Yemen

Asia/Pacific
287	Asia, East
207	Asia, South
262	Asia, South East
194	Asian Wildlife, Southeast
272	Australia
206	Bali Baru
246A	Bangkok
234A	Beijing
247B	Calcutta
234	China
247A	Delhi, Jaipur, Agra
169	Great Barrier Reef
196	Hong Kong
247	India
212	India, South
128	Indian Wildlife
143	Indonesia
278	Japan
266	Java
203A	Kathmandu
300	Korea
145	Malaysia
218	Marine Life in the South China Sea
272B	Melbourne
211	Myanmar
203	Nepal
293	New Zealand
205	Pakistan
222	Philippines
250	Rajasthan
159	Singapore
105	Sri Lanka
272	Sydney
175	Taiwan
246	Thailand
278A	Tokyo
255	Vietnam
193	Western Himalaya

are close friends. Thus Ko Kau Reng will never call his friend "Ronnie," but will address him as "Ko Ronnie" or "Maung Ronnie." Similarly, Nancy would be called "Ma Nancy." Ko Kau Reng expects that he, too, will be similarly addressed.

The Economy

Burma's gross national product is US$9.3 billion (1988), a per capita GNP of US$235. It is growing by about 6.4 percent p.a. The national labor force numbers 15 million, of whom 67 percent are employed in agriculture and 13 percent in industry.

Government

The Union of Burma (in Burmese, Myanma Naing-Ngan; in the future Pyidaungsu Thamada Myanmar Naung-Ngan-Daw) is at present in the state of adopting a new constitution. Once that has happened, a newly elected People's Assembly (*Hluttaw*) will convene. Until then the "State Law and Order Restoration Council" headed by General Than Shwe rules by decree.

The National Flag

The Burmese national flag is red in colour with a dark blue canton in the top left corner. Within the blue field are a white pinion and ears of paddy rice, surrounded by 14 white stars. The pinion represents industry, the rice symbolizes agriculture, and the stars correspond to the 14 administrative districts of Burma. The three colours of the flag represent decisiveness (red), purity and virtue (white) and peace and integrity (blue).The state flag was adopted in 1974.

Temple Etiquette

A Buddhist place of worship is very unlike a similar place in the West. You might find a devout Buddhist in deep meditation on any temple platform, but you might also find whole families eating their lunches in front of a Buddha image. You will see lines of monks walking slowly and consciously around the stupa, but you also may see hordes of children running around merrily and haphazardly. The temple ground is where every Burmese village or city neighbourhood congregates in

the evening. But don't let the "everydayness" fool you. This is sacred ground, and there are certain rules you must keep to show your respect.

Throughout Burma, wherever you enter or leave religious grounds, you must remove your shoes (or sandals) and socks. Many shrines will have a sign posted to remind you: "Footwear Prohibited." You'll have to plod with naked soles over marble plates scorched by the mid-day sun, up long flights of stairs (the whole of Mandalay Hill, for example, is sacred ground), or even over thorn-studded fields if they lie within the enclosure that marks a temple ground.

You can also show your respect for Burmese religion by wearing proper clothing at a temple – especially, no short skirts for women, and no short pants. Those who come for meditation and contemplation do not want to be distracted by "shocking" Westerners: Theravada Buddhists have a strong "anti-flesh" attitude, an equally strong desire for virtue, and a refined awareness of beauty.

If you watch the pious Buddhists who climb to the terrace surrounding a stupa, or who wander through the passageways leading around a temple's central cella, you will notice that they always turn to their left. By keeping the sanctuary on the right, they follow a universal "law," moving in the same direction as the sun across the sky.

At the Shwedagon Pagoda and other shrines with planetary posts on their terraces, the pilgrim walks from one season to another: by visiting monuments to the last four Buddhas, he walks through different worlds and different times. This reminds him of his smallness compared to the universe, and awakens in him pure Theravadain spirit. He may stop at planetary posts corresponding to his birthday and the current weekday; he may pause (especially at older shrines) to study the terracotta friezes describing the Buddha's former lives; he might make an offering of flowers or candles at a Buddha image, and perhaps wash it for additional merit. You will see him murmur the "Three Gems": "I take refuge in the Buddha, I take refuge in the Dhamma, I take refuge in the Sangha."

Pagodas and temples are usually beautifully decorated, and most Bur-

mese show great pride if you are inspired to photograph their shrine. But photos should be your only souvenirs. Although many Buddhist structures seem to have a surplus of small Buddha statues that no one appears to care about, these are still venerated images. Leave them alone.

Planning The Trip

Electricity

In Burma, the standard electrical current is 230-volt, 50 hertz.

What To Wear

Dress in Burma is casual but neat. Unless you are conducting business in Yangon, you won't be expected to wear a tie. Long pants for men and dress or long skirt for women, lightweight and appropriate to the prevailing climatic conditions, is the generally accepted mode of dress for Westerners. Quick-drying clothes are a good idea for visits during the rainy season or Thingyan (the "water festival"). There is no law against shorts or mini-skirts, but this type of clothing is not welcomed by the Burmese. A sweater or jacket should be carried if you plan a visit to the hill stations or Shan Plateau, especially in the cool season. Open footwear, such as sandals, is acceptable, but remember to remove footwear when entering religious institutions. If you forget your umbrella and arrive during the rainy season, a worthwhile investment would be one of the highly-colored hand-painted Burmese umbrellas.

Entry Regulations

Visas & Passports

Visitors to Burma must present a valid passport and a tourist or business visa obtained at one of Burma's overseas embassies or consulates. An entry visa for tourists (ETV) is valid for 28 days. These visas can now easily be prolonged for another four weeks at the Yangon immigration office. It is also possible to obtain a **Multiple Journey Entry Visa** for those operating a business in Burma. A visa for a longer stay, a so-called **stay permit**, can be issued for a duration of up to one year and extended upon application; there is also a visa that permits multiple entries during the time of one year. Stay permits must be endorsed by the Foreign Investment Commission or the ministry concerned.

Children above seven years of age, even when included on their parents' passport, must have their own visas.

Individual travel that was possible in the 1970s and 1980s is now possible again.

Official Registration

Officially, as a foreign tourist, you must register either with immigration authorities or police whenever you move around the country. This obligation is automatically fulfilled by staying overnight at any tourist hotel. An overnight stay at a monastery, pagoda or private home, especially if it is not in a principal tourist region, is likely to present complications.

Many new regions have been opened since 1994. To visit them you need to be accompanied by a liaison from the information ministry, but in most cases a registered tourist guide will also do. The many new travel agencies know how to arrange such trips and are able to organize the official permission, the necessary transport and the guide. The fees, though, they charge, are not too small.

Health officials require certification of immunization against cholera, and against yellow fever if you arrive within nine days after leaving or transiting an affected area. Proof of smallpox vaccination is no longer required.

Since 1994 the entry and exit procedures have become more or less the same as in any other Southeast Asian country and Burma has overseas embassies in the following cities:

North America: Washington, D.C., Ottawa, New York (mission to the United Nations).
Europe: Belgrade, Bern, Bonn, London, Moscow, Paris, Prague, Rome.
Asia: Bangkok, Calcutta (consulate), Colombo, Dacca, Hanoi, Hong Kong (consulate), Islamabad, Jakarta, Kathmandu, Kuala Lumpur, Manila,

New Delhi, Beijing, Singapore, Tokyo, Vientiane.
Middle East: Tel Aviv, Cairo.
Australia: Canberra.

Customs

Tourists are allowed duty-free import of limited quantities of tobacco – 400 cigarettes, 100 cigars, or 8 ounces of pipe tobacco as well as two litres of alcoholic beverage, and a ½-litre bottle of perfume or eau de cologne.

A passenger may bring in one unit or one set each of the following articles (declared on the property list and taken out again on departure):
– 1 camera and accessories with 3 rolls of film
– 1 tape recorder
– 1 portable radio
– 1 video cassette recorder
– 1 portable computer
– 24 diskettes
– 1 pair of field glasses
– 1 set of golf clubs
– 1 portable typewriter
– declared articles of personal jewelry
– 1 electric shaver
– 1 hair dryer
– 1 pocket calculator
– personal effects in actual use
– two tennis rackets
– medicine for personal use
– 1 travelling blanket
– 1 portable musical instrument
– 20 records/1 dozen unrecorded tapes
– 1 unrecorded video tape
– professional/technical equipment according to requirement

You will be required to fill out a customs form declaring your camera, jewellery, tape recorder, radio, typewriter and similar effects. This declaration must be returned to customs officials upon departure to assure that you haven't sold any of these items in Burma's black market. Contrary to the regulation in force during the 1970s and 1980s you are now permitted to bring in your video camera.

Artefacts of archaeological interest cannot be taken out of the country, nor can any precious stones – unless they've been purchased from the Tourist Department Stores, the airport duty-free shop, or with special government permission. There is no enforced restriction on the export of souvenirs of genuine tourist interest. For inquiries, call the Customs House at 84533.

The following articles cannot be exported:
– Stone Age implements and artefacts
– fossils
– ancient coins
– Burmese bronze and brass weights
– bronze and clay pipes
– palm leave manuscripts and *Parabaike* (folding manuscripts)
– inscribed stones and bricks
– inscribed gold and silver plates and other inscribed objects
– historical documents
– religious images and statues
– carvings or sculptures of bronze, stone, stucco and wood
– frescoes and fragments thereof
– porcelain and pottery
– Burmese regalia and paraphernalia

On arrival at Yangon airport, after having your customs declaration stamped and if you have no goods to declare, you can pass through the "Green Channel." If you have any doubts, use the "Red Channel."

Formalities both on arrival and departure are now quite easy. Do not lose the various forms you have been given upon entry, otherwise you will face problems on departure.

Leaving through Mingaladon Airport, there is a US$6 airport tax. You will have to queue at the tax counter before checking in.

Health

All visitors to Burma should take appropriate anti-malaria precautions before entering the country, and should continue to take medication throughout their stay. The risk is highest at altitudes below 1,000 metres (3,000 ft) between May and December. Many upcountry hotels have mosquito nets, but they're worthless if they have holes in them. It can be a worthwhile investment to carry your own mosquito net and pack mosquito coils to burn while you sleep.

Perhaps the two most common hazards to Burma visitors are sunburn and "Delhi Belly." The best way to prevent sunburn, especially if you're not used to the intense tropical sun, is to stay under cover whenever possible at midday and if you do go out, wear a hat or carry an umbrella. You'll see many Burmese, especially women and children, with yellow *thanaka*-bark powder applied to their faces to help shut out the sun. If you find yourself sweating a lot and feeling weak or dizzy, sit down (in the shade!) and eat some salt, either in tablet form or by mixing salt in a soft drink or tea.

North Americans sometimes know "Delhi Belly" as "Montezuma's Revenge." No matter what it's called, sooner or later, nearly every Westerner traveling in Asia and eating local food comes down with diarrhoea. This can be uncomfortable and inconvenient. A good solution is to carry Lomotil tablets. Another solution is to stay away from less familiar foods when possible.

Health standards in much of Burma are still relatively low. Under no circumstances should you drink water unless you know it has been boiled. All fruit should be carefully peeled before being eaten, and no raw vegetables should be eaten. Amoebic dysentery is a danger to those who are not careful.

In the event that you get sick in spite of all precautions, several hospitals in Yangon can cater to Westerners' medical needs. These include:

Hospitals

Diplomatic Hospital (Kandawgyi Clinic), Kyaikkasan Road. Tel: 50149.
Eye, Ear, Nose and Throat Hospital, Alanpya Road. Tel: 72311.
Infectious Diseases Hospital, Upper Pansodan Street. Tel: 72497.
Yangon General Hospital, Bogyoke Aung San Street. Tel: 81722.
University Hospital, University Avenue. Tel: 31541.
Kandawgyi Clinic, Natmauk Road. Tel: 50149.
Lake View Clinic, Kan Yeiktha Road, 6.5 mile. Tel: 30083.
Central Women Hospital, Minye Kyawzwa Road. Tel: 73944.
Aye Yeiktha Polyclinic, 340, Shwe Bon Tha Street. Tel: 77242.

Upcountry, in case of an emergency, the best bet is the nearest military hospital.

Money Matters

When entering Burma every visitor has to exchange US$300 into FECs (Foreign Exchange Currency, commonly called tourist money). Children up to 12 years and members of package tours are, however, exempted. One FEC has a value of 100 kyats (the official exchange rate, however is still 6 kyats

to US$1). These 300 FECs cannot be reconverted when leaving the country. The visitor can exchange as many dollars into FECs as he needs during his stay and can reconvert the surplus. This system has now made the former black market somehow obsolete.

Among the required documents is a currency form. There is no limit to the amount of foreign currency you can bring into Burma, as long as it is declared upon entry. However, the import and export of Burmese kyats is forbidden, and the export of foreign currency is limited to the amount declared upon entry.

The currency form must be presented whenever money is converted into FECs, and again when you leave the country.

Customs officials will probably also check to see that the foreign currency you declared coming into the country is accounted for upon your departure. Whenever you change your money at a bank or pay your hotel, train or plane tickets with foreign exchange (as required), you'll have an entry made on your currency form.

You have to make your first official currency exchange at the Myanmar Foreign Trade Bank (MFTB) counter at the airport. Thereafter, US$ and UK Pounds and a variety of other currencies can officially be exchanged into FECs at the Foreign Trade Bank (in Yangon, it's on Barr Street; in Mandalay, on B Road at 82nd Street), or at major hotels. Traveler's cheques will bring a slightly better return than cash. The following currencies will be accepted for exchange into FECs: the US Dollar, British Pound, German Mark, French Franc, Swiss Franc, Australian Dollar, Singapore Dollar, Malaysian Ringgit, Hong Kong Dollar and Japanese Yen. FECs are issued in notes of one, five and ten FECs.

The following Traveller's Cheques are accepted: Master Card, American Express, Bank of Tokyo, City Corp., Visa, Bank of America, National Westminster Bank, First National City Bank, Swiss Bankers and Commonwealth Bank of Australia.

Remember that it is illegal to take kyats into or out of Burma, the government appears to be stiffening its controls.

Burmese coins come in a variety of interesting sizes and shapes. They are

in denominations of 1, 5, 10, 25 and 50 Pyas and 1 Kyat. Notes are in denominations of 1, 5, 10, 15, 25, 45, 50, 90, 100 and 200, marked with both Arabic and Burmese numerals. Due to present inflation however, you will rarely find any coins in circulation.

At the time of press, the official exchange rate of the Kyat was 6.30 to the US Dollar and 3.60 to the German Mark.

Credit Cards

American Express and Master Card are accepted at Myanmar Travels & Tours as well as in all the major hotels and the Tourist Department Stores.

Getting There

By Air

Most of Burma's visitors arrive by air at Yangon's Mingaladon Airport. Situated 19 kilometres (12 mi) northwest of the capital, it is where most scheduled international flights arrive. In the near future, however, the planned Mandalay International Airport will also accept international flights. A newcomer, Silk Air, flies three times a week to and from Singapore. The largest number of international flights connect Yangon and Bangkok. Burma's international carrier, Myanmar Airways International (MAI) operates daily flights between Yangon and Bangkok, two flights a week to Hong Kong and three flights to Singapore. Thai International flies daily to Bangkok; Biman, the national carrier of Bangladesh, flies once a week from Chittagong via Yangon to Bangkok and back. Air Mandalay, the new domestic airline, started a bi-weekly services to Chiang Mai, Chiang Rai and Phuket. Air China (CAAC) has a weekly flight between Yangon and Kunming (Yunnan).

Air service between Delhi and Yangon is to start in 1996. Lufthansa has also started a co-sharing route together with Thai International to Yangon.

Myanmar Airways, UB, the domestic carrier, handles bookings for the following airlines: Air India, British Airways, Czechoslovak Airlines, Cathay Pacific, Japan Air Lines, Lot-Polish Airways, Lufthansa, Royal Nepal and Scandinavian Airlines. For a listing of airline offices in Yangon, check the "Useful Addresses" section.

Travelers from the United States, Australia, Europe and other locations probably will find it easiest to reach Burma via Bangkok. Some 30 international airlines connect Bangkok with other world capitals.

By Sea

The only option to traveling to Burma by air is to arrive by ship. Freighter travel, or arrival by a cruise ship, is now possible due to the prolonged visa period but a confirmed itinerary is still necessary for the visa. The M.V. Ocean Pearl, the M.V. Leo Tolstoi and the Song of Flowers are cruise ships that dock regularly in Yangon. Information is available from shipping lines. The **Myanmar Five Star Line**, 132/136 Theinbyu Street, Yangon. Tel: 1221, Fax: 00951-89567, is the agent for all foreign lines calling in Burma. It has offices in Japan, Singapore and the United Kingdom and agents in Malaysia, Thailand, Indonesia, Australia, Bangladesh, India, Sri Lanka, Pakistan, South Korea, Honk Kong, in the Peoples Republic of China, in Germany, Holland, Italy and Egypt. (Details under "Useful Addresses".)

Entry Note: Burma's frontiers have long been closed to overland international travel, due primarily to the continuing rebellions by various ethnic groups in the border areas. Since a short while ago it is, however, possible to visit Tatchilek and Kyaing Tong in the Shan State from Mae Sai in northern Thailand. For a day trip the visa is available at the border post. By special arrangement you can proceed on to Kyang Hong in Yunnan through Mai-lar. Similarly, the island of Kawthaung (the former Victoria point) in the Mergui archipelago can be reached from Ranong in southern Thailand. On the Burma-Yunnan border new border posts have been opened at Lwe-ge from where you can go to Bhamo, Ruili, Muse, Nam-Kham and Kun-lone. Organized groups are also permitted to continue via Lashio to Yangon.

The Thai and Burmese governments are constructing a bridge across the Moei river between Mae Sot and Myawaddy which soon should permit land travel between the two countries. If the present development plan is carried through it should be possible to travel by car from Singapore through Burma to India or China and on to Europe.

Useful Addresses
Airline Offices

The following international airlines have offices in Yangon:
Biman Airline, 106 Pansodan Street. Tel: 75882.
Aeroflot, 501/503 Pyay (Prome) Road. Tel: 20295.
Air France, 69 Sule Pagoda Road. Tel: 74119.
Myanmar Airways, 104 Strand Road. Tel: 80710.
Myanmar Airways International, 104, Strand Road. Tel: 84566.
Air China (CAAC), 67-A Pyay (Prome) Road. Tel: 75714.
Pakistan International Airways, 510 Merchant Street.
Thai Airways International, 441-445 Maha Bandoola Street. Tavoy House. Tel: 75988.
North West Orient Airlines, 36 Shwebonta Street. Tel: 81638.
Silk Air, 537 Merchant Street. Tel: 84600.

Business Addresses

While Burma was "Socialist Burma" all businesses were nationalized. These strict rules have now been lifted. The government encourages small private businesses, joint ventures and even 100 percent foreign ownership of factories. The former 11 "trade corporations" have now become "State-owned Economic Enterprises" run by different ministries.

Chambers Of Commerce

The Union of Myanmar Chamber of Commerce and Industry, 74/86 Bo Son Pet Street. Pabedan Township. Tel: 70749.

For those who want to set up joint ventures in Burma, the government has published a booklet, *Guide to Foreign Investment in Myanmar*, that can be ordered at UMFIC, 653/691, Merchant Street Yangon. It contains a wealth of interesting information about the new state of the economy after the socialist system has been abolished. Business Centre: Secretarial services etc. MCC Business Centre, 31 (A) Park Lane, Kokkine. Tel: 51851.

International Organizations In Yangon

United Nations Children's Fund (UNICEF), 132 University Avenue. Tel: 31107, 31895, 31287.
United Nations Development Program (UNDP), 6 Natmauk Road, Yangon. Tel: 92911.
United Nations Program for Drug Abuse Control, Myanmar (UNPDAC), 557A Pyay (Prome) Road. Tel: 32301.
World Health Organization (WHO), 39, Shwetaungyar Road, Yangon. Tel: 31135.
FAO, 56 Shwetaunggya Road. Yangon. Tel: 31281.

Practical Tips

Weights & Measures

Burma has retained many of the old weights and measures in use during the British colonial period.
1 viss (peith-tha) – 1,633 grams, 3.6 lbs
1 tical – 16.33 grams
1 cubit (tong) – 0.457 metres, 18 inches
1 span (htwa) – 0.23 metres, 9 inches
1 lakh – 100,000 (units)
1 crore – 100 lakh

The tin, or basket, is used to measure quantities of agricultural export goods. The kilogram equivalent differs for rice, sesame, and other goods.

Business Hours

Most government offices, including the post office and the Myanmar Airways office, are open 9.30am to 4.30pm Monday through Friday.

Banks are open to the public 10am to 2pm weekdays. The Central Telegraph Office stays open from 8am to 9pm weekdays, and from 8am to 8pm, Sunday and holidays.

The information counter at the Myanmar Travels & Tours office is open seven days a week from 8am to 8pm.

Most restaurants close by 10pm, although some tea and coffee shops will stay open later. Drug stores have staggered days off, so that shops dealing in medicine are always open somewhere.

Tipping is not a common practice in Burma. It is becoming less unusual in Yangon at major tourist hotels; a waiter might probably come running after you to return the change you had intended to leave as a tip! If you wish to show your appreciation for some small service, a gift such as a ball-point pen or a cigarette lighter will be more readily accepted, and perhaps more appreciated, than a monetary tip.

Religious Services

Despite a heavy emphasis on Buddhism, Burma is a country of great religious freedom. The following list of non-Buddhist places of worship in Yangon is indicative.

Roman Catholic

St Mary Cathedral, 372 Bo Aung Kyaw Street. Tel: 72662.
St Augustine's Church, 64 Inya Road. Tel: 30620. Sunday masses at 7 and 9.30am.

Anglican

Cathedral of the Holy Trinity, 446 Bogyoke Aung San Street. Sunday services: communion 7am, communion and sermon 8.30am, Sunday school (children) 9.45am, evensong 5pm.
Church of the Holy Cross, 104 Inya Road. Tel: 30658. Holy communion and sermon at 8am Sunday.

Methodist

Methodist-English Church, 65 Signal Pagoda Road. Tel: 72808. Sunday school 8.30 to 9.30am, morning service 9.45am, Methodist youth fellowship 3.30 to 4.30pm Sunday.

Baptist

Immanuel Church, corner of Maha Bandoola and Barr streets. Tel: 75905. Sunday school 8am, Sunday worship 5pm.

Armenian

St John the Baptist Armenian Church, 113 Bo Aung Gyaw Street at the corner of Merchant Street. Sunday service 9 to 10.30am.

Judaism

There is a Jewish synagogue in 26th Street in Yangon. Call the Israeli Embassy for a current schedule of services.

Islam

Khoja Mosque, Shwebontha Street.
Shia Mosque, 30th Street.
Sunni Mosque, Shwebontha Street.
Sunni Mosque, Maung Taulay Street.
Sunni Mosque, Sule Pagoda Road
Surathi (Sunni) Mosque, Mogul Street.
    Prayers are offered five times daily at all mosques.

Hindu

Hindu Temple, Anawratha Street, near to Thein Ghyi Zei market.
Sri Sri Durga Temple, 307 Bo Aung Gyaw Street.
Sri Sri Siva Krishna Temple, 141 Pansodan Street. Open daily 10 to 11am and 3 to 8pm.

Sikh Temple

Sikh Temple, 256 Theinbyu Road.

Media

Newspapers

The daily English language newspaper is called *The New Light of Myanmar* and is available on newsstands and in all hotels.
    The International Press Club is at 245-247, Anawratha Street. Tel: 22023.

Radio & Television

The **Voice of Myanmar** broadcasts in Burmese, English and eight national languages on 314 MHz and 520 MHz Medium Wave and 30.85 MHz, 50.13 MHz and 63.49 MHz Short Wave.
    Of interest to the linguist might be the "nationalities program" presented daily from 5 to 9.15pm on 63.49 MHz Short Wave. It broadcasts in Kachin, Kayah, Sgaw Kayin (Karen), Pwo Kayin (Karen), Chin, Mon, Bamar, Arakanese and Shan. If they are not jammed, you can listen to the Voice of America and the BBC as many Burmese do.
    Television was introduced to Burma in 1981. The system used is NTSC. Most hotels catering for foreigners in Yangon, Bagan and Mandalay can receive Star TV and a few other foreign

programmes via satellite, and better hotels have TV sets in the room.

Postal Services

The **Yangon General Post Office** (Tel: 85499) is located on Strand Road at the corner of Bo Aung Gyaw Street. All post offices in Burma are open 9.30am to 4.30pm Monday through Friday, and 9.30am to 12.30pm Saturday. They are closed Sunday and public holidays.
    The only exception is the Mingaladon (Yangon) Airport mail sorting office. It is open round-the-clock daily, including Sunday and holidays, for receipt and dispatch of foreign mail. Ordinary letters and postcards will be accepted here at any time. Registered letters can be taken at the airport postal counter only during normal government working hours.
    Foreign postage rates are:
    Aerogrammes, 1.25 *Kyat* to all destinations.
    Postcards, 85 to Asia, 1.30 *Kyat* to Europe and Australia, 1.60 *Kyat* to North America.
    Letters up to one ounce, 1.25 *Kyat* to Asia, 2.15 *Kyats* to Europe and Australia, 2.70 *Kyats* to North America.
    For parcels and other postal rates, the post office should be consulted for a complete rate schedule.
    Inland postage is negligible. Letters are 15 *Pyas* for the first half-ounce, 10 *Pyas* for each additional half-ounce; postcards are a standard 10 *Pyas*.
    Commemorative stamps are occasionally issued. All can be purchased at Yangon's GPO.

Telephone & Telegram

Communication services in Burma are rendered through 1,115 post offices, 65,419 telephones, 310 telegraph offices and 138 telex services (1990). Automatic exchanges are in 24 towns and 195 towns have manual exchanges. Burma has direct satellite links to seven countries: Japan, Hong Kong, Singapore, Thailand, India, UK and Australia. Siemens of Germany has installed additional satellite communication lines that should bring telecommunication connections up to western standard. Most of the new hotels now offer an IDD telephone and fax service to foreign countries. It is cheaper if you telephone or send your fax through the nearest post office, but you will have to wait for a few hours until you get a connection.

The area code for Yangon (Rangoon) is 01; Mandalay is 02; for Bagan it is 35; and for Taunggyi 81. Local calls are free of charge.

Call 101 for an overseas or inland booking between 7am to 7pm, and the operator will call you back at your hotel (or wherever else you may be) when the trunk line is open for your call. For further information, call the information line, Tel: 103, or the trunk supervisor, Tel: 72001.

The **Central Telegraph Office** (Tel: 81133), located one block east of the Sule Pagoda on Maha Bandoola Street, is open from 8am to 9pm Monday through Saturday, and from 8am to 8pm Sunday and public holidays.

If you encounter problems with any of the communications systems, direct your queries to the Myanmar Posts and Telecommunications, 43 Bo Aung Gyaw Street, Tel: 85499.

Tourist Information Service

Train, bus and flight schedules. Yangon, Tel: 75328 or 82075; Mandalay, Tel: 02-22540; Bagan, Tel: 89001; Taunggyi, Tel: 081-21601.
Myanmar Railways: Yangon, Tel: 74027.
Road transport: Yangon, Tel: 76957.
Immigration: Yangon, Tel: 86434.
Customs: Yangon, Tel: 84533.
Yangon Airport: Tel: 62657.
Police: Yangon, Tel: 199/82511.
Fire Brigade: Yangon, Tel: 74211.
Ambulance: Yangon, Tel: 192/71111.
Myanmar Airways: Yangon, Tel: 62712.
Myanmar Airways International: Yangon, Tel: 75988.
Limousine: Yangon, Tel: 64472.

Embassies

Australia, 88 Strand Road. Tel: 80711.
Austria, 16(G), Thallawaddy Road, Myangon. Tel: 73098.
Bangladesh, Kaba Aye Pagoda Road. Tel: 51174.
Belgium, 18B Inya Road. Tel: 32775.
China, 1 Pyidaungsu Yeiktha. Tel: 21280.
France, 102 Pyidaungsu Yeiktha. Tel: 82122.

Germany, 32 Natmauk Street. Tel: 50477, 50603.
India, 545/547 Merchant Street. Tel: 82933.
Indonesia, 100 Pyidaungsu Yeiktha. Tel: 81714.
Italy, 3, Inya Myaing Road, Golden Valley. Tel: 30966, 30474.
Japan, 100 Natmauk Road. Tel: 52288, 52640.
Korea (North), 30 Thantaman (Tank Road) Street. Tel: 73394.
Korea (South), 591 Pyay (Prome) Road. Tel: 30497, 30655.
Laos People's Democratic Republic, A1, Diplomatic Quarters, Tawwin Street. Tel: 22482.
Malaysia, 82,Pyidaungsu Yeiktha Road. Tel: 20284.
Nepal, 167 Natmauk Yeiktha. Tel: 50633.
Netherlands, 53/55, Maha Bandoola Garden Street. Tel: 71495.
Norway (consulate), 48A Komin Kochin Road. Tel: 50011.
Pakistan, A-4 Diplomatic Quarters, Pyay Road. Tel: 22881.
Philippines, 56, Pyay Road. Tel: 64010.
Russian Federation, 38, Sagawa Road. Tel: 72427.
Singapore, 287, Pyay Road. Tel: 33200.
Sri Lanka, 34 Taw Win Street (Fraser Road). Tel: 22812.
Sweden, 80, Strand Road. Tel: 81700.
Thailand, 91 Pyay (Prome) Road. Tel: 82471.
United Kingdom, 80 Strand Road. Tel: 81700.
United States of America, 581 Merchant Street. Tel: 82055.
Vietnam, 40 Komin Kochin Road. Tel: 50361.

Photography

The time when foreign goods were scarce in Yangon's shops is now in the past. For FECs or Dollars you can now get film nearly everywhere. There are also a few automatic film developing shops in Yangon and Mandalay where you can have your film developed within an hour.

Getting Around

From The Airport

There are two ways to get from Mingaladon Airport to downtown Yangon, a distance of 19 kilometres (12 mi). As you pass through the terminal exit, taxi drivers will besiege you in a bid to drive you into the city. What were once huge middle-of-the-century conveyances are now mostly modern taxis with metres. The government has permitted the duty free import of taxis (running with a special number and marked as such) to solve the individual transport problem in the city. Taxis should charge 20 *kyats* per mile. They can also be hired on an hourly or daily basis.

In past years Myanmar Airways (UB) was supposed to provide a bus to its city office for incoming flights, but it was often not available. Due to a SLORC order, however, this has now become a regular service in both directions. The fare is five *Kyats*. Limousines are available at the Tourist Information Service in the arrival hall or through the transport division at the Inya Lake Hotel. Tel: 64472

Domestic Travel

Myanmar Airways controls an intricate network of air routes to 37 localities within Burma. The airline's fleet consists of three Fokker F-28 jets, Fokker F-27s, and Havilland Twin Otter aircraft for routes into smaller airstrips. (A new set of aircrafts is now on order and should soon facilitate domestic travel.) Western tourists, however, will see few of these airports. Without showing a special permit, UB will sell tickets to foreigners only for flights to Mandalay, Bagan, Taunggyi (Heho), and on rarer occasions to Thandwe (Sandoway) and Mawlamyine (Moulmein), plus return flights to Yangon.

Tickets for UB domestic flights could be purchased overseas, but it is probably better to wait until you arrive in Burma. Tickets may be cheaper overseas, but because Myanmar Airways UB (domestic) is not a member of the International Air Transport Association (IATA), it is not bound to honor tickets sold at those prices. Therefore, upon arrival at Yangon, you should try as soon as possible to book an air passage to your next destination; and upon reaching that destination, you should confirm – in person at a UB office – your return flight. Since 1994 you can also fly with Air Mandalay. A new era of comfortable domestic air travel came with the launching of Air Mandalay, a joint venture with a Singaporean company. Air Mandalay serves several domestic destinations with French ATR 72-210 planes and offers western standard service, check-in procedures and flight safety.

Visitors can purchase domestic flight tickets (with foreign exchange only) at Myanmar Travels & Tours offices. The main offices are located at 73, Sule Pagoda Road, just south of the pagoda itself and across the street from Maha Bandoola Park. There are other Myanmar Travels & Tours offices in Bagan, Mandalay and Taunggyi, but Yangon is the most reliable. Since there are only a few flights (and scheduled only during the dry season), most tourists are sent by train to Mandalay.

Despite all precautions, it is still possible that you might get bumped from your seat on the plane. The Burmese government runs an unofficial but nevertheless rigid priority list which can disrupt flight bookings right up to the last minute. Burmese VIPs, of course, have first priority. Behind them, in order, come tour parties, individual foreign visitors, foreign expatriate residents, and – last and least – native residents of Burma.

Water Transport

Burma's rivers provide over 8,000 kilometres (5,000 mi) of navigable routes, and as a result, shipping is the most important means of transportation for much of the country.

The Ayeyarwady (Irrawaddy) River, Burma's lifeline, is navigable from its delta to Bhamo throughout the year, and all the way to Myitkyina during the rainy season. The Twante Canal links the Ayeyarwady to Yangon. The Chindwinn (Chindwin) River – the Ayeyarwady's most important tributary, joining it a short distance above Bagan – is navigable in shallow-bottomed boats for 792 kilometres (492 mi) from Yesagyo to Hkamti.

In the east, the Thanlwin (Salween) River is suitable for shipping only as far as 89 kilometres (53 mi) from its mouth near Mawlamyine to Shwegun. Strong currents funneling through its narrow chasm block further progress. In Rakhine (Arakan), the Kaladan River and the Saing Tin are the most important routes of transportation. The Kaladan is navigable for 177 kilometres (110 mi) from Sittwe (Akyab) to Paletwa and the Saing Tin for 129 kilometres (80 mi) from Sittwe to Buthidaung.

The red-and-black coloured passenger vessels and cargo steamers of the Inland Water Transport are a common sight throughout Burma. Still, the government network is only a little more than half of what it was under the British-owned Irrawaddy Flotilla Company prior to 1948. Equipment is antiquated, and timetables offer only the roughest idea of when boats will arrive and depart. Present boats plying between Yangon and Pyay, Pyay and Mandalay and between Mandalay and Bhamo are of the refitted P-Class type, equipped with 150 and 250 hp diesel engines that have steerable propeller shafts that enable them to free themselves when they get stuck on submerged sandbanks. Three new triple decker boats from China have been introduced in 1995. They will run on the Ayeyarwady, one of them serving the rivers around Mawlamiyne.

The most interesting river route of tourist interest (under present political conditions) is the stretch of Ayeyarwady between Mandalay and Bagan. A boat leaves Mandalay at 5am, arriving in Bagan (Nyaung-U) in the evening. You can travel deck class on the boat, sharing open quarters with monks, soldiers, nursing mothers, chicken and fruit baskets; or you can step up to the "first class" section – a cabin in the prow of the upper deck with four wooden benches and a table. Either way, you should outfit yourself with a blanket or sleeping bag, especially during the winter months, and with mosquito netting or repellent.

The sheer romance of this particular river journey is enough to repay the loss of comfort in triplicate. With the prolonged visa period you can now also take the upriver voyage to Mandalay. It fits better into the UB flight schedule with a daily round-trip Yangon-Bagan-Mandalay-Heho-Yangon.

It is theoretically possible to continue downriver from Bagan to Pyay, and from there take the train to Yangon. This would require several days of travel. A round-trip river journey between Yangon and Mandalay would take up to 21 days. Since 1995 the former "Elbresidenz," a boat that plied the Rhine, is now serving the Ayeyarwady in all colonial splendor as the "Road to Mandalay" between Mandalay and Bagan. Trips are sold as packages starting and ending in Bangkok.

The ultimate adventure trip on the river is, however, flying to Bhamo and taking the boat through the second and third defile down to Mandalay. For this trip one still needs an official permission. This, however, can be obtained through U Myo Yee, Zone Express Tours, 145, 74th Street between 29th & 30th Street, Mandalay, Tel: 22752, priv. 21429. This company ownes a 45-foot boat that can be chartered for trips to Bhamo.

Considerably less time is needed, however, to make the voyage from Yangon to Pathein (Bassein) via the Twante Canal, touching Myaungmya, Maubin, Pyapon and Kyaiklat, all of them typical delta cities with their own charm and lifestyle.

Since July 1989, a new express boat, the Banyardala, leaves Yangon on Monday, Thursday and Saturday for Pathein-Chaungtha. It has 30 modern cabins for tourists. You can also cruise the Yangon River on the *Golden Seagull*, Riverine Pleasure Cruise, and enjoy the city from the water. Tel: 91083.

Ferry service between Yangon's Htinbonseik Jetty and Syriam operates on a commuter basis. Once an hour between 5.30am and 9.45pm, triple-deck boats shuttle back and forth across the Bago (Pegu) River at its confluence with the Yangon River. The trip takes about 45 minutes. Since the construction of the new bridge, however, most people go by car or bus to Syriam.

Another popular ferry trip for tourists is the one across the Ayeyarwady between Mandalay and Mingun. Boats leave from Mandalay's B Road Jetty at 7.30am and 8.30am every day for the one-hour voyage.

The Myanmar Five Star Line (MFSL) manages all overseas routes with a fleet of 25 vessels. Four smaller company ships also link Yangon with Thandwe, Kyaukpyu, Sittwe in Rakhine and Dawei, Myeik and Kawthaung in Tanintharyi.

Rail Transport

Myanmar Railways (Tel: 74027) – like all other important means of transportation, run by the state – has a network of more than 4,000 kilometres (2,500 mi) of track. Yangon's Central Railway Station, of course, is the nation's hub. By day and night, express trains, mail trains and local trains depart on journeys of varying length.

Ordinary (second class) and Upper Class (first class) seating is available on all trains. Upper Class seats cost almost three times Ordinary Class. Sleepers are not readily available for overnight trips. Foreigners must purchase their tickets through Myanmar Travels & Tours, advisably 24 hours in advance if possible. The tourist office has a quota on tickets available during its business hours.

For the main route most often used by tourists, the **Yangon-Mandalay Line** the government has recently bought new Korean coaches. This is the country's finest railway and is highly recommended for the varied view of Burmese village life it offers from its windows. Most tourists will have to use it anyhow, since during peak season there are not enough airplane seats available. Passengers must be willing to put up with a little bump and grind; however, the journey conforms roughly to European expectations. The following departure times are more or less estimates and should be rechecked before planning an onward journey within Burma.

There are three services daily between Yangon and Mandalay. The fastest is the 7am express, which covers the 621 kilometres (386 mi) in 12.5 hours, making only four stops (Bago, Toungoo, Pyinmana and Thazi) along the way and arriving in Central Burma's metropolis at 7.30pm, just in time for you to find a room and a meal. Other trains leave Yangon at 11.45am

(arriving in Mandalay at 4.45am the next day) and 6.45pm (arriving in Mandalay at 7.45am the next day).

The return schedule from Mandalay to Yangon is much the same, with an identical 7am express. The 11.45am from Mandalay arrives in Yangon at 5.05am the next day, and the 6.45pm from Mandalay reaches Yangon at 7.45am the next day.

These times, however, are only those listed on Burmese timetables, which are not always strictly adhered to. Problems of climatic, technical or bureaucratic nature often cause long delays in rail journeys. Nevertheless, the Yangon-Mandalay service is certainly the most reliable in Burma.

From Mandalay, there are train connections to the hill station of Pyin-U-Lwin (Maymyo), 61 kilometres (38 mi) east, from where you are now permitted to continue across the famous Gokteik viaduct to Kyaukme and Lashio. The five-hour rail journey is twice what the trip takes by jeep collective. Other rail trips of interest to tourists might include the following:

Yangon-Thazi Line. Leaves Yangon 3.35pm daily, arriving Thazi 4.55am. Local trains connect Thazi with Shwenyaung, the nearest rail terminus to Taunggyi and Inle Lake; there are also buses which travel west to Bagan from Thazi. The southbound train leaves Thazi 7.50pm, arriving in Yangon 8.15am. Passengers can disembark the Yangon-Mandalay express here, but to board the main line in Thazi might be more difficult: it is usually full.

Yangon-Pyinmana Line. Leaves Yangon 8.07am, arriving in Pyinmana 8.45pm. Local trains cover the 225 kilometres (140 mi) between Pyinmana and Kyaukpadaung. Buses connect Kyaukpadaung with Bagan, about 50 kilometres (31 mi) further west. This rail and bus link is not suggested, however, as it is an exceedingly slow trip that can last up to 36 hours. The southbound train leaves Pyinmana at 4.10am, arriving in Yangon at 6pm. The Yangon-Mandalay train makes a stop in Pyinmana.

Visitors to Toungoo can disembark at that town when any of the three above-mentioned lines stops at the Toungoo station.

Yangon-Martaban Line. Express leaves Yangon 6am, arriving in

Martaban 12.20pm. Local trains leave Yangon 7.20am, arriving in Martaban 5pm; and 6.30am, arriving in Martaban 3.25pm. A train ferry across the Thanlwin River carries travellers from Martaban to Mawlamyine on the opposite bank. The most direct return train from Martaban to Yangon leaves at 1.50pm, arriving in the capital 8.10pm. Other trains depart from Martaban 7.20am, arriving in Yangon 4.20pm, and 8.45am, arriving in Yangon 7.10pm.

Stops can also be made in Kyaik-to or Thaton on this line. This and all previously mentioned lines pass through Bago, and day trippers can embark there as well.

Yangon-Pyay Line. Leaves Yangon 2.30pm, arriving Pyay 8.15pm. Return train leaves Pyay 6am, arriving Yangon 11.50am. A local train also departs from Yangon's Kemendine Station 8.45am daily, arriving Pyay 7.50pm; the southbound local leaves Pyay 7.15am, arriving in Kemendine 6.55pm.

Long-distance rail travellers in Burma will find vendors pushing fruits, curries and soft drinks through the windows of the train at every stop. Burmese trains don't have diners, with the exception of the daytime Yangon-Mandalay express. Therefore, you would be well advised to carry your own food and beverage with you, especially during the dry season.

Journeys outside of the normal tourist areas are not expressly forbidden by government edict. However, they are in practice quite difficult to undertake. Station masters are not allowed to sell tickets to foreigners without special authorization, and Myanmar Travels & Tours avail tickets only for certain routes. For one foreigner's experience in bucking the Myanmar Railways Corporation, see Paul Theroux's *The Great Railway Bazaar*.

Yangon city has a suburban local train service which connects to the national routes. Of greatest interest to the visitor is the **Circular Line**, running both clockwise and counter-clockwise through Yangon Central Station to Insein and Mingaladon in the north, and stopping at all smaller stations in between. The route takes about three hours to complete, but should be avoided during rush hours. Tickets are less than two *Kyats* for the full trip.

Public Transport

Public bus travel, as long as it is not with one of the newly established airconditioned buslines that travel to Bagan and Mandalay, is not recommended for long-distance journeys. Though there are now new Japanese Hino buses in service, most roads are poor, vehicles are overcrowded, and in the event a bus breaks down, it can be hours before mechanical assistance becomes available. However, there are a few routes with which tourists should be acquainted.

The longest journeys are aboard the Road Transport vehicles that ply regular routes from Yangon to Mandalay and to Magway (Magwe) via Pyay. Both routes are also linked with Bagan.

Bagan via Kyaukpadaung, but that's a tedious 16-hour trip. Preferable would be the 10-hour bus ride to Bagan from Mandalay. Buses depart at 4am daily from the corner of 29th Road and 82nd Street.

It's also possible to travel by bus to Taunggyi, capital of the Shan State, from both Bagan and Mandalay. In both cases, it's a fatiguing 12-hour journey. The Taunggyi bus leaves Mandalay between 4 and 5am daily, and leaves Bagan at the same time from near the Myanmar Travels & Tours office. In addition, buses leave hourly for Taunggyi from the rail junction at Thazi, and direct service between Bagan and Taunggyi is available. Check with Myanmar Travels & Tours.

Visitors to Mandalay can reach the ancient capitals of Amarapura and Innwa (Ava) by taking the No. 8 bus south from the city.

From Yangon, buses run the 80 kilometres (50 mi) to Bago on a regular half-hourly basis. The terminal is on 18th Street, near the Chinese quarter west of downtown.

Yangon city is served by an extensive network of local buses which connect Yangon with the new satellite towns that have been created after 1989.

Private Bus & Limousine Service

The Rainbow Express Company runs comfortable air-conditioned buses between Yangon and Mandalay and Yangon and Bagan. (Yangon: 96/98 Pansodan Street. Tel: 72250/Manda-lay: 262 (B) 29th Street, between 82nd & 83rd streets. Tel: 02-28809.)

Other Local Transport

Bicycle trishaws are the most popular means of getting around the streets of the larger cities. Easily available and cheap, they take their passengers – who sit back to back – anywhere in the city they want to go.

For longer trips in the vicinity of Yangon, Mandalay and other large population centers, jeep collectives or "pick-ups" – not unlike the collectivos of Latin America – do yeoman's work carrying large numbers of riders. They don't follow a set schedule; instead, they take off whenever the last seat is taken. For journeys from Yangon to Bago and from Mandalay to Pyin-U-Lwin, this is a cheap, fast means of transportation.

In Burma's dry central plain, especially in the areas of Mandalay and Bagan, there are many horse-drawn cabs, or *tongas*. They are slow moving, but are well-suited for sightseeing trips. In smaller towns and villages, high-wheeled ox carts often are counted upon for transportation.

Taxis

Cab drivers wait in front of all the big tourist hotels in Yangon, anxious to carry visitors to their destinations. Private vehicles are no more the largely oversized remnants of America autos of the 1950s, they have mostly been substituted by newer Japanese models.

Taxis with meters charge 20 kyats per mile. Although Myanmar Travels & Tours has fixed rates for most regular routes, you'll probably have to haggle with the drivers of taxis without metres to bring their rates down to a reasonable level. Still, taxis are probably the best way to explore the countryside surrounding Yangon, especially if one is able to share the fare with other passengers. Limousines are available through the transport division at the Inya Lake Hotel. Tel: 64472.

Where To Stay

Hotels

Burma is fast becoming a premier tourist destination. After only 32,000 tourists in 1989 and 100,000 in 1994, the present estimate for 1996, named the Visit Myanmar Year, is 500,000. Since 1992, many huge hotel construction projects are on their way to being finished. Except for a multitude of smaller private hotels, 17 large hotel projects are now being carried out, 13 of them in Yangon, scheduled to cater for the onslaught of tourists before, during and after Visit Myanmar Year. In Yangon, it's the Summit Park View Hotel on Ahlone Road with 265 rooms, the Floatel at the Wadan Jetty with 132 rooms, the rebuilt Baiyoke Kandawgyi Hotel with 231 rooms, the Sedona Yangon Hotel on Kaba Aye Pagoda Road with 450 rooms, the Nawarat Hotel on Insein Road with 120 rooms, the Emerald Rose Garden on Bo Min Gaung Road with 315 rooms, the Shangri-La Hotel on Kan Yeikhta Road with 700 rooms, the Traders Hotel Yangon on Sule Pagoda Road with 496 rooms and the Central Hotel on Bogyoke Aung San Street with 82 rooms. Also both the prestigious Strand and the Inya Lake Hotels, as well as the old Thamada Hotel, are now renovated and enlarged.

In Mandalay, the Mandalay Hotel with 104 rooms has been upgraded and will have a swimming pool and a tennis court, and the new Yadanabon Hotel at the foot of Mandalay Hill will have 200 plus rooms. According to plan, by 1996 there should be 5,000 rooms available in Yangon, more than 2,000 in Mandalay and up to 400 in Bagan and Taunggyi.

The **Paradise Resort** at the Burmese-Thai-Laos border is run in cooperation with Vitavas International of Thailand, the **Thahtay Kyun Resort Hotel** on Thahtay Kyun (an island once known as Palo Ru in the Mergui archipelago, just off the Thai port of Ranong) is a joint venture with Thailand's Union Farm Engineering. An 80-room chalet type hotel in Bagan and a 60-room hotel on Inle Lake are to be built in collaboration with the French company Asia Voyages.

In the following list of accommodations, you can expect to pay US$80 and more a night (double) at luxury hotels, about half that at first-class and private hotels, and as little as US$2 or US$3 a night at hostels.

Since the change over to a free market economy, many private hotels have opened in Yangon, Mandalay and Bagan. They charge between US$20 and 80 for a double room. They are often affiliated with some of the private tour organizations, have only a few rooms and are rarely in the town centre. Nevertheless, they offer an inexpensive way to stay for a prolonged period. You'll find most of their addresses at the end of the list after the official MT&T controlled hotels. Representatives of tour agencies and private hotels are normally at the airport when the flights from Bangkok come in. Some of them even have stalls in the arrival hall.

Yangon

Inya Lake Hotel, 229 rooms, standard to deluxe suite. Kaba Aye Pagoda Road. Tel: 62866. Restaurant, cocktail lounge, swimming pool, tennis, putting green, barber shop, beauty salon, conference facilities. Opened 1961.

Kandawgyi Hotel, Kanyeiktha Road. 35 rooms, standard, superior and chalet. Tel: 82255, 82327. On lakeshore; located on the site of former Museum of Natural History and the Orient Boat Club.

Strand Hotel, At present 32 suites (US$280) with another 40 rooms when the Strand Annex is completed. 92 Strand Road. Tel: 81533. Restaurant, bar. Opened 1901.

Thamada (President) Hotel, 58 rooms, economy to suite. 5 Signal Pagoda Road. Tel: 71499. Restaurant, bar. Opened 1972.

Summit Parkview, 252 rooms. One of the first modern hotels in Yangon. 350, Ahlone Road.

Nawarat Hotel, 80 rooms, western standard and comfort. 275, Insein Road. Tel: 65794, Fax: 65971.

Dagon (Orient) Hotel, 12 standard and economy rooms. 256 Sule Pagoda Road. Tel: 71140. Restaurant, bar.

Garden Hotel, 16 standard and economy rooms. Sule Pagoda Road, South Block. Tel: 71516. Opened 1979.

Sakhanta Hotel, 13 standard rooms, with or without air-conditioning. Central Railway Station. Tel: 82975.

YMCA, 19 rooms. 265 Maha Bandoola Road. Tel: 71408.

View Kan Taw Yeik Hotel, 11 rooms. 21 (A) Natmauk Lane 2. Tel: 51313.

Jade Pavilion Myanmar, 17 rooms. 126 (A) Dhammazedi Road, Bahan. Tel: 86021.

Tropical Comfort, 5 rooms. 4 Shwe Lee Street, Kamayut. Tel: 33370.

Fair View Inn, 5 rooms. 16, Saw Maha Street. Tel: 53526.

Inya Villa, 6 rooms. 9/3 Martin Yeikhta, 0.5 mile, Hlaing. Tel: 33941.

Asia Villa, 55 Inya Maing Road, Bahan. Tel: 33536.

Bright Corner Inn, 38 Bawdi Yeiktha, Bahan. Tel: 31958.

Capital Motel, 45, Parami Yeiktha, Yankin. Tel: 65829.

Comfort Inn, 4, Shweli Road. Tel: 33377.

Cozy Guest House, 126, 52nd Street. Tel: 91623.

Crown Inn, 38 (B), Bawdi Yeiktha, Golden Valley. Tel: 32081.

Decent Gate Lodging House, 6 rooms. 133(F), Mawyawaddy Street, Block 5, Mayangone. Tel: 61383.

Euro Asia Hotel, 374, Strand Road. Tel: 96731.

Golden Inn, 14, Pyay Road. Tel: 30014.

7 Mile Inn, 12(F), Pyithu Lane, Mayangone. Tel: 62484.

Green Hill Inn, 12, Po Sein Street, Natmauk Yeiktha. Tamwe. Tel: 50330.

Guest Care Hotel, 107(A), Dhammazedi Road. Tel: 83171.

Happy Inn, 7, Pyay Road. Tel: 32009.

Happy Journey Hotel, 56, Saya San Road. Tel: 50997.

Highland Inn, 9(A), Kone Myint Yeiktha Road. Tel: 63855.

Highland Lodge, 1, Highland Avenue. Tel: 61642.

Jupiter Inn, 102, Dhammazedi Road. Tel: 81846.

Lace Inn, 26, Kaymar Street, Sanchaung. Tel: 22669.

Lotus Villa Inn, 8, Kanthayar Lane, Ngwe Kya Yan Yeikhta. Tel: 58292.

Mo Mo Villa Inn, 81(A) 11, Supaung Lane, Inya Maing, Bahan. Tel: 30814.

Windermere Inn, 15 (A) Aungmyngaung Ave. Tel: 33846.

Aungban

Myat Ma Naw Guest House, Taunggyi Road, Aungban. Tel: 164.

Bago (Pegu)

Shwewatun Hotel, 40 rooms, economy and standard. (air-conditioned, plus 25 percent). Tel: 052-21263.

Chaungtha

Chaungtha Beach Hotel, 14 rooms, superior and suite. Tel: 042-22587 or 01-89589.

Mandalay

Mandalay Hotel, 112 rooms, economy to suite. Corner of 26th Road and 68th streets. Restaurant, bars, beer garden, bakery. Tel: 02-22499.

Innwa Hotel, 54 rooms. Corner of 66th and 23rd streets. Tel: 02-27028.

Myamandala Hotel, 48 standard air-conditioned rooms. Corner of 27th and 69th streets. Tel: 02-21283. Restaurant serves Burmese, Chinese and European cuisines. Bar, coffee-shop, swimming pool.

Mannmyo Hotel, 12 rooms. Recently opened economy class hotel. 78th Street, near railway station. Tel: 02-26889.

Hotel Sapphire, 223, 83rd Street, between 28th and 29th streets. Tel: 02-24129.

Silver Cloud Hotel, 40 rooms. Corner of 73rd and 29th streets. Tel: 02-27059.

April Moon Hotel, 133, 31st Street between 76th and 77th streets. Tel: 02-27710.

Central Hotel, 156, 27th Street, between 80th and 81st streets. Tel: 02-25856.

Emerald Land Inn, 9, 14th Street, between 87th and 88th streets. Tel: 02-22813.

Gold Star Hotel, 149, 84th Street, between 30th and 31st streets. Tel: 02-24374.

Kaung Myint, 21 rooms. 502, 80th Street between 39th and 31st streets. Tel: 02- 22790.

King Hotel, 543, 36th Street, between 81st and 82nd streets. Tel: 02-22149.

Hotel Venus, 27 rooms. No. 22, 28th Street between 80th and 81st streets. Tel: 02-25612.

Golden Express Hotel, 10 rooms. Salain 34, 9th Street.

Tiger Hotel, 628, 28 rooms. 82nd Street between 36th and 37th streets. Tel: 02-23134.
Sabai Byu, 62 rooms. No. 58, 81st Street between 25th and 26th streets. Tel: 02-25377.

Bagan

Thiripyitsaya Hotel, 68 rooms, superior. Tel: 89000. Restaurant, gardens, swimming pool, conference facilities.
Ayeyar Hotel, 45 rooms. The former Irra Inn, on the banks of the Ayeyarwady. Tel: 25, near Bupaya Pagoda.
Golden Express Hotel, 15 rooms. Wekyi-in Village. Tel: 37.
Co-operative Hotel, 22 rooms. Bagan. Tel: 40.

All the old resthouses in the center of Bagan were torn down when the village had to move out of the temple area to a place about 8 kilometres (5 mi) south. Most of the resthouses have been rebuilt there.

Paradise, **Sithu**, **Mya Thida**, **Burma**, **Min Chan Myei**, **Aung Tha Haya**, **Bagan**, **Moe Moe**, **Zar Nee**, **Mother** and **Kyi Kyi Mya**. Since 1991 there are also private travel agents in Burma. Two of them have already bought land in New Bagan where they intend to build hotels that can be booked without using the services of Myanmar Travels & Tours.

Kalaw

Kalaw Hotel, 24 rooms, economy to superior. Tel: 47.

Kawthaung

Kawthaung Motel, 31 rooms.

Kyaing Tong

Kyaing Tong Hotel, 12 rooms.

Kyaikhtiyo

Kyaikhtiyo Hotel, 24 rooms. Can be used by groups of above five on their way to the Kyaik-tiyo Pagoda (trip of 2 days/1 night package at US$400).

Letkhokkon

Letkhokkon Hotel, 30 rooms.

Mawlamyine

Mawlamyine Hotel, 24 rooms. Strand Road. Tel: 032-22560.
Thanlwin Hotel, 15 rooms. Lower Main Road, Bo Lone. Tel: 032-21518.

Meiktila

Meiktila Hotel, Yangon – Mandalay Road. 10 rooms, superior and chalet. Tel: 064-21892.
Wunzin Hotel, Fine view of the lake. 30 rooms, standard, with/without air-conditioned suites. Nandaw Gone Qr. Tel: 064-21559.

Monywa

Monywa Hotel, 24 chalets. Ah-Lone Road. Tel: 071-21549.

Muse

Muse Hotel, 40 rooms.

Nyaung Shwe

Inle Khaung Daing Hotel, 30 rooms, dormitory to suite.
Inle Inn, Yone Gyi Road, Yaungshwe. Tel: 16.
Golden Express Hotel, 11 rooms. No. 19, Foungtawpyan Road. Tel: 37.

Pathein (Bassein)

Pathein Hotel, Pathein – Monywa Road, 15 rooms. Tel: 042-21162.
Pathein New Hotel, Kanthonesint. Tel: 042-21783.

Pindaya

Pindaya Hotel, 23 rooms, superior.

Pyay

Pyay Hotel, 20 standard rooms. Strand Road. Tel: 053-21890.

Pyi-U-Lwin

Nanmyaing Hotel, 30 rooms, standard. Tel: 2047.
Thiri-Myaing Hotel. It is the former Candacraig, also known as Maymyo Inn. 12 rooms, dormitory to standard. Tel: 2118.
Cherry Myaing Hotel, (State Guest House No. 1) 12 suites.
Yuzana Myaing Hotel, (State Guest House No. 2) 5 superior rooms.
Thazin Myaing Hotel, (State Guest House No. 3) 6 standard rooms.
Gandamar Myaing Hotel, (State Guest House No. 4) 5 standard rooms.

Shwedaung

Shwedaung Guest House, 10 standard rooms. Not far from Pyay. Tel: 053-21890.

Sittwe

Sun and Moon Rest House.

Taunggyi

Taunggyi (Strand) Hotel, 56 rooms. Tower Road. Restaurant, bar.
Sarmaing Hotel, Economy hotel close to the Taunggyi hotel. There are some other hotels and guest houses in Taunggyi. They are, however, rarely used by foreigners.
Bawzia Hotel, May Kyu Inn, Myo Daw Guest House, San Pya Inn, Shan States Hotel, Thee Thant Hotel.

Thandwe

Ngapali Beach Hotel, 34 rooms. Tel: 10128.
Shwewargyaing Hotel, 26 rooms, standard and economy.

Thazi

Moon Light, 15 rooms. Meiktila – Taunggyi Road. Tel: 56.

Toungoo

Toungoo Hotel, 14 Rooms. Tel: 054-21764.

Any traveller moving off the normal tourist routes should always carry a sleeping bag or blankets, as pagodas, temples and monasteries will usually make floor space available for a night or two. The proverbial hospitality of the Burmese may also come to the rescue: it isn't all that unusual for Burmese to invite a total stranger to spend the night in their home. In this case, however, you'll have to report to the nearest authorities.

Many towns that served as regional administrative centers during the period of British rule have "circuit houses." Then as now, these are primarily reserved for traveling state officials. However, if the tourist has been granted official permission to travel outside the normal tourist areas, there is a good chance of finding overnight accommodation at these inns.

Eating Out

What To Eat

Below is a categorized list of food items and their respective English translations easily available on any Burmese restaurant menu.

Soups

Ah Nyar Hin Cho. Upper Burma lentil soup.
Chin Ye Hin. Spicy fish soup.
Bu Thee Hin Khar. Clear soup with vermicelli and gourd.
Kin Mone Ywet Hin Khar. Clear soup with herbal leaves.

Appetizers

Pa Zun nga paung kyaw. Deep fried prawns with onions.
Ginn Thoke. Pickled ginger salad with fried condiments.
Nga Paung Kyaw. Deep fried beansprouts with fish.
Bu Thee Kyaw. Fried gourd with batter.
Ah Kyaw Sone. Selection of deep fried appetizers.

Salads

Pe Thee Thoke. Long bean salad.
Dha – wei Tha – nat Sone. Mixed vegetable salad (Dawei speciality).
Pa Zun Thoke. Prawn salad.
Myin Khwar Ywet Thoke. Herbal leaves salad.
Ngar Phe Thoke. Pounded fish salad.
Kyet Thar Thoke. Burmese chicken salad.

Vegetables

Ah Sone Kyaw. Mixed-fried vegetables.
The Sone Hin. Vegetables in curry sauce.
Kha Yan Thee Hnat. Eggplant curry with shrimps.
Mho Ne Ka Zun Ywet Kyaw Chet. Mushrooms with watercress.

Curries

Kyet Tha Hin. Chicken Curry.
Wet Tha Hin Lay. Pork Curry.
Ah Mae Tha Hnat. Beef Curry.

Ngar See Pyan. Fish Curry with tomatoes.
Bae Tha Hin. Duck Curry.
Pa Zun Ne Ahloo Hin. Prawn Curry and potatoes.

Seafood

Ngar Doke Kha. Red snapper with garlic and parsley.
Pa Zun Oh Kat. Shrimp with chili.
Nga Su See. Yangon fish fillet.
Mawlamyine Nga Thalauk Paung. Fish steamed in lemongrass, ginger and garlic.

Meat Dishes

Wet Tha A Sat Kyaw. Pork with chilies and onions.
Sin Gaw Hut. Minced meat sauteed with mint and ginger.
Kyet Tha Cho Chet. Chicken with basil.

Desserts

Rakhine Nget Pyaw Paung. Steamed banana with coconut milk.
Mote Kyar Sae. Sticky rice, lotus seeds and syrup.
Thaku Pyin. Sago with coconut milk.

Where To Eat

Chinese, Indian and European food – and, of course, the spicy curries and fish dishes typical of Burmese cuisine – are available at restaurants throughout the country. Here's a listing of some of them:

Yangon

EUROPEAN FOOD

Inya Lake Hotel, Kaba Aye Pagoda Road. Tel: 50644.
Strand Hotel, 92, Strand Road. Tel: 81533.
Michiko Furusato Restaurant, 137, West Shwegondaing Road. Tel: 52265.

WESTERN AND JAPANESE FOOD.

Golden View Restaurant on the southern approach to the Mahawizaya Pagoda. Tel: 80425.

BURMESE AND CHINESE FOOD

Mya Kan Tha, 70, corner of Natmauk Road and Pho-Sein Rd. Tel: 52712.
Burma Kitchen, 141 Shwegondine Road. Tel: 50493.
Nan Yu Restaurant, 81, Pansodan Street. Tel: 77796.

Nagani Restaurant, 148, Pyay Road. 8.5 mile. Tel: 60871.
Panda Restaurant, 205, Wadan Street, 177 Min Ye Kyaw Swa Road. Tel: 21152.
Ruby Restaurant, 50, Bo Aung Kyaw Street. Tel: 71106.
Yadana Garden Restaurant, at the foot of Southern Stairway of Shwedagon Pagoda. Tel: 77351.
Yankin Restaurant, 1a, Kan Be Road, Yankin. Tel: 64127.
Yin Swe Restaurant, 137, University Ave. Kamayut. Tel: 30316.
People's Park Restaurant, Pyay Road. Tel: 87022.
Danubyu, Anawrahta and 28th streets.
Karaweik Restaurant, East Shore Royal Lake. Tel: 52352.
Kyaiklat (*mohinga shop*), Myenigone, West Yangon.
U Than Maung Daw Dwe May, 33-12th Street.
Chung Wah Restaurant, 162 Sule Pagoda Road.
Hai Yuan Restaurant, 29 University Avenue.
Hwan Chyu Restaurant, 98 Kaba Aye Pagoda Road.
Kan Bow Za Restaurant, 120 Sule Pagoda Road.
Kwan Lock Restaurant, 67-22nd Street.
Nam Sin Restaurant, 120 Pyay (Prome) Road, 8th Mile.
Nan Yu Restaurant, 81 Pansodan Street.
New Oi Hkun Restaurant, 75 Latha Street.
Palace Restaurant, 84-37th Street.
Star Garden, Wingate Road.
Thamada Hotel, 5 Signal Pagoda Road. Tel: 71499.
Wah Min Restaurant, 79 Godwin Road.
Panda Restaurant, 205, Warden Street. Tel: 21152.

There are also street stalls selling Burmese food at numerous locations throughout Yangon.

THAI FOOD

Sala Thai, 56, Saya san Road. Tel: 50997.

INDIAN FOOD

Dagon (Orient) Hotel and Restaurant, 256/260 Sule Pagoda Road. Tel: 71140.
Hotel de City, 232 Anawrahta Street.

Also, the Indian quarter has many small restaurants and food stalls. Try the Biryani chicken shop on the street level of the Surathi Mosque in Mogul Street.

SNACK SHOPS

Mya Sabe Cafe, 71 Pansodan Street.
People's Patisserie, 345 Bogyoke Aung San Street. Tel: 76579.
Yatha Confectionery, 458/460 Maha Bandoola Street. Tel: 70281.

As a consequence of the new economic policy a series of new restaurants have opened all over the country. Some of the Yangon restaurants are supposed to be very good but they have to stand the test of time. Here are a few of the newly opened restaurants that offer Burmese and western food and cater especially to tourists:
Croissant Bakery House, 779, Maha Bandola Street. Tel: 25414.
Ever Green Restaurant, 85/87, Theibyu Street. Tel: 75832.
Green Garden Restaurant, 23, Sinkan Road. Tel: 056-25032.
Jimmy Restaurant, 150(A) New University Avenue Road. Tel: 30510.
My Other Place Restaurant, 28, A-1 Kokkine Swimmingpool Road. Tel: 50586.
Oriental House Restaurant, 126 (A) Myoma Kyaung Road. Tel: 84068.
Royal Rose Restaurant, 221, Shwegondine Road. Tel: 52707.
Sylvan European Restaurant, 71 Pansodan Road. Tel: 89178.

An open-air roof-top restaurant, is atop the Peoples Department Stores, Shwedagon Pagoda Road.

Mandalay

BURMESE AND CHINESE FOOD

Tu-Tu Lay Shop, corner of 74th Street and 28th Street.
Nyaung Bin Yin, 278-29th Road.
Sa Khan Thar Restaurant, 24, 72nd Street, between 27th and 28th streets. Tel: 02-21066.

EUROPEAN FOOD

Kanbawza Restaurant, 502-80th Street.
Kin Kyi Restaurant, 189-29th Road.
Mandalay Hotel, corner 26th Road and 3rd Street. Tel: 4.
Meiktila Parker, 191-29th Road.
Shan Pin Restaurant, 199-29th Road.

Shanghai Restaurant, 172-84th Street.
Shwe Wah, 80th Street between 32nd and 33rd roads.

SNACK SHOPS

Nylon Ice Cream Bar, 83rd Street between 25th and 26th roads.
Olympic Cafe, 83rd Street between 25th and 26th roads.

SHAN FOOD

Khan Shwe Wa, corner 25th Street and 84th Street.

Pyi-U-Lwin

CHINESE FOOD

Lay Ngoon Restaurant, Mandalay-Lashio Road.
Shanghai Restaurant, Mandalay-Lashio Road.

Bagan

EUROPEAN FOOD

Thiripyitsaya Hotel, Tel: 28.

BURMESE FOOD

Aye Yeik Tha Ya, Nyaung U.
Mya Yatana, Wetkyi-in.
Nation, Nyaung U.
Yar Zar, Myinkaba.

TEA SHOPS

Nay Pyi Taw, New Bagan.
Yar Kyaw, New Bagan.
Bagan Tea shop, New Bagan.

Tauynggyi

EUROPEAN

Taunggyi (Strand) Hotel. Tel: 21127.

If you'd like to eat good home-style Burmese food, you should visit the **Mandalay Restaurant** in Bangkok, 23/17 Soi Ruam Rudee. Tel: 255-2893. The owner, a Burmese, takes pride in keeping the haute cuisine of Burma alive.

Drinking Notes

Western-style nightlife has been non-existent in Burma. However, most of the better hotels make it possible for visitors to imbibe spirits, both domestic and imported, and to sample Mandalay Beer from the People's Brewery. The bar of the Inya Lake Hotel has

become the 'in place' where resident foreigners meet every evening. There are Karaoke Lounges at the Thamada Hotel and at the New Park Restaurant on Theinbyu Road (Tel: 82267), and the new Nawarat Hotel is even supposed to have a discotheque. Soon Yangon will have a series of western style meeting places for the 'after dark' hours. During these times of change a little inquiry will let you know where people meet.

The Inya Lake Hotel has also a formal cocktail lounge, while the Strand, Thamada and Dagon hotels have pleasant bars. The Nanthida Pub, adjacent to the Strand, has a beer garden, and the Win Bar, across the street from the Dagon Hotel, also serves drinks.

In Mandalay, and in other provincial cities, beer and spirits are sold only through government hotels (although some guest houses buy from the bigger hotels and resell to their patrons for a higher price). The foreigner's meeting place in Mandalay is the bar of the newly renovated, joint venture Mandalay Hotel.

In addition to the local beer, there is also rum, whisky and gin made in Burma. You'll see bottles of many imported liquors, particularly Scotch whisky, for sale in night markets, but this is considerably more expensive here than if you were to buy it outside of the country.

Attractions

Things To Do

The Myanmar Hotels and Tourism Services' subsidiary, Myanmar Travels & Tours, has full information on all activities the government feels ought to be of interest to tourists. The **Myanmar Travels & Tours** office is located in downtown Yangon at 77-79 Sule Pagoda Road, and is open normal government business hours. There are branch offices in the other three tourist destinations actively promoted by the government – Mandalay, Bagan and Taunggyi.

During the last few years over 100 private tour operators have gone into business in Yangon and Mandalay. They are more flexible than MT&T but have less possibilities. Anyhow, you will need a tour operator if you want to visit an outlying destination. The tour operators will get the permits and will most probably have the guide to accompany you. Most of them can accommodate you in Yangon and Mandalay and they all have cars to venture across the country.

Other destinations than those on the classic round trip fall into two classes: those forbidden for travel, and those accessible but not encouraged.

Forbidden areas are the rebel-held regions of Burma's northeast and south. There, civil war continues between the rebellious ethnic minorities (Shan and Kayin) and government troops. (The government has signed peace agreements with 15 ethnic groups during the early 1990s). Military roadblocks mark the end of areas of government control; beyond there, anyone could step on unmarked land mines or fall prey to an ambush.

However, there are many places which, although not on the list of routes actively promoted by Myanmar Travels & Tours, are not on the "main itinerary" of the government tourist bureau, but which, for a price, and accompanied by a guide, can be visited. These include towns like Pathein, Pyay, Toungoo and Mawlamyine, Myitkyina, Bhamo, Mogok, etc. The list becomes longer and longer every month. Nonetheless, if you make your own arrangements, you will probably encounter obstacles.

The present official list which distinguishes between individual (I) and package tours (P) include the following places:

Kachin State: Mohnyin, Hopin, Indawgyi, Mogaung, Myitkyina, Putao, Bhamo (P) – Myitkyina, Bhamo (I).
Northern Shan State: Up to the Chinese border via Lashio, Muse, Namkhan and Kutkai or Lashio via Konlone. Coming from China to Mandalay, Yangon via Lashio (P) – Lashio (I).
Southern Shan State: Up to Kyaing Tong and Tachilek (P) Up to Kalaw, Pindaya, Inle Lake, Taunggyi and Lawksawk (I)

Coming from Thailand: Up to Kyaing Tong (P, I)
Coming from China: Up to Kyaing Tong and Tachilek via Mai Lar and up to Tachilek via Wun Pon Jetty (P).
Kayah State: Up to Loikaw (P, I).
Rakhine State: Sittwe, Myohaung, Taungkoke, Thandwe, Ngapali and Gwa. Nga Tine Chaung-Gwa motorway and Pyay Taungkoke motorway (P, I).
Kayin State: Up to Pa-an and Hlaing Bwe (P).
Mon State: Kyay-tyio, Thaton, Belugyun (P) – Kyaikmaraw, Thanpyu, Zayat and Kyaikkami (I).
Tanintharyi Division: Da We, Maungmakan, Lanpi Island, Zadatgyi Island (excluding Navy base) (P) – Myeik, Kawthaung (I).
Ayeyarwady Division: Myaung Mya, Pathein, Chaungtha, Nge Thine Chaung and Bogalay (P).
Sagaing Division: Monywa, Kyaukka, Butalin, Twin Taung, Phowin Taung, Yinmarpin, Flooding Wells and Alaungtaw Kathapa. Kale, Homalin, Khanti (P).
Chin State: Falam, Haka and Tiddim (P).
Gems mines area: Mogok, Phakant, Mai Shoo and Pearl Island (P).
Along the Ayeyarwady: Bhamo-Mandalay-Bagan-Yangon-Delat area (P).

Tour Packages

Trips to Burma have always been controlled by Myanmar Travels and Tours (the former Tourist Burma) which until recently had a monopoly on tourist related business in the country. Since the summer of 1991, however, other private tour operators are now permitted to organize trips to and around Burma. For the time being they still have to rely on the available hotel rooms which are controlled by Myanmar Hotels and Tourism Services, the parent company of Myanmar Travels and Tours. For some time, until more privately owned hotels are built in Burma, their tour offers will not be much different from what the government tourist organization arranges.

The larger foreign travel agencies still work together with Myanmar Travels and Tours, buying packages from them that include, transport, accommodation, food and sightseeing. Of those companies outside of Burma two operators from Bangkok have the longest experience:

Diethelm Travel, 544 Ploenchit Road, Bangkok; and **Skyline Travel Service**, 491/39-40 Silom Plaza, Silom Road, Bangkok. Tel: 233-1864; Fax: 237-6696.

Skyline offers diverse tour schedules, and direct links to the tourism authorities in Yangon make it the ideal operator for individuals who'd like to travel to Burma.

Mandalay Myanmar Tours, a subsidiary of Skyline Travel Service in Bangkok (same address), organizes also special tours from Yangon to: Myohaung (Mrauk-U), Syriam and Kyauktan, by boat along the Twante Canal, to Pyay and Sri Ksetra, to the Phaung Daw U Pagoda Festival, to Sandoway, to Mt Popa, to Bago, to the Kyaik-tiyo Pagoda (the Golden Rock) and to Chaungtha Beach Resort. They also arrange special programs for certain festivals in Burma. Special group tours are conducted for 5 to 12 participants.

The least expensive way to travel in Burma is to just book the flight and use the mandatory exchanged FECs to pay for accommodation and travel.

This, however, is only recommended to seasoned travelers, otherwise you are better off buying the whole package already before entering the country. At peak season you might have difficulties arranging for your onward stay.

Packages to Burma normally include flight to Yangon, airport tax (Bangkok US$8, Yangon US$6), transfer airport – hotel – airport, accommodation sharing twin in economy hotels, three meals (budget tours only breakfast), domestic transport, sightseeing and entrance fees.

A typical 15-day tour would be: Bangkok-Yangon-Mandalay-Pyin-U-Lwin-Mandalay-Bagan-Kalaw-Pindaya Caves-Lake Inle-Taunggyi-Thazi-Yangon-Bangkok. The economy price would be around US$1,500 and the budget price US$1,000.

The fares for an 8-day trip which includes Mandalay and Bagan would be in the region of US$800 and US$530 respectively.

Myanmar Travels & Tours offers a tour to Thandwe, the beach resort on Rakhine's Bay of Bengal coast, during the dry season (November to February). While not a likely destination for a first-time visitor to Burma, Thandwe is an attractive alternative. Occasionally, especially if called for by a group of Japanese war veterans, Myanmar Travels & Tours will arrange a tour to Mawlamyine. Excursions to Mount Popa, the Pindaya Caves, the Golden Rock and other off-the-beaten-track locations can also be arranged. Special pilot tours have been run to Rakhine.

Myanmar Travels & Tours also conducts half-day tours of Yangon city, and full-day excursions to Bago and Syriam from Yangon.

As an individual traveler to Burma you have two choices within the context of a two-week stay. You can travel through the country, taking in as many sights as possible; or you can dawdle in one or two locations, soaking up the culture and atmosphere.

Generally speaking, groups have an easier time traveling in Burma than individuals. Myanmar Travels & Tours pre-plans all group travel, including hotels and flight or train arrangements.

The individual traveller, however, will better be able to absorb the "lost, old-time travel feeling" of which Somerset Maugham stories are a reminder. Financially, the individual's trip won't be as costly as that of the group traveler, but taking the upcoming growth in tourism into account there will be complications in finding accommodation and transportation.

Many new private travel agencies have opened during the last few years, mostly run by openminded young entrepreneurs they often can arrange for accommodation and transport when MT&Ts hotels and means of transportation are fully booked.

Akai Travels and Tours, 131/3 42nd Street. Tel: 94751.
Ambika Tour Agency Ltd., 243, 39th Street. Tel: 83496.
Ayeyarwady Travels and Tours, 57/59 Yaw Myin Gyi Street. Tel:84142.
Colourful Land Tours Co., 118, Myanma Gonyi Road.
Cozy Travels and Tours, 12 (A) Shwe Hnin Zi Road.
Free Bird Tours, 213, Bo Myat Tun Street. Tel: 71031.
Golden Express Ltd., 56, Wardan Street. Tel: 21479.
Golden Land Travel Services, 214 (2A) Bo Aung Gyaw Street. Tel: 83827.
Lion Star Tours and Travel Co. Ltd., 54 G/F Yegyaw Street. Tel: 95095.

Mya Thiri Tourism and Tours, 507, Pyay Road.
Princess Tours Co., Ltd., 213, Bo Myat Htun Street. Tel: 94586.
Rubyland Co. Ltd., 90, Upper Pansodan Street. Tel: 81216.
Thutya Tours and Travels, 192, 39th Street. Tel:72912.

GUIDE SERVICES

Yangon:
U Mya Win Maung (German and English). Tel: 64777.
U Soe Myint (French). Tel: 85116.
Ms Htay Htay Tin (French and English). Tel:81391, 65068.
Ms Rose Martha (English and Japanese). Tel: 53109.
Khin Myat Thu Mary (English). Tel: 87792.

ENTRANCE FEES

The Chinese have not only been an example (Peking/Beijing) when many English language names were changed in accordance with the local pronunciation, they also invented the idea that a tourist should pay additionally wherever there is an extraordinary sight. Since April 1989 the Burmese have copied these awkward rules. Entering the sacred Shwedagon or the Maha Muni Pagoda, Burmese enter freely since it is a place of worship, foreigners, however, have to pay four or five dollars.

One of the joys of staying in Yangon is to visit the Shwedagon several times a day, according to the time of the day and the mood you are in. This becomes a very costly undertaking.

Yangon
Shwedagon	US$5
National Museum	US$4

Mandalay
Mandalay Palace	US$5
Maha Muni Pagoda	US$4
Shwenandaw Monastery	US$3
Mandalay Museum	US$3
Mandalay Hill	US$3
Mingun	US$3
Sagaing	US$3

Bagan
Archaeological zone (for every extra night exceeding 2 nights)	US$10
	US$3
Archaeological Museum	US$4

Taunggyi
Inle Lake/Phaungdaw Oo	US$5
Pindaya Cave	US$3

Tickets can be bought at Myanmar Travels & Tours, the museums and at hotels.

The Eras

Burmese date their years by four different systems. Most frequently seen is the calendar based on the Christian Era, but you may see any of these other three as well:

The Buddhist Era began in 544 BC with the death of Gautama. According to this system, the Christian year 1992 is the Buddhist year 2536.

The Prome Era began in AD 78. A large amount of epigraphical data of interest to archaeologists is dated by this system. The year 1992 is 1914 of the Prome Era.

The Bagan (Pagan) Era is considered to have begun in AD 638. Linked to Burmese royalty, it is rarely in use today. The year 1354 of the Bagan Era parallels 1992 of the Christian Era.

Pagodas & Temples

There are two main types of Buddhist monuments in Burma: pagodas and temples.

A pagoda consists of a stupa and its surrounding enclosure. The stupa (also known as a *zedi*, *cetiya* or *dagoba*) is a monument of commemoration containing a relic chamber beneath (or sometimes over) the bell-shaped central structure. Burmese stupas are generally built on several terraces; these are passages on which devotees should walk in a clockwise direction.

The term "temple" is applied to Buddhist structures in Burma only because a more specific terminology does not exist in English. In Theravada Buddhism a temple is not a place of worship of a higher being; the Buddha is not a god, and Theravada Buddhism in its pure form does not recognize any form of divine worship. The temple is instead seen as a place of meditation. The Burmese word is *ku*, derived from the Pali guba, which roughly translated means "cave." This word also reflects the cultural heritage of the edifice – these buildings were formerly constructed as artificial caves used by monks where there were no overhanging slopes.

The main feature of a *ku* is that it is dark and cool inside. This feature characterizes the Mon-style ("hollow cube") Bagan temples, into which only a little light is able to enter through the perforated stone windows. The Bamar-style ("central pillar") temples are totally different: they were built with huge entrances and two tiers of windows to make the interiors bright and airy.

One can trace the development of the "central pillar" type from the stupas. During festivals, it was the custom to stretch huge awnings from the stupa to the surrounding wall of the enclosure to offer protection from rain and sun. As a result, a covered walkway surrounds the central sanctuary. When this was copied in solid materials, it gave the impression that the upper part of a stupa had been built on the temple roof. The same principle applies to the multi-storied Bamar-style temples.

The "hollow cube" type of temples are not actually hollow inside; they may seem to be so, but the majority have a central supporting pillar. From the outside, their pointed, bell-shaped domes resemble Gothic buildings. But the temples of Bagan could not be more different. Instead of spanning the greatest possible space, the Buddhist temple interiors consist of a multitude of walls enclosing narrow passageways and chambers, thereby satisfying the *ku*'s original purpose as a sanctuary for inner peace and meditation. The exterior of these temples – white, and invariably decorated with a gold finial – represent Mount Meru and the devout Buddhist's striving for a spiritual goal via the ever-valid Dharma, the law of life.

The Mudras

Just as temples and pagodas are created in different styles, so are Buddha images. The various body postures and hand and leg positions have symbolic meanings, each of considerable importance to students of Buddhism. These positions, called the mudras, are thousands of years old. As religion and art form an inseparable unity in Burmese life, they constitute the basis of dance and of the *yokethe pwe*, or marionette theater.

There are four basic body posture in which an image might appear. The **standing posture** depicts the descent of the Buddha from the Tavatimsa heaven where, according to legend, he traveled to preach the Buddhist doctrine to his mother.

The **walking posture** represents the Buddha's taming of the Nalagiri elephant.

The **seated posture** is the most common. It can represent any of three events: the Buddha calling upon Mother Earth to stand witness to his enlightenment; his preaching of the Sermon of the Wheel of the Law; or the Buddha in deep meditation. There are three different seated postures: legs crossed with both soles out of sight; legs crossed with soles turned upward and resting on thighs, in the lotus position; and legs upright in almost a European style of sitting.

The Buddha might also be in a **reclining posture**. If his head is pointed north, the position depicts his death and transition into nirvana. If his head is pointed any direction but north, he is sleeping.

In addition to the body and leg postures, there are six different hand gestures, each conveying a clear message. These are demonstrated in the following:

THE BHUMISPARSA MUDRA

In this mudra, the left hand lies palm upward on the Buddha's lap, and the right hand rests palm downward across his right knee, with the fingertips touching the ground below. This is the most common mudra; it shows the Buddha calling upon Mother Earth to stand witness to his moment of enlightenment.

According to the Buddha legend, Mara, the god of destruction, tried to subdue the Buddha by sending his army of demons to attack the Buddha as he meditated under the Bodhi tree, and by sending his three daughters – Desire, Pleasure and Passion – to tempt the Buddha. But the Buddha called upon Vasumdarhi, the Earth goddess, to bear witness that he had found perfect knowledge. With this, the ground began to shake, and Mara took flight.

THE DHYANA MUDRA

This position, said to represent many events in the life of the Buddha, has the palm of his right hand placed flat in the palm of the left, with both hands laid in his crossed legs. Objects placed in the palms, or figures standing to the side of an image in this position, specify which event is being depicted.

THE DHARMACAKRA MUDRA

In this mudra, both of the Buddha's hands are held in front of his breast. The tips of the middle finger and thumb of the left hand are joined with the tips of the index finger and thumb of the right hand to form a circle. This gesture recalls the Buddha's first sermon (at Sarnath, India); the hand sign is said to set the Wheel of the Law in motion.

THE ABHAYA MUDRA

This posture, found only in a standing Buddha, has the figure's right hand raised and the left pointed downward. It represents the promise of tranquility, protection and fearlessness given by the Buddha to his followers. It is also a reminder of the attempted assassination of the Buddha by his cousin Devadatta, who sent the Nalagiri elephant against him.

THE VARADA MUDRA

The arms of the standing Buddha are half out-stretched in front of the body in this pose. The palms are opened out, and the tips of the fingers point downward. This mudra depicts the bestowal of the Buddha's blessing on followers.

THE ABHAYA & VARADA MUDRAS

The Buddha's right hand is in the raised position of the Abhaya Mudra, and his left hand is out-stretched as in the Varada Mudra. This posture signifies protection and blessing, and at the same time recalls the Buddha's descent to earth after preaching in the Tavatimsa heaven.

All makers of Buddha images in Burma today must follow the specific mudras outlined here, as well as other strict rules. A list of 108 characteristics which all Buddha images must exhibit are laid down in the Digha Nikaya, found in the Buddhist scriptures.

Monasteries

If the temples and pagodas of Burma haven't exhausted you, and you're still enthused about exploring more Buddhist buildings in Yangon before departure from Burma, the Burmese government has compiled a list of "impressive monasteries" in Yangon. Many of them feature ornate wood carving and fine Buddhist artefacts. Visitors should make it a point to obtain permission to enter the monasteries from their respective *sayadaw*, or abbots.

Aletawya Kyaungtaik, Dhamma Zedi (Boundary) Street.

Bagaya Kyaungtaik, Bagaya Road, Kemendine.

Bahan Kyaungtaik, Bahan.

Kyaunggyi Kyaungtaik, Kemendine.

Mingun Tawyar, Inyamyaing (Louis) Street.

Mya Theindan Kyaungtaik, Kemendine.

Naw-man Kyaungtaik, Pazundaung.

Ngadatkyi Kyaungtaik, Nagadatkyi Road.

Payagyi Kyaungtaik, Schwegondine Road.

Pazundaung Kyaungtaik, Pazundaung.

Pyinnya Ramika Maha, Theinbyu Road.

Salin Kyaungtaik, Lower Kemendine Road.

Shin Ah-deiksa-wuntha Kyaungtaik, Pazundaung.

Theinbyu Kyaungtaik, Theinbyu Road

U-Kyin Kyaungtaik, Bagaya Road, Kemendine.

Weluwun Kyaungtaik, Kemendine.

Zeyawaddy Kyaungtaik, Kemendine.

The Six Buddhist Synods

Theravada and Mahayana Buddhists are not in complete agreement about the dates of Buddha's life. While Mahayana reckons his birth at 556 BC and his death at 476 BC, Theravada chronicles specify the years 623 BC to 544 BC. The latter date is the starting point for the Buddhist calendar valid in Southeast Asia.

Whichever calendar may be correct, the First Synod took place three months after Gautama Buddha's seath and entry into nirvana. It was held in the Satta Panni Cave in Rajagriha in the present-day Indian state of Bihar. The Second Synod was convened in Vesali in northern Bihar not long after. King Ashoka convened the Third Synod – the last joint meeting between the divided sects – in 253 BC in Pataliputra. Then the two schools of thought went their separate ways.

The Fourth Synod, summoned by King Kanishka, took place in AD 78 in northern India. Theravadins later denied the validity of this synod, maintaining that the Fourth Synod took place in Lanka (Sri Lanka) between 29 and 13 BC.

The Fifth Synod, at which the entire text of the *Tipitaka* (Buddhist scripture) was committed to stone tablets for the first time, was held in Mandalay in 1871–72 (see Mandalay chapter)

Modern legend has it that Prime Minister U Nu, who in the early 1950s took a pilgrimage to Buddhism's most important religious sites, had a vision while sitting under the Bodhi tree in Bodhgaya, India. He saw that on the 2,500th anniversary of Gautama's death – a date that would also represent the halfway point of the Buddha's 5,000-year world regency – faithful Buddhists from all over the world would meet in Burma to hear the message of peace and light in a world of hate and war.

Upon his return to Burma, U Nu ordered the work be started immediately on the maha Pasana Guha artificial cave. It was completed in 1954, three days before the official opening of the Sixth Synod on May 17, the day on which the Theravada Buddhists celebrate the birth of the Buddha. The synod – which recited, interpreted and amended the *Tipitaka* – lasted for two years, until the next one but one full moon day in May, the 2,500th anniversary of Buddha's death.

Museums

Burma's myriad pagodas and temples are her finest museums. These museums have also assembled various items of historical and anthropological interest:

National Museum, Pansodan Street between Strand Road and Merchant Street, Yangon. It contains the Mandalay Regalia from Burma's last royal court and various artefacts of ancient history. Open 10am to 3pm, Sunday through Thursday and 1 to 3pm, Saturday. Closed Friday and holidays. (The National Museum is about to move to a new location).

National Museum and Library, 24th Road and West Moat Road, Mandalay. Contains a variety of memorabilia from many eras of Burmese history, and a fine collection of Buddhist literature.

Bagan Museum. Near Thiripyitsaya Hotel, Bagan. A good introduction to the images and architectural styles of this ancient city.

Taunggyi Museum, Main Road, Taunggyi. Displays traditional costumes and cultural artefacts of the 30-plus ethnic groups living in the Shan Plateau region.

Theatres

The best place to view a Burmese *pwe* is on the city street or pagoda grounds at festival times. For those whose visit doesn't coincide with a festival, however, there are two public theatres in Yangon which have irregular performances of various types. They are:

Garrison Theatre, U Wisara Road.

Open-Air Theatre, Lanmadaw (Godwin) Road.

Myanmar marionette, Mandalay Marionette, Garden Villa Theatre, 66th Street, between 26th and 27th streets, Mandalay.

Cinemas

The Burmese love movies. There are more than 50 "cinema halls" in Yangon, about a third of them in the downtown area. In addition to Burmese language films, the Motion Picture Corporation shows carefully selected foreign features on a regular basis, including movies from North America, Europe, India and Japan.

The following seven cinema halls present English-language and other foreign films on a regular basis:

Bayint, 321 Bogyoke Aung San Street. Tel: 75368.

Gon, 223/229 Sule Pagoda Road. Tel: 72982.

Pa Pa Win, Sule Pagoda Road. Tel: 7227.

Thamada, 5 Signal Pagoda Road. Tel: 70282.

Waziya, 327 Bogyoke Aung San Street. Tel: 73468.

Wizaya, 224 U Wisara Road. Tel: 30660.

Yei Yint, corner Sule Pagoda Road and Bogyoke Aung San Street. Tel: 70945.

Literature

LIBRARIES

Sarpay Beikman Public Library, 529 Merchant Street at the corner of 37th Street. It has more than 11,000 English-language books among its 35,000 volumes. Of particular interest are the contemporary Burmese language books translated into English.

University Central Library. Located on the Yangon University campus, it is Burma's largest library. Some 170,000 books in Burmese, English and many other languages are kept here.

The library at the **International Institute of Advanced Buddhistic Studies**, Kaba Aye Pagoda, has a large selection as well. Among its holdings are more than 10,000 volumes in English. The collection also includes about 9,000 sets of ancient palm-leaf manuscripts and 2,412 museum objects.

The **National Library** in the Yangon City Hall houses an interesting collection of rare books and palm-leaf manuscripts. There are libraries in the **United States Embassy**, 581 Merchant, and at the **British Embassy**, 80 Strand Road. Both embassies carry current magazines as well as a variety of books.

In addition, the **Information and Broadcasting Department** operates 110 libraries and reading rooms through the country. Many of them, especially in major towns, have English-language literature. The department's headquarters in Yangon, near the Strand Hotel on Pansodan Street, has a wide selection of newspapers and periodicals, as well as official publications.

BOOKSELLERS

Sarpay Beikan, the public library at 529, Merchant Street, also has a book sales section. This is probably the best place of government controlled bookshop where you can find contemporary Burmese works in English.

Paperbacks and foreign journals can generally be found at two shops operated by the **Paper**, **Stationery**, **Books and Photographic Stores Trading**. They are located 232, Sule Pagoda Road and 98, Pansodan Street. It has also shops dealing in general literature at the corner of Merchant and Pansodan streets, and in medical literature at 181/189 Sule Pagoda Road.

The first private English language bookshop that opened in Yangon is the **Innwa Book Store**, 232, Sule Pagoda Road, with an acceptable selection of English language books and magazines.

Rare book collectors will find it worthwhile to browse through the many book stalls set up along main streets in both Yangon and Mandalay. Bookinists have their stalls on Pansodan Street and 37th Street, where original and photocopied, long-sought out-of-print books can often be found. There are two outstanding used book shops in Burma: In Yangon, book collectors should seek out the **Pagan Bookshop**, 100-37th Street; and in out-of-the-way Taunggyi, a charming surprise is the **Myoma Book Stall**, 390, Main Road.

Festivals

Full Moons and Festivals

When the moon waxes full, there is a Burmese celebration, the mood of which varies from season to season: frivolity during the water dousings of the New Year in April, solemnity of Buddhist Lent in July, joyousness during the October Festival of Light.

Thingyan – the Changing Over: The year's biggest party is the *Thingyan* Festival in the month of *Tagu* (March/April). This is when the Burmese celebrate their New Year. For three or four days (the length of the celebration is determined annually by *ponnas*, or Brahman astrologers), farm labor, business and government come to a virtual standstill.

Thingyan is best known as the "water throwing festival." The old year must be washed away and the new year anointed with water. No one, Burmese or foreign visitor, is safe from the deluges which seem to appear from nowhere out of the hot blue sky. From the sweet-smiling maiden carry-

ing her water pot on her head, to the skinny street cleaner labouring with his bucket, everyone is a potential prankster who might at any moment drench you from head to toe. For those without buckets or pots, water pumps and hoses are set up wherever there are roadside stalls. When out in the streets during this time, it is best to have your camera covered with a sheet of plastic or else...

Thingyan begins when Thagyamin, king of the *nat*, descends to earth to bring blessings for the new year. He also carries two books with him: one bound in gold to record the names of children who have been well-behaved in the past year, and one bound in dog skin with the names of naughty children.

Thagyamin comes riding a winged golden horse and bearing a water jar, symbolic of peace and prosperity in Burma in the coming year. Every house greets him with flowers and palm leaves at their front doors. Guns fire in salute and music resounds from all corners of the land. Gaily decorated floats parade up and down the streets of the cities and larger towns.

Yet there are times of tranquility in the midst of this exuberance. All revelers find a quiet moment each day to make offerings at pagodas and at the homes of their elders. Buddha images are given a thorough washing on this holiday by devout elderly women.

In medieval times, *Thingyan* was observed with a public hair-washing by the Burmese king, a ritual purification.

The Day of Buddha: *Kason* (April/May) is a month of anticipation, as the annual monsoon could break at any time. On the full moon, the birth, enlightenment and death of the Buddha is celebrated. Citizens join in a procession of musicians and dancers to the local pagoda. There, the participants pour scented water not over each other, but over the roots of the sacred Bodhi tree, under which the Buddha gained enlightenment.

In addition to this annual occasion, Buddha Day observances are held once a month at local temples on the day of the new moon.

The Scriptures Exam: During the full moon day of *Nayon* (May/June), after the rains have begun and the hot dry months are at an end, Burmese students are tested on their knowledge of the *Tipitaka*, the Buddhist scriptures. *Sayadaw* lecture before large crowds, schools operated by monasteries are opened to the public, and the best scholars exhibit their knowledge and win public acclaim. The huge open Assembly Hall at the Shwedagon is a good place to be at this time.

The Beginning of Lent: For the next three months, the country is soaked in water as the monsoons gain strength. This is the beginning of the Buddhist Lent season. On *Dhammasetkya*, the full moon day of *Waso* (June/July), the people of Burma celebrate the Buddha's conception, his renunciation of worldly goods, and his first sermon after enlightenment. A majority of *shinpyu* are staged at this time, and full ordination of those who wish to devote their lives to the Sangha takes place.

During the following three months, all members of the Sangha go into deep retreat for study and meditation. Monks are not permitted to travel, and all devout Buddhists enter a period of fasting.

The "Draw-a-Lot" Festival: Since no marriage or other secular celebration is permitted during the Lenten season, the full moon of *Wagaung* (July/August) is observed as a festival of food offering. This is purely a religious time for merit-making. The name of each member of the local Sangha is written on a piece of paper, which is then rolled up and deposited in a large basket. A representative from each household of the community draws a slip of paper from the basket, and the next day, provides an elaborate feast for the *pongyi* named on the piece of paper. One layman will have drawn a paper containing the name of the Gautama Buddha. He is the most fortunate of all, for he will have the opportunity to host the Buddha.

The Boat Racing Festival: By the time of *Tawthalin* (August/September), Burma's rivers are full and flowing majestically. Throughout the land, boat races are held in rivers and lakes. At Inle Lake, the Phaung Daw U Festival is held this month or next, with leg-rowing competitions and the voyage of a recreated royal *karaweik* barge.

The Festival of Light: Buddhist Lent comes to an end with the long-awaited arrival of the full moon of *Thadingyut* (September/October), indicating the approach of clear blue skies and relatively low temperatures.

On this full moon night, the Burmese celebrate the descent of the Buddha and his followers to earth from *Tavatimsa* heaven where, according to legend, he travelled to preach the doctrine to his mother. Just as the Buddha's return to this plane was illuminated by his radiance, millions of candles and lamps now light up monasteries, pagodas, houses, even trees. Everyone tries to stay awake until dawn, and an air of joyousness pervades the country. Especially happy are engaged couples, who can marry now that the taboo of the Lenten season is over.

The Weaving Festival: In the month of *Tazaungmone* (October/November), the Weaving Festival is held. Unmarried girls sit under the full moon in the pagoda grounds, engaged in weaving competitions as they make new robes for the monks. In the early morning hours, their finished products will be ceremoniously presented to the *pongyi* in the nearby *kyaung*.

The month of *nat* festivals: In *Nadaw* (November/December), when the full moon arrives, most *nat* festivals take place, and villages dedicate celebrations to the spirit world.

National or regional *nat* festivals, however, are held in other months over a period of several days, before, during and after the full moon. Among the most important are the Mount Popa Festival in *Nayon* (May/June), the Taungbyon Festival north of Mandalay in *Wagaung* (July/August), the Manao Festival in Myitkyina in *Pyatho* (December/January), and the Shan Festival in Kyaukme in *Tabaung* (February/March).

The month of temple festivals: *Pyatho* (December/January) was formerly a time when Burmese royalty displayed its strength with military parades. Nowadays, however, this particular period is reserved mostly for local pagoda festivals.

These local festivals are religious affairs, with gifts presented to monks and offerings made for temple upkeep. But even more so, they are occasions for merrymaking, lasting three or more days. A wide-ranging bazaar, boat and pony races, magic acts and side shows, and evening *pwe* performances are common activities. The full assortment of Burmese culinary delicacies are also offered.

A few major temple festivals are held in *Pyatho*. The Ananda Temple festival in Bagan falls at this time, and the Shwedagon Pagoda festival in Yangon is held either in *Pyatho* or in *Tabaung* (February/March). Other important festivals are at Pathein's Shwemokhpaw Pagoda in *Kason* (April/May), Bago's Shwesandaw Pagoda in *Tazaungdaing Festival* (October/November), Nyaung U's Shwezigon Pagoda in *Nadaw* (November/December) and Pyay's Shwenattaung Pagoda in *Tabaung* (February/March). These national celebrations can last up to four weeks.

The harvest festival: When the month of *Tabodwe* (January/February) arrives, it is time to harvest the paddy and celebrate the harvest festival. As in every land where farming is the mainstay of the population, it is a time of joy. After the first harvest is offered to the monastery, elaborate meals are prepared, and Burmese women have a chance to show off their cooking prowess to neighbours and monks. The celebration is named *Htamane* after a food offering of rice, sesame, peanuts, ginger and coconut.

The month of serenity: *Tabaung* (February/March), the last month of the Burmese year, is a time of romance and quiet thoughts. On the full moon day, Burmese travel to tranquil lakes or rivers where they can relax under the stars and spend the evening playing music, singing and reciting poetry. It is a fitting close to the year, displaying the simple joys of life by people far from Western influence.

The festival calendar: The Burmese calendar subscribes to both the solar and the lunar months, thus requiring an intercalary 30-day 13th month every second or third year.

Tourists should keep this in mind when planning their visit , and consult the Myanmar embassy to synchronize their schedule with the Burmese calendar. Visits should ideally be timed to coincide with the full moon.

The holiday schedule: In addition to the festival schedule, there are several secular and public holidays during which all offices are closed. The dates for these holidays follow the Western calendar.

Independence Day is observed on January 4, commemorating the date in 1948 that Burma left the British Commonwealth and became a sovereign independent nation.

Union Day is celebrated on February 12, marking the date in 1947 that Aung San concluded an agreement with Burma's ethnic minorities at Panglong in the Shan State.

The Union of Burma flag, which has been carried by runners to each of Burma's state capitals, would on this day be returned to Yangon amidst the roar of hundreds of thousands of people from all over the nation.

Peasants' Day, March 2, and **Workers' Day**, May 1, honour the working population of Burma.

Resistance (*Tatmadaw*) **Day**, March 27, commemorates the World War II struggle against the Japanese. It is celebrated with parades and fireworks. Ironically, Burma spent most of the war on the Japanese side fighting Allied forces, but switched allegiance in early 1945.

May Day, on May 1, is the working people's holiday. **Martyrs Day**, July 19, is a memorial to Burma's founding father, Aung San, and his cabinet ministers who were assassinated on this fateful day in 1947. Special ceremonies take place at the Martyrs Mausoleum in Yangon.

Non-Buddhist religious holidays: Because of Burma's policy of religious freedom, various minority groups celebrate important holidays which do not fall on the Burmese calendar. These include the Hindu festival *Dewali* in October, the Islamic observance of *Bakri Idd* with changing dates, the Christian holidays of Christmas (December 25) and Easter (late March or April), and the Kayin (Karen) New Year Festival on or about January 1.

Shopping

Shopping Areas

Burma's markets and bazaars are the most interesting, and at the same time the most reasonable places to shop for native arts and crafts. In Yangon, the **Bogyoke Aung San Market** is open from 9.30am to 4.30pm Monday through Saturday. It is the place where most tourists do their last shopping before leaving the country. Some of the shops in the market with reasonable prices and a large selection are listed here:

Lacquerware, Daw Chit Khin Lacquerware, Shop 43, East (C) Block

Jade, Colourful Jade Store, Shop 42, West "D" Arcade

Mother of Pearl, Myanmar Variety Store, Shop 75, Center Arcade

Silverware, William Tan, Shop 33, Main Line. This shop offers beautiful hammered silverware for US$0.90 cents per gram.

Other markets, including Mandalay's **Zegyo Market**, generally open early in the morning and remain open until dark. The best shopping for laquerware is done in New Bagan, the residential area about 8 kilometres (5 mi) from the archaeological zone. There are also separate night markets which set up on specified streets after dark; the best ones are in Yangon's Chinese and Indian quarters, and in Mandalay on 84th Street between 26th and 28th roads.

Bazaars and markets thrive in Yangon city. There are open-air markets across Bogyoke Aung San Street from the Bogyoke Market; at the corner of St John's Road and Pyay Road; and east of the Botataung Pagoda. The **Thein Gyi Zay** Indian market is just off Anawrahta Street, and there's a Chinese market at the corner of Maha Bandoola Street and Lanmadaw Road.

The entrances to the **Shwedagon Pagoda** are also bazaars – of some length, in fact, covering both sides of the stairways. The bazaar at the east entrance is possibly the most interesting; among the items frequently sold are puppets, drums, masks, toys, brassware, and metal goods including swords. The bazaar at the pagoda's south entrance is notable for wood and ivory carvings.

Wood carvings are also sold in quantity and quality at the **New Carving Shop**, 20 University Avenue. For other types of art work, try the **Loka Nath Art Gallery**, 62 Pansodan Street, or the **Aung Zeya Art Gallery**, 90 Kaba Aye Pagoda Road; and **Curio de City**, 35 Bahan Road, for antiques. In Mandalay, a variety of art work is sold during exhibitions at the **State School of Fine Arts, Music and Drama**.

OTHER SHOPS

Jewellery:
Myanmar VES Joint Venture Co. Ltd., 66 Kaba Aye Pagoda Road. Tel: 61902.
Sein Yadana, 134, Shwebonte Street. Tel: 72467.
Golden Owl, Jewelry and Gem Laboratory, Jewel Palace II, counter 19, Bogyoke Aung San Market.
Nat Nan Taw, Jewelry and Gems, corner of Parami & Kaba Aye Pagoda Road. Tel: 60530.
Art:
Golden Valley Art Centre, 54 D, Golden Valley. Tel: 33830.
Nang Aung Art Gallery, Bldg. 5, Bothataung Lane (2).
Traditional Arts and Sculpture Sales Shop, 188 To 192, East Wing Bogyoke Aung San Market. Tel: 87604.

If you are looking for a special producer or distributor, look into the Myanmar Business Directory. Chamber of Commerce, 74-86, Bo Sun Pat Street. Tel: 77103.
Antiques:
Charlie Antique, 17, Kaba Aye Pagoda Road.
Furniture:
Hla Gabar, Burmese furniture, 166, Maha Bandoola Road. Tel: 91311.
Myanmar Elephant House, 24 A. Aung Min Khaung Ave. Tel: 32773.

Longyis:
Pan Sa Gar Longyi, 386, Mahabandoola Panchan Upper Street. Tel: 74870.

A pricey selection of all types of Burmese handicrafts is always for sale at the **Tourist Department Stores**, 143-144 Sule Pagoda Road in Yangon. Open 10am to 4pm Monday through Friday and 10am to 1pm Saturday, the stores will accept only foreign exchange in its transactions.

There are gift shops at the Inya Lake and Strand hotels. Both are open 9.30am to 5pm daily except Sunday.

Sports

As in every country of the world, sports are a popular amusement and diversion in Burma. Soccer is often played at Aung San Stadium in Yangon, and on small fields throughout the country. Other sports familiar to Westerners are also played. Uniquely Burmese, however, are the sport of chinlon and traditional boxing.

Spectator
Burmese Boxing

To the unfamiliar Westerner, Burmese boxing appears to be a needlessly vicious sport. Boxers may use any parts of their bodies in attacking their opponents, and a match is won by whoever draws first blood. But there are specific rules and courtesies which keep a match from getting out of hand, and musical accompaniment by a Burmese percussion orchestra, or *saing-waing*, lends an air of unreality to the event.

The following description of Burmese boxing is taken from *Forward* magazine (August 1, 1964), as quoted by author Helen Trager in her book *We, The Burmese*:

"The head is used for butting, either to stop an opponent's rush or to soften him up while holding him fast in a tight grip. The hands are used not only for hitting but also for holding. The el-

bows are used to parry an opponent's blow or to deliver one in the opponent's side. The knees are used for hitting an opponent who is held fast, or they may be used to deliver blows while the boxers are apart. The feet may trip an opponent or at least keep him off balance, or they may be used to stop an opponent's rush with a well-executed flying kick.

"These tactics are commonly employed by Burmese boxers. To deliver the blows effectively, however, the boxer has to master his footwork, which is also considered important in another branch of art of self-defense, Thaing. A Burmese boxer has to know where to place his feet, how to advance, how to retreat, from what position to jump into the attack, and how best to evade the blows of the opponent. In close combat the Burmese boxer has to be well acquainted with techniques of wrestling.

"...To safeguard the boxers from accidents, there are rules against scratching, biting, pulling hair, and hitting or kicking an opponent in the groin. The fingernails and toenails of boxers have to be kept properly trimmed. A boxer who is down may not be kicked or hit in any way...

"The match is decided at the sign of blood. Each boxer is allowed to wipe away the blood three times before he is declared the loser. A match may also be decided when one of the boxers is too hurt to continue although he may not be bleeding."

Chinlon

Chinlon is Burma's national game. Said by some to have originated in ancient Pyay in the 7th century, its object is to keep a caneball in the air for as long as possible, using no part of the body except the feet and knees.

Although the game is played for fun by any number of people throughout the country, the All-Burma Chinlon Association has set up rules for team play that is increasing in status. A team of six players stand within a boundary circle 6.5 metres (21 ft) in diameter, passing the ball back and forth among themselves. Points are scored according to the difficulty of the footwork used and the skill with which it is executed; specific point values are assigned to certain "strokes." Points are subtracted if the ball hits the

ground, or if a player steps outside the boundary circle.

The chinlon, or caneball, is made of six leaves of sugar cane interwoven and dried, forming a circular ball with holes about an inch and a half apart. The standard-size ball is 40 centimetres (16 in) around.

Clubs

The following private clubs might be of interest to visitors, who generally will be welcomed:
Myanmar Golf Club, Pyay Road, 9th Mile. Tel: 61702.
Growers Club, Myepadethakyun, Kandawgyi. Tel: 50288.
Kokine Swimming Club, 34 Saya San (Goodliffe) Street. Tel: 50034.
Orient Club, 169 Shwegondine Road. Tel: 50869.
Yangon Golf Club, Danyingone Mingaladon. Tel: 40001.
Yangon Sailing Club, 132 Inya Road. Tel: 31298.
Yu Nandar Myint, Aerobics Club, 63, Thukhawaddy Street. Tel: 58937.

Beauty Parlors
Vilas Beauty Salon, 64, Latha Street. Tel: 78064.
Fashion Cut Terry. Make Up and Hairstyle, 165, Room 12, 1st Floor, corner of Seik Khan Tha Street and Mahabandola Street.

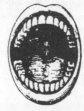

Language
General

The Burmese language is a member of the Tibeto-Burman language family, which is in turn a sub-group of Sino-Tibetan. While 80 percent of Burma's diverse peoples speak this language, there remain more than 100 distinct languages and dialects spoken in different parts of the country. The great variation in cultural histories of the ethnic groups can be seen in their languages.

Burmese is thought to have originated in the Bamar's ancestral central Asian homeland. The language spread rapidly among Burma's Thai (Shan) and Mon-Khmer peoples during the 19th century, when the last Mon Empire had declined and the Ayeyarwady Delta was opened to rice cultivation, attracting many hill Kayin.

Burmese script has an origin quite different than the written tongue. It derives from the Pali language of south India, and has strong similarities with the Telugu written language. The Mons had adopted the scripts during their interactions with Theravada Buddhist priests from south India, and the Bamars absorbed it after King Anawrahta's conquest of the Mon capital of Thaton in the 11th century.

The Burmese alphabet consists of 44 letters: 32 consonants, eight vowels and four diphthongs. It is written and read from left to right, top to bottom.

The Burmese numerical system, although written in typically Burmese script, is based upon the Arabic and decimal systems in common use in the West.

An-Ah-Deh

Every language contains some expressions which don't lend themselves to translation. Burmese is no exception.

The noble art of Burmese courtesy and persuasion lies behind the principle of "an-ah-deh." This entails never using the word "No," and never putting anyone else in the position of having to use it. At the same time, "an-ah-deh" allows a Burmese to convince another person that the thing that person wants but cannot achieve is, in fact, not worthy of aspiration.

"An-ah-deh" must be learned and felt inwardly. It is true art to meet another person at a halfway point where neither side will lose face in the confrontation.

There is a difference between a lie and a statement that is not exactly true. Drawing the fine line in the right place is, for the Burmese, indicative of good manners and upbringing.

Because this principle is integral to the Burmese social graces, the people of Burma find it difficult to exclude foreign visitors from "an-ah-deh." It is indicative of Burma's deep-rooted culture - an expression of a view of life

both tolerant and compromising, often the very antithesis of the West's "down-to-earth" mentality.

In the Westerner's dealings with Burmese officialdom, he will often encounter this "an-ah-deh" approach to problems, coupled with a marked aversion for making decisions. In some cases, it can lead to considerable delays. The Westerners must be patient and try to understand the underlying reason for the Burmese behaviour.

Survival Burmese

The Burmese language is tonal, like Chinese. The way in which a word is pronounced affects its meaning: a single syllable, given different kinds of stress, may carry several distinctly different meanings.

In the following list of words and phrases, the following accent marks are used:

(no mark) – low even tone/(:) – long falling tone/(.) – short falling tone/(') – glottal stop or creaky tone.

Numerals

one/*tit*
two/*nit*
three/*thone*
four/*lay*
five/*ngar*
six/*chak*
seven/*kun nit*
eight/*shit*
nine/*ko*
ten/*ta sair*
eleven/*sair tit*
twelve/*sair nit*
twenty/*na sair*
thirty/*thone sair*
forty/*lay sair*
fifty/*ngar sair*
sixty/*chak sair*
seventy/*kun na sair*
eighty/*shit sair*
ninety/*ko sair*
one hundred/*ta yar*
one thousand/*ta taung*

Conversation

How are you?/*Nay gaun the lah?*
I am well./*Nay gaun ba day.*
I am not well./*Nay magaun ba boo.*
How's it? (informal)/*Be low lay?*
That's good./*Kaun day.*
Do you understand?/*Na lay the lah?*
I understand./*Na lay ba day.*
I do not understand./*na malay ba boo.*

Yes (male)./*Kamyah.*
Yes (female)./*Shin.*
Yes (polite)./*Hout ke(t).*
Yes, that's right./*Hour bah day.*
No, that's not so./*Ma hout bah boo.*
What are you saying?/*Bah pyaw the lay?*
Please repeat./*Byan pyaw ba own.*
Speak clearly./*Byaya byay pyaw bah.*
Why?/*Bah pyit lou lay?*
Never mind./*Nay bah zay.*
It doesn't matter./*Keit sa ma shi bah boo.*
What is it?/*Bah lay?*
Do you know Burmese?/*Bamah lou dat the lah?*
Only a little./*Neh neh beh dat ba day.*
he speaks well./*Gaun gaun dat day.*
Are you English?/*Ing gah lay lah?*
No, I'm not English./*Ing gah lay ma hout ba boo.*
Where do you come from?/*Beh gah lah the lay?*
I come from America./*Amay yi kah pyay gah lah day.*
Please./*Jay zu pyaw bah.*
Thank you very much./*Amyah ee jay zu tin ba day.*
Goodbye./*Thwa may.*

Dining

What do you want to eat?/*Bah tamin sah jin the lay?*
Is there...?/*...shee the lah?*
I'll eat.../*...sah meh.*
Pork curry/*Wet thah hin*
Chicken curry/*Chet thah hin*
Beef curry/*Amay thah hin*
Fish curry/*Ngah hin*
Shrimp curry/*Bazoon hin*
Egg/*Chet oo*
Shrimp paste/*Ngapee*
Noodles with curry soup/*Kaut sway*
Vegetables/*Hin thee hin youwet*
Fruit/*Thit thee*
I don't want to eat./*Bah thaut ma lay?*
I'll drink.../*...that may.*
Coffee/*Kahpee*
Black tea with milk and sugar/*Lapay*
Plain green tea/*Lapay yay john*
Hot tea/*Yay nway*
Water/*Yay*
Beer/*Beeyah*
Hot soup/*Hin joe*
I don't want to drink./*Bah hmat ma thaut ba boo.*

Directions

Where is the...?/*...beh hmah lay?*
Where are you going?/*Beh gou thwa melay?*
Railway station/*Mee yatah yown*

Hospital/*Say yown*
Theatre/*Yout shin bwe*
Hotel/*Ho tay*
Post Office/*Sah daik*
Bank/*Ban daik*
Barber/*Sabin hnyat the mah*
When will you go?/*Beh daw thwa me lay?*
When will it start?/*Beh a chain pyat me lay?*
When will it leave?/*Beh a chain twet ma lay?*
One o'clock./*Ta nai yee.*
Two o'clock./*Na nai yee.*
How much is it? (price)/*Beh laut lay?*
One kyat five pyas./*Ta jat ngar byaz.*

Further Reading

General Interest

Bixler, Norma. **Burma: A Profile**. New York: Praeger, 1971. A well done general survey.

Burma Research Society. **50th Anniversary Publication** (two volumes). Rangoon: 1961. Highlights of 50 years of scholarly writings.

Collis, Maurice. **Lords of the Sunset**. New York: Dodd Mead, 1938. A tour of the Shan States.

Donnison, F.S.V. **Burma**. New York: Praeger, 1970. The country from a patronizing British standpoint.

Enriquez, C.M.D. **A Burmese Loneliness**. Calcutta: Thacker, Spink 1918. Travels in the Shan States.

Esche, Otto von. **Burma: Land und Leute**. Leipzig: Brockhaus, 1963.

Henderson, John W., and others. **Area Handbook for Burma**. Washington, D.C.: American University Foreign Area Studies, 1971. An overview.

Kessel, Joseph. **Mogok: La Vallé des Rubis**. Paris: Gallimard, 1955.

Keyes, Charles F. **The Golden Peninsula: Culture and Adaptation in Mainland Southeast Asia**. New York: Macmillan, 1977. An anthropologist studies changes in the region's Buddhist societies.

Kipling, Rudyard. **Letters From the East**. London: 1889. The author's travels through Asia.

Maring, Joel M. and Ester G. **Historical and Cultural Dictionary of Burma**. Metuchen, N.J.: The Scarecrow Press, 1973.

Maugham, Somerset. **The Gentleman in the Parlour**. Garden City, N.Y.: Doubleday, Doran & Co., 1930. Subtitled: A Record of a Journey From Rangoon to Haiphong.

Nash, Manning. **The Golden Road to Modernity: Village Life in Contemporary Burma**. New York: Wiley, 1965. A study of peasant agricultural society.

Scott, Sir James G. **Burma: From the Earliest Day to the Present Day**. New York: Alfred A. Knopf, 1924.

Shway Yoe (Sir J.G. Scott). **The Burman: His Life and Notions**. London: Macmillan, 1882. Two volumes. A gold mine of cultural information from a 19th Century British colonial official.

Storz, H.U. **Birma: Land, Geschichte, Wirtschaft**. Wiesbaden: Otto Harrassowitz, 1967. German-language survey.

Theroux, Paul. **The Great Railway Bazaar: By Train Through Asia**. New York: Random House, 1975. Amusing account of the author's railway adventures.

Trager, Helen G. **We the Burmese**. New York: Praeger, 1969. Burmese life and culture through its people's eyes.

General History

Bennett, Paul J. **Conference Under the Tamarind Tree**. New Haven, Conn.: Yale University Southeast Asian Studies, 1971. Three essays on Burmese history.

Cady, John F. **A History of Modern Burma**. Ithaca, N.Y.: Cornell University Press, 1958. The standard history of Burma since the 18th Century.

Hall, D.G.E. **Burma**. London: Hutchinson's University Library, 1960. A brief but complete history.

Hall, D.G.E. **A History of Southeast Asia**. New York: St. Martin's Press, 1968. Third edition. The most comprehensive book yet published about this exotic region.

Harvey, Godfrey E. **History of Burma**. London: Longmans, Green, 1925. Reprinted 1967. A detailed treatment from ancient times to 1824.

Htin Aung. **A History of Burma**. New York: Columbia University Press, 1967. A Burmese view of the nation's history.

Phayre, Sir Arthur P. **History of Burma**. London: Trübner, 1883. Reprinted 1967. The first formal history of Burma by a Westerner.

Trager, Frank N. **Burma From Kingdom to Republic**. New York: Praeger, 1966. A historical and political analysis.

Ancient History

Htin Aung. **Burmese History Before 1287**. Oxford, England: Asoka Society, 1970. "A defence of the Chronicles."

Humble, Richard. **Marco Polo**. New York: G.P. Putnam's Sons, 1975. Easy-reading survey of the travels of Polo.

Luce, Gordon H. **Old Burma-Early Pagan**. Ascona, Switzerland: Artibus Asiae, 1970. Three volumes. The crowning achievement of a lifetime of study of the art and architecture of 10th to 12th Century Bagan.

Pe Maung Tin and Gordon H. Luce. **The Glass Palace Chronicle of the Kings of Burma**. Oxford England: Oxford University Press, 1923. Also, Rangoon: Burma Research Society, 1960. English translation of the royal chronicle of Burma, first written in 1829.

Yule, Sir Henry. **The Book of Ser Marco Polo**. London: John Murray, 1929. Polo's journal edited by Yule.

Aung-Thwin, Michael. **Pagan, the Origins of Modern Burma**. Honolulu, 1985.

European Contact

Anderson, John M.D. **English Intercourse With Siam in the 17th Century**. London: Kegan Paul, Trench, Trubner, 1890.

Cox, Hiram. **Journal of a Residence in the Burmahn Empire, and more particularly at the Court of Amarapoorah**. London: John Warren and G. & W.B. Whittaker, 1821. Establishes a pattern of anti-Burmese writing by British authors.

Collis, Maurice. **The Land of the Great Image**. New York: Alfred A. Knopf, 1943. The experiences of Friar Manrique of Rakhine.

Dalrymple, A. **Oriental Repository**. London: Ballantine and Law, 1808. The East India Company in Burma, 1695 to 1761.

Fitch, Ralph. **"The Voyage of Mr. Ralph Fitch, Merchant of London, to Ormuz & so to Goa in the East Indies, 1583 to 1591."** In Volume IX of John Pinkerton, editor, A general collection of the best and most interesting voyages and travels..., London, 1808–1814.

Hunter, W.A. *A Concise Account of the Kingdom of Pegu*. Calcutta: John Hay, 1785. From the East India Company viewpoint.

O'Connor, V.C. Scott. *Mandalay and Other Cities of the Past in Burma*. London: Hutchinson, 1907.

Sangermano, Father Vicentius. *Description of the Burmese Empire*. Westminister, England: Archibald Constable, 1893. Third Edition. (First published in Rome in 1833.) A Barnabite missionary in Burma, 1783 to 1803.

Symes, Michael. *An Account of the Embassy to the Kingdom of Ava sent by the Governor-General of India in 1795*. London: W. Bulmer, 1800. Keen observations on all aspects of Burmese life.

Symes, Michael. *Journal of his Second Embassy to the Court of Ava in 1802*. London: George Allen and Unwin, 1955.

Yule, Henry. *A narrative of the mission sent by the Governor-General of India to the Court of Ava in 1855*. London: Smith, Elder, 1858. An intelligence report with excellent plates and sketches.

The British Colonial Era

Anderson, John M.D. *Mandalay to Moulmein*. London: Macmillan, 1876. Reprinted 1979. Subtitled: A narrative of the two expeditions to western China of 1868 and 1875 under Col. Edward B. Sladen and Col. Horace Browne. Good data about Shan and Kachin areas.

Banerjee, A.C. *Annexation of Burma*. Calcutta: A. Mukherjee, 1944. British policy towards Burma.

Bigandet, Father Paul A. *An Outline of the History of the Catholic Burmese Mission From the Year 1720 to 1887*. Rangoon: 1887. A study by a French missionary.

Bird, George W. *Wanderings in Burma*. London: Simpkin, Marshall, Hamilton, Kent, 1897. British travel book.

Browne, Horace A. *Reminiscences of the Court of Mandalay*. Woking, England; Oriental Institute, 1907. Extracts from the diary of England's last resident at the Court of Mandalay.

Bruce, George. *The Burma Wars, 1824–1886*. London: Hart-Davis MacGibbon, 1973. A review of the three Anglo-Burmese wars.

Chong, Siok-hwa. *The Rice Industry of Burma 1852–1940*. Kuala Lumpur: University of Malaya, 1968. Scholarly treatment of the industry's growth.

Collis, Maurice. *Into Hidden Burma*. London: Faber and Faber, 1953. Autobiography of a British colonial administrator.

Cooler, Richard M. *British Romantic Views of the First Anglo-Burmese War, 1824–26*. DeKalb, Ill.: Northern Illinois University, 1977. Catalogue of prints for an Asian exhibition.

Crawfurd, John. *Journal of an Embassy From the Governor-General of India to the Court of Ava in 1827*. London: Henry Colburn, 1829. Narrative with ethnic and social commentaries.

Crosthwaite, Sir Charles. *The Pacification of Burma*. London: Edward Arnold, 1912. The end of Burma's traditional village governments.

Foucar, E.C.V. *Mandalay the Golden*. London: Dennis Dobson, 1963. First published in 1946 as *They Reigned in Mandalay*. The city's royal era.

Furnivall, J.S. *Colonial Policy and Practice*. New York: Cambridge University Press, 1948. How the British ran Burma.

Fytche, Albert. *Burma Past and Present*. London: Kegan Paul, 1878. Two volumes. Burma during the British era.

Gouger, H. *A personal narrative of two years imprisonment in Burma 1824–1826*. London: John Murray, 1860. A British merchant's account.

Hall, Gordon L. *Golden Boats from Burma*. Philadelphia: Macrae Smith, 1961. The life of Ann Hasseltine Judson, the first American woman in Burma.

Htin Aung. *The Stricken Peacock*. Den Haag: Martinus Nijhoff, 1965. Anglo-Burmese relations between 1752 and 1948.

Moscotti, Albert D. *British Policy in Burma, 1917–1937*. Honolulu: University Press of Hawaii, 1974.

Orwell, George. *Burmese Days*. London: Secker and Warburg, 1934. Reprinted 1975. Bittersweet novel about British colonial rule.

Rawson, Geoffrey. *Road to Mandalay*. New York: Harcourt Brace and World, 1967. A popular account of the end of Burmese royalty and British takeover.

Singhal, D.P. *The Annexation of Upper Burma*. Singapore: Eastern Universities Press, 1960.

Stewart, A.T.Q. *The Pagoda War*. London: Faber, 1972. Subtitled: "Lord Dufferin and the fall of the Kingdom of Ava, 1885–86."

McCrae, Alister. *Scots in Burma*. Edinburgh, 1990.

World War II

Collis, Maurice. *Last and First in Burma*. London: Faber and Faber, 1956. An account of the country during and after the war.

Fellowes-Gordon, Ian. *Amiable Assassins: The Story of the Kachin Guerrillas of North Myanmar*. London: Robert Hale, 1957. Freedom fighters take on Japanese invaders.

Jesse, Tennyson. *The Story of Burma*. London: Macmillan, 1946. A wartime account.

Kinvig, C. *Death Railway*. London: 1973.

Morrison, Ian. *Grandfather Longlegs*. London: Faber and Faber, 1946. The biography of Major H.P. Seagrim, who stayed behind Japanese lines in Burma.

Nu, Thakin. *Burma Under the Japanese*. London: Macmillan, 1954. An important account of the occupation.

Seagrave, Gordon S. *Burma Surgeon*. New York: W.W. Norton, 1943. An important work about the life of a wartime doctor.

Seagrave, Gordon S. *Burma Surgeon Returns*. New York: W.W. Norton, 1946. More of the same.

Slater, Robert. *Guns Through Arcady: Burma and the Burma Road*. Madras, India: Diocesan Press, 1943. An account of events leading to the Japanese invasion.

Slim, W.J. *Defeat Into Victory*. London: Cassell, 1956. A good autobiographical account of the war, by the British military leader.

Stilwell, Joseph. *The Stilwell Papers*. Edited and arranged by Theodore H. White. New York: William Sloane Associates, 1948. "Vinegar Joe" in his own words.

Takeyama, Michio. *Harp of Burma*. Tokyo: Charles E. Tuttle, 1966. First published in Japanese in 1949. Novel about the Japanese experience in wartime Burma.

Tuchmann, Barbara W. *Stilwell and the American Experience in China, 1911–1945*. New York: Macmillan, 1971. A very important history and biography.

Williams, J.H. *Elephant Bill*. Garden City, N.Y.: Doubleday, 1950. An autobiography by the commander of a World War II elephant brigade.

Contemporary Burma

Butwell, Richard. *U Nu of Burma*. Stanford, Calif.: Stanford University Press, 1963. Second edition, 1969. Political biography.

Maung Maung, editor. *Aung San of Burma*. Den Haag: Martinus Nijhoff, 1962. Collected writings by and about the nation's founding father.

Maung Maung. *Burma and General Ne Win*. Bombay, India: Asia Publishing House, 1969. A Burmese interpretation of the nationalist movement.

McAlister, John T. Jr., editor. *Southeast Asia: The Politics of National Integration*. New York: Random House, 1973. A collection of 30 interpretive essays, several specifically on contemporary Burma.

McCoy, Alfred W. *The Politics of Heroin in Southeast Asia*. New York: Harper & Row, 1972. A fascinating expose of the web of international involvement in the Gold Triangle.

Nu, U. *U Nu: Saturday's Son*. New Haven, Conn.: Yale University Press, 1975. The former prime minister's autobiography.

Pye, Lucian W. *Politics, Personality and Nation Building: Burma's Search for Identity*. New Haven, Conn.: Yale University Press, 1962. An analysis of events in postwar Burma.

Silverstein, Josef. *Burma: Military Rule and the Politics of Stagnation*. Ithaca, N.Y.: Cornell University Press, 1977. An analysis of Ne Win's politics.

Silverstein, Josef, compiler. *The Political Legacy of Aung San*. Ithaca, N.Y.: Cornell University Press, 1972.

Silverstein, Josef. *Independent Burma at Forty Years: Six Assessments*. Ithaca, 1989.

Steinberg, David. *The Future of Burma – Crisis and Choice in Myanmar*. New York, 1990

Sitte, Fritz. *Rebellenstaat in Burmadschungel*. Graz, Austria: Verlag Styria, 1979. A German-language study of Burma's ethnic rebellions.

Tinker, Hugh. *The Union of Burma*. London: Oxford University Press, 1967. Fourth edition. A study of Burma's first years of independence.

Lintler, Bertil. *Outrage*. Hong Kong, 1989.

Lintler Bertil. *Aung San Suu Kyi and Burma's Unfinished Renaissance*. Bangkok, 1990.

Lintler Bertil. *The Rise and Fall of the Communist Party of Burma*. Ithaca, 1990.

Aung San Suu Kyi. *Aung San*. University of Queensland Press, 1984.

Aung San Suu Kyi. *Let's Visit Burma*. London, 1985.

Aung San Suu Kyi. *Burma and India*. New Delhi, 1990.

Tin Maung Latt. *City of Yangon*. Modernization Record, Yangon, 1990.

State Law and Order Restoration Council. *Senior General Saw Maung's Addresses*. Yangon, 1990.

State Law and Order Restoration Council. *Burma Communist Party's Conspiracy to Take Over State Power*. Yangon, 1990.

State Law and Order Restoration Council. *The Conspiracy of Treasonous Minions Within the Myanmar Naing-Ngang and Traitorous Cohorts Abroad*. Yangon 1989.

State Law and Order Restoration Council. Different brochures regarding the new laws published in 1990: *Myanmar Tourism Law, The Union of Myanmar Foreign Investment Law and the State-Owned Economic Enterprises Law*.

The Central Commitee for Drug Abuse Control. *Myanmar Narcotics Report*. Yangon, 1990.

Ethnic Minorities

Cochrane, Wilbur W. *The Shans*. Rangoon: Government Printing Office, 1915. Reprinted 1978. A missionary's account.

Colquhoun, Archibald R. *Amongst the Shans*. New York: Scribner and Welford, 1885. Reprinted 1970. Of historical interest.

Enriquez, C.M.D. *A Burmese Arcady*. London: Seeley, Service, 1923. Reprinted 1978. An account of the Burmese hill tribes.

Enriquez, C.M.D. *Races of Burma*. Calcutta: Government of India Central Publication Department, 1924. Reprinted 1978. Descriptive account for British military recruiting purposes.

Gilhodes, Charles. *The Kachins: Religion and Customs*. Calcutta: Catholic Orphan Press, 1922. Strong on folklore and mythology.

Hanson, Ola. *The Kachins, Their Customs and Traditions*. Rangoon: American Baptist Mission Press, 1913. A missionary account.

Head, W.R. *Handbook of Haka Chin Customs*. Rangoon: Government Printing Office, 1917.

Leach, Edmund R. *Political Systems of Highland Burma*. Cambridge, Mass: Harvard University Press, 1954. A study of Kachin social structure. An anthropological classic.

Leber, Frank, Gerald C. Hickey and John K. Musgrave. *Ethnic Groups of Mainland Southeast Asia*. New Haven, Conn.: Human Relations Area File Press, 1964. Standard reference volume.

Lehman, Frederick Y. *The Structure of Chin Society*. Urbana, Ill.: University of Illinois Press, 1963. Contemporary anthropological study.

Marshall, Harry I. *The Karens of Burma*. London: Longmans, Green, 1945.

McCall, Anthony G. *Lushai Chrysalis*. London: Luzac, 1949. A study of the Chins of the Indian border region.

McMahon, A.R. *The Karens of the Golden Chersonese*. New York: 1978.

Milne, Leslie. *The Home of an Eastern Clan*. New York: Clarendon Press, 1924. Reprinted 1978. A study of the Palaungs of the Shan States.

Milne, Leslie. *Shans at Home*. London: Murray, 1910. Reprinted 1970. Descriptive account.

Scott, Sir James G. *Burma: A Handbook of Practical Information*. London: Daniel O'Connor, 1921. Third edition. Reference book on ethnic minorities.

Yegar, Moshe. *The Muslims of Burma*. Wiesbaden: O. Harrassowitz, 1972.

Religion

Appleton, George. *Buddhism in Burma*. London: Longmans, Green, 1943.

Bigandet, Father Paul A. *The Life or Legend of Gautama, the Buddha of the Burmese*. Two volumes. London: Kegan Paul, Trench, Trübner, 1911. Reprinted 1978.

Bode, Mabel Haynes. *The Pali Literature of Burma*. London: Royal Asiatic Society, 1909. Reprinted 1965.

Fielding-Hall, H. *The Soul of a People*. London: Macmillan, 1909.

Htin Aung. *Folk Elements in Burmese Buddhism*. London: Oxford University Press, 1962.

King, Winston L. *A Thousand Lives Away: Buddhism in Contemporary Burma*. Oxford, England: Bruno Cassirer, 1964. One of the best modern studies by an American scholar.

Lester, Robert C. *Theravada Buddhism in Southeast Asia*. Ann Arbor, Mich.: University of Michigan Press, 1973. Good basic survey.

MacGregor, Allan. *Die Religion von Burma*. Breislau, Germany: 1911. (Reprinted as The Religion of Burma and Other Papers by Ananda Maitreya. New York: 1978.)

Mahasi Sayadaw. *Mahasi Abroad*. Rangoon: 1979.

Mendelson, E. Michael. *Sangha and State in Burma*. Ithaca, N.Y.: Cornell University Press, 1975. Relations between the government and Buddhist monks.

Pe Maung Tin. *Buddhist Devotion and Meditation*. London: Pali Text Society, 1964.

Ray, Nihar-ranjan. *Brahmanical Gods in Burma*. Calcutta: University of Calcutta Press, 1932. Study of iconography by a Sanskrit scholar.

Ray, Nihar-ranjan. *An Introduction to the Study of Theravada Buddhism in Burma*. Calcutta: University of Calcutta Press, 1946. Reprinted in 1978. Historical treatment.

Ray, Nihar-ranjan. *Sanskrit Buddhism in Burma*. Calcutta: University of Calcutta Press, 1946.

Sarkisyanz, Emmanuel. *Buddhist Backgrounds of the Burmese Revolution*. Den Haag: Martinus Nijhoff, 1965.

Smith, Donald E. *Religion and Politics in Burma*. Princeton, N.J.: Princeton University Press, 1965. Excellent study of the impact of Buddhism on the nationalist movement.

Soni, R.L. *A Cultural Study of the Burmese Era*. Mandalay: Institute of Buddhist Culture, 1955. Burmese history from the viewpoint of Buddhist cosmology.

Spiro, Melford E. *Buddhism and Society*. New York: Harper and Row, 1970. Scholarly treatment.

Spiro, Melford E. *Burmese Supernaturalism*. Englewood, N.J.: Prentice-Hall, 1967. Expanded edition, 1977. A fascinating study.

Temple, Sir Richard C. *The 37 Nats*. London: W. Griggs, 1906. Interesting work, especially valuable for its illustrations.

Uhlig, Helmut. *Auf den Spuren Buddhas*. Berlin: Safari Verlag, 1973.

Warren, Henry Clarke. *Buddhism in Translations*. Cambridge, Mass.: Harvard University Press, 1896. Reprinted 1953, 1962, 1976. Perhaps the best translation of the most important Buddhism scriptures.

Arts & Culture

Allott, Anne. "Burmese Literature" in *A Guide to Eastern Literatures*, edited by David M. Lang. New York: Praeger, 1971.

Brandon, James R. *Guide to Theater in Asia*. Honolulu: The University Press of Hawaii, 1976. What to see, where to go.

Franz, H.G. *Von Gandhara bis Pagan*. Graz, Austria: 1979.

Frederic, Louis. *The Art of Southeast Asia*. New York: 1965.

Griswold, Alexander B. *The Art of Burma*, Korea, Tibet. New York: Methuen, 1964.

Htin Aung. *Burmese Drama*. Calcutta: Oxford University Press, 1937.

Htin Aung. *Burmese Folk Tales*. Calcutta: Oxford University Press, 1948.

Htin Aung. *Burmese Monks' Tales*. New York: Columbia University Press, 1966.

Htin Aung. *A Kingdom Lost for a Drop of Honey and Other Burmese Folk Tales*. With Helen G. Trager. New York: Parents Magazine Press, 1968.

Htin Aung. *Thirty Burmese Tales*. London: Oxford University Press, 1958.

Khin Myo Chit. *The 13-Carat Diamond and Other Stories*. Rangoon: Sarpay Lawka, 1969.

Lustig, Freidrich von. *Burmese Classical Poems*. Rangoon: Rangoon Gazette, 1966.

Munsterberg, Hugo. *Art of India and Southeast Asia*. New York: H.N. Abrams, 1970.

Myhint Thein. *Burmese Folk Songs*. Oxford, England: Asoka Society, 1969.

Myint Thein. *When at Nights I Strive to Sleep*. Oxford, England: Asoka society, 1971.

Rawson, Philip. *The Art of Southeast Asia*. New York: Praeger, 1967.

Swaan, W. *Lost Cities of Asia*. New York: G.P. Putnam's Sons, 1966. A

view of Kampuchea's Angkor Wat, Burma's Pagan, and three sites in Sri Lanka through art and architecture.

Thomann, Thomas H. *Pagan: Ein Jahrtausend Buddhistischer Tempelkunst*, Stuttgart: Walter Seifert, 1923. "A thousand years of Buddhist temple art." One of the few art books on Pagan.

Withey, J.A., and Kenneth Sein. *The Great Po Sein: A Chronicle of the Burmese Theater*. Bloomington, Ind.: Indiana University Press, 1965.

Burmese Publications

Aung Thaw. *Historical Sites in Burma*. Rangoon: Rangoon University, 1972.

Burma Gazetteers. Rangoon: Government Printing Office, 1907 through 1967. Regional studies of Akyab, Amherst, Bassein, Bhamo, Henzada, Insein, Kyaukse, Lower Chindwin, Mandalay, Myitkyina, Northern Arakan, Pegu, Yangon, Ruby Mines, Salween, Sandoway, Shwebo, Syriam, Tharrawaddy, Toungoo, Upper Burma and Shan States, Upper Chindwin, and Yamethin districts.

Directorate of Archaeological Survey. *The Mandalay Palace*. Rangoon: Government Printing Office, 1963.

Directorate of Archaeological Survey. *Pictorial Guide to Pagan*. Rangoon: Government Printing Office, 1963.

Directorate of Information. *The Golden Glory: Shwedagon Pagoda*. Rangoon: Government Printing Office, 1956.

Directorate of Information. *A Handbook on Burma*. Rangoon: Government Printing Office, 1968.

Directorate of Information. *Rangoon: A Pocket Guide*. Rangoon: Government Printing Office, 1956.

E Maung. *Burmese Buddhist Law*. Rangoon: New Light of Burma Press, 1937. Reprinted 1978.

Duroiselle, Charles. *Guide to the Mandalay Palace*. Rangoon: 1925. Interesting as a pre-World War II account.

Khin Myo Chit. *Anawrahta of Burma*. Rangoon: Sarpay Beikman, 1970. Historical novel.

Lu Pe Win. *Historic Sites and Monuments of Mandalay and Environs*. Rangoon: Government Printing Office, 1960.

Lu Pe Win. *Historic Sites and Monuments of Pagan*. Rangoon: Government Printing Office.

Ministry of Union Culture. **Manao-Kachin Festival**. Rangoon: Government Printing Office.

Bibliographies

Aung Thwin. **Southeast Asia Research Tools: Burma**. Honolulu: University of Hawaii Asian Studies Program, 1979. Trager, Frank N. **Burma: A Selected and Annotated Bibliography**. New Haven, Conn.: Human Relations Area Files Press, 1973. The most complete bibliography available.

Other Insight Guides

Insight Guide: Singapore explores this island-city's multi-racial culture, unique food, exciting shopping and modern yet warmly exotic atmosphere in this colourful guidebook.

Insight Pocket Guide: Vietnam brings you to the diverse attractions of this exotic, historical land, now emerging as one of Asia's top tourist destinations. Hanoi, Ho Chi Minh City, the beaches, and the nightlife are all explored in detailed itineraries and a new pull-out map.

Insight Guide: Thailand brings you to this exotic destination of ancient temples, majestic rivers, and friendly smiles.

Insight Guide: Philippines captures the country's warm, friendly people and their unique culture, while exploring in-depth, the country's breathtakingly varied landscapes, both natural and modern.

Insight Guide: Indonesia. The romantic islands of this Southeast Asian archipelago have long been an irresistable draw to travellers from all around the world. Come experience Bali, Java, Sumatra and more in this fascinating guidebook.

Insight Guide: Malaysia is for the traveller seeking colonial elegance, tropical adventure, modern luxuries and welcoming peoples, all in one beautiful, exciting country.

Index

L

M